THE UNIVERSITY OF
WINCHESTER

Martial Rose Library
Tel: 01962 827306

To be returned on or before the day marked above, subject to recall.

Resetting the Stage
Public Theatre Between the Market and Democracy

Dragan Klaic

intellect Bristol, UK / Chicago, USA

First published in the UK in 2012 by
Intellect, The Mill, Parnall Road, Fishponds, Bristol, BS16 3JG, UK

First published in the USA in 2012 by
Intellect, The University of Chicago Press, 1427 E. 60th Street,
Chicago, IL 60637, USA

A catalogue record for this book is available from the
British Library.

Cover designer: Holly Rose
Copy-editor: MPS Technologies
Production manager: Melanie Marshall
Typesetting: Planman Technologies

ISBN 978-1-84150-547-3

Printed and bound by Hobbs the Printers Ltd, UK

Contents

Contents

Preface

A long-standing involvement with theatre has to a great extent shaped my sense of Europe and its fascinating cultural diversity. As a theatre professional and academic, I have been observing the upsurge in commercial theatre and its advanced professionalism with growing concern for the implications for the non-commercial stage. In view of the competition, proximity and even enmeshment of these two realms – one profit-chasing and the other sustained by public subsidies – I want to plead in this book for their firm demarcation. My analysis of the performing arts as an artistic domain sketches a system of interconnected public institutions, created across Europe for public service and for the delivery of the public good. The question I am posing is how these companies, venues, festivals, studios and the supporting and intermediary facilities on which they rely can be sustained against the competition of commercial entertainment and the weakened support of public authorities. Globalisation, migration, European integration and the digital revolution are altering the lifestyles of city and country dwellers and putting pressure on public theatre to adjust and modify its role, or risk marginalisation and irrelevance.

An early impulse to write this book came from an invitation from the young interns of the Dutch government to speak at their annual seminar on the public finances, some time around the start of the new millennium. I recall my surprise at how ignorant these prospective civil servants were about Dutch cultural policy and the cultural infrastructure, maintained as it is by public subsidy. Moreover, they failed to see why the national government was subsidising theatre companies and festivals while Joop van den Ende, the famous commercial producer, was putting on his musicals and other popular productions without subsidy, and even making a profit on them. A long and complicated argument was involved in explaining on that occasion that there are different sorts of stage products and that only some of them can earn enough to cover their expenses and hopefully generate a profit, and why others cannot. It was especially difficult since I was flanked on the panel by a cultural economist, who after his years in the United States had become a staunch opponent of any government subsidies to culture, and argued that those who have cultural needs and passions should support cultural organisations of their choice with donations, just as religious people support churches. He advocated this without regard to the fact that in the Netherlands, as in most European countries, the government supports religious organisations in many ways and maintains their buildings if they are listed historic monuments. As the economist pitched the usual arguments, I was thinking how, in 10–15 years, those interns would have risen to positions of power and influence in the national civil service without an understanding and appreciation of the values of non-commercial public culture, and in the belief that cultural production and distribution should be left entirely to market forces.

Now, several years later, when I have finally written this book on the specific values and benefits of non-commercial theatre in a deliberative democracy, I have no illusion that it will be read by those former interns, now making their careers in the upper echelons of the Dutch civil service. In the past few months they must have been preoccupied with calculations of how to eliminate 18 or more billion euros from the national budget in the next four years, as required by the coalition programme of the new cabinet that emerged from the June 2010 Dutch elections and the subsequent long negotiations. Among the far-reaching cuts of this minority Liberal/Demo-Christian coalition, dependent on the support of the PVV (an anti-immigration, anti-Islamic and anti-cultural party) is the announced reduction of €200 m in the national budget for culture (totalling some €840 m); this is planned mainly to affect creative projects, especially the performing arts. These political intentions, coinciding with subsidy cuts for public culture elsewhere in Europe, add some urgency to my topic and argument[1].

The belief that the market should be left to regulate itself was discredited in the banking crisis of autumn 2008, when many governments intervened to rescue major banks and nationalise their losses, thus becoming their majority shareholders. In the ensuing recession, the worst since the Great Depression of the 1930s and global in its widespread impact, many governments dropped their neo-liberal convictions and embraced Keynesianism for a short while, restoring state capitalism. As Europe slowly pulled out of recession, at least in the statistical sense, albeit with a shaky, uncertain recovery, sluggish growth and protracted high unemployment, politicians across Europe dropped Keynesian ideas and turned to savage budget cuts, supposedly in order to reduce the national debt and its servicing, alarmed by the proportions of the Greek, Irish, Spanish and Portuguese public deficits and the implicit risks to the euro. In the autumn of 2010, economic protectionism and global monetary wars returned to the world stage.

In the 2008–2009 recession commercial theatre suffered from slow ticket sales and the difficult formation of the capital needed for investment in new productions. Consequently, in New York some Broadway playhouses went dark for a long period and in 2009 London West End shows offered tickets on the Internet at a 60 per cent discount, just as restaurants and hotels in all major European tourist destinations did. But at the end of 2010 an eagerly awaited musical, *Spider-Man* (spidermanonbroadway.marvel.com), went into delayed previews on Broadway, with a record pre-premiere investment of $60 m (over €46 m) and weekly running costs of over $1 m. This constituted a sign of optimism in show business, even though risky acrobatic numbers caused injuries to the performers and repeatedly postponed the official premiere (Healy 2010c–g; Edgecliffe-Johnson 2010).

In European non-commercial theatre there was much nervousness about the implications of the recession, but 2009 public subsidies were already more or less decided when the crisis erupted. Very few public venues reported a dramatic drop in ticket sales in 2009. Some complained about the disappearing donations of private foundations and vanishing potential sponsors, but most non-profit companies lacked sponsors and all were used to being understaffed, underfunded and overworked, so they believed that they would somehow pull through the recession. In 2010 they expected to be able to sigh with relief, but budgetary reductions induced new anxieties about the prospects for public theatre.

Meanwhile in Iceland, hit harder by the recession than any other European economy because of deregulation and lack of governmental supervision, the banking system collapsed and currency dramatically devalued, non-commercial theatre experienced an unprecedented growth in demand. Iceland (population 317,000 with 118,000 in the capital Reykjavik) has persistently had the highest rate of theatre attendance in Europe, but the Reykjavik City Theatre went from 500 subscriptions to 9,700, a stunning increase of 1,940 per cent, encompassing 3 per cent of the country's total population. The total audience went from 132,000 to 207,000. The National Theatre and the Reykjavik Symphony Orchestra also experienced a dramatic increase in subscriptions and tickets sold. This unprecedented jump in interest, occurring from an already very high level of cultural participation, indicates that a troubled and confused society, its spending and speculation binge curtailed along with frequent holidays abroad, turns to the public theatre for an artistic, but also social and intellectual experience, for collective soul-searching, critical insight and some self-assurance.

This book is not about the survival of theatre in the economic recession – although its shadow looms heavily over the following chapters – but about the notion of public theatre, non-commercial and thus subsidised, its distinct virtues, values and benefits. The argument I will put forward is that, under increased competition from commercial theatre and the profit-making cultural industry, public theatre needs to reinforce the specific features that qualify it for public support. Why? So that its critical stance can galvanise civil society and shape various communities of concern. Each non-commercial performing arts organisation needs to stress its unique character, make its products and service as specific as possible, as well as challenging and confrontational, in order to create rich educational, discursive and social opportunities for the public around its productions. Standardisation of the programme, repertoire and product, as well as imitation of commercial theatre and its practices, deprive public theatre of its distinctiveness and ultimately de-legitimise its claim to public support. At the same time, I will also argue against an automatic entitlement to public subsidy on the part of performing arts organisations, just because they claim a high artistic quality or a venerable history. Instead, public subsidies should be allocated on the basis of firm criteria that go beyond artistic excellence, in a tough but fair competition. A new covenant between politics and public culture would be quite demanding on performing arts organisations because public support would not be based on tradition and historic relationships with the government and not on an abstract idea of public-service mission or representational concerns but on systemic investment in and the encouragement of synergies, partnerships, mobility, innovation and audience development.

My standpoint is European and my evidence is derived from the numerous European national theatre systems I have observed and studied on my travels. Despite substantial differences – which I also try to point out – the public performing arts systems in Europe are quite similar, and confronted with the same essential pressures and challenges. A systematic analysis of national cultural and theatre systems is offered in the Compendium of Cultural Policies and Trends in Europe (www.culturalpolicies.net), an initiative of the Council of Europe and ERICarts, and further data is to be found in the studies of major European networks, such as PEARLE (Performing Arts Employers Associations League Europe, www.pearle.ws), IETM (Informal European Theatre Meeting www.ietm.org), ENCATC (European network on Cultural Management and Cultural Policy education, www.encatc. org) and Culture Action Europe (www.cultureactioneurope.org). The essential similarities among the national models enable me to focus on the big picture, on the major processes and issues, and avoid technical matters and managerial advice, for which I have no expertise and which is available in numerous culture-management handbooks.

Instead, I deal with artistic profiling, programming range and strategies, local and international cooperation and partnership, contextual dynamics, public-space activation and policy articulation that would consolidate the public theatre in Europe and make it clearly distinguishable from the commercial theatre and other for-profit forms of entertainment. There is no sense in fulminating against commercial theatre as such. With all its reliance on consumption and on market trends and forces in the provision of entertainment, commercial theatre has a vested interest in a strong public theatre as its own research and development laboratory, sustained by the subsidy of public authorities – which, incidentally, often themselves forget that commercial theatre could not make its profits without all the talent, products, styles, and aesthetic innovations generated and nourished in the realm of public theatre.

My intellectual debts are chiefly to Raymond Williams and his linkage of theatre and emancipatory processes in cultural democracy; to Jürgen Habermas's notion of public space; to Zygmunt Bauman's critique of globalisation and consumption; and to theatre practitioners and theorists who have stubbornly believed that the stage can improve society, or at least sharpen a critical attitude towards it. Today, it seems to me, the stage is a privileged public space in which to confront complexity, alter ingrained attitudes, challenge the imagination and probe difficult issues, in contrast to the haste, flippancy and inevitable superficiality of most electronic media, where one-liners and invective commonly replace arguments.

I hope this book will be read by present and future performing arts professionals, but also by board members of cultural organisations and civil servants, politicians and officers of private foundations, who all determine support for public theatre, shape objectives, insert criteria and design procedures; by corporate executives buried under an avalanche of sponsorship requests; and also by journalists who in their coverage of the performing arts might miss the cultural-policy context and a comparative European perspective. My aim has not been to write an academic book but a polemical one. Consequently, I sought to keep references to a minimum and yet insert a range of examples and cases from all four corners of Europe and refer to ongoing theatre developments as reported by the media. These examples are offered in order to support and specify my argument, but a reader in search of a quick overview may want to ignore them and avoid being distracted by them. For this reason they are given in a different font from the main text. By rethinking the prospects for public theatre in Europe, I am returning to my favourite topic, explored elsewhere in my writing (Klaic 2005, 2007a): the emergence of an integrated public space in Europe, dynamic and inclusive, as well as sensitive to the local contingencies and aware of the larger world, reinforcing the link between the experience of culture and citizenship. Theatre has been exploring this relationship since its origins in Athens 2500 years ago. It has experienced formidable importance and public loyalty in some periods, whenever it questioned and reshaped values, probed the modes and rules of social life and rejected fatalism in the name of imagination. Hopefully, theatre can continue to perform all these functions in our globalised world of digital culture and electronic communication, integrated world markets and casino capitalism.

Amsterdam, February 2011

Note

1 In the meantime the political landscape in the Netherlands has changed and the position of the arts, especially the performing arts, looks, if anything, even grimmer than at the time of writing.

Acknowledgements

In writing this book I benefited from the generosity of many universities, cultural organisations, publications and colleagues and friends.

At the University of Bologna, Professor Luca Zan invited me in 2007 to teach a yearly compact course on European theatre systems in the GIOCA Master Program. The University of Amsterdam, University of Kent, Stockholm Drama Institute, Hogeschool voor de Kunsten Utrecht, ArtEZ Arnhem, the University of Leeds, Leeds Metropolitan University, the Goethe-Universität Frankfurt, University of Hildesheim, Universität der Kunste Berlin, Theatre University Shota Rustaveli in Tbilisi, the Academy of Dramatic Arts of the University of Sarajevo and the University of Arts in Belgrade have invited me for guest lectures, seminars, workshops and conferences that prompted me to pursue some of the ideas later developed in this book. The Centre d'études théâtrales at Louvain-la-Neuve, the Centre of Performance Research in Aberystwyth, Vlaams Theater Instituut and Koninklijke Vlaamse Schouwburg (KVM) in Brussels, Office National de Distribution Artistique (ONDA) and Relais Culture Europe in Paris, the Danish Ministry of Culture and Danish Art Agency, Arts Council England, Fondazione Fitzcarraldo in Torino, Cinema Teatro Lux in Pisa, Interarts Barcelona, Shadow Casters Zagreb, Arts Palace in Budapest, Intercult in Stockholm, Deutsche Bühnenverein, Frascati and Stichting Internationale Culturele Activiteiten (SICA) in Amsterdam offered opportunities to test my ideas in debates and professional conversations. Professional networks and consortia, such as Informal European Theatre Meeting (IETM), European Theatre Convention (ETC), Eunet, Kedja and European Festivals Organisation (EFRP) and festivals such as Divadelna Nitra in Nitra, the Avignon Festival, Fabbrica Europa in Florence, Golden Mask and Big Break in Moscow, Sterijino pozorje in Novi Sad, Dubrovnik Summer Festival and others, have offered valuable insights into the diversity of performing arts conditions and practices across Europe. In a preliminary form, some key ideas in this book appeared in articles published in *Performance Research, Cahiers Théâtre Louvain, Courant, Boekman, Die Deutsche Bühne* and *Theatermaker*.

A grant from the Performing Arts Fund NL gave me some condensed and productive time to write this book.

Dialogue with many performing arts professionals, artists, producers and presenters provided a constant reality check for my notions and hypotheses. Special thanks to

Vesna Čopič, Milena Dragićević Šešić, Cornelia Dümcke, Rudy Engelander, Christopher Gordon, Sanja Jovićević and Yana Ross, generous friends who read the earlier versions of the manuscript and offered critical comments; to Aleksandar Brkić for research assistance and fact-checking; and to Patricia Marsh-Stefanovska for the English-language editing. Writing a book on the topic of the performing arts, I feel gratitude to my early theatre teachers and mentors, hardly any of them still alive, who inspired my interests, orientations and affinities. And I hope that my former and future students in various programmes, courses and seminars will use this book to argue for their own theatre dreams.

Dragan Klaic

PART I

A Blurred Role

Chapter 1

Public and Commercial Theatre: Distinct and Enmeshed

P ublic theatre, as we know it in Europe today, artistic in orientation and subsidised by public authorities, has its roots in the nineteenth-century ideology of nationalism. The concepts of a nation and nation state postulated national theatre as an emblematic institution and as a privileged ideological platform. It was a common argument that, if the nation needs a national theatre for its own elucidation and consciousness of self, the nation state must be capable of paying for it. Hence, public commitment grew to establish and sustain a national theatre as a representative institution and a pillar of the nation state – in some cases paid for by members of the national community in anticipation of a nation state that still had to be created. This was the case with the Poles, Czechs, Serbs, Croats and Hungarians, who all articulated their national theatre projects as a preparatory phase for the emergence of their nation state (Wilmer 2008).

Today's prevailing models of public theatre could also be linked to the small venues of the Paris avant-garde in the 1880s–1890s, created in penury but with a surplus of passion and conviction, and supported by small coteries of avid followers. André Antoine's Théâtre Libre (1887) inaugurated naturalism on stage, supported by Zola and a few prominent naturalist authors whose plays were staged there. The short-lived Théâtre d'Art of Paul Fort (1892) and Le Théâtre de l'Oeuvre (1893–1898), led by Aurélien Lugné-Poë, ushered symbolism onto the stage and sought to create a dreamlike poetic reality, elusive and minimalist in its material properties. These pockets of the avant-garde at the edge of Paris, far removed from the official status of the Comédie-Française (established as a court and state theatre company in 1680), and the hustle and bustle of the commercial boulevard theatre and its demi-mondaine and popular audiences, provided a model for an entire movement of *independent* theatres that sprang up soon afterwards in Berlin, London and other large European cities (Brown 1980). While business-minded managers operated large theatres as commercial enterprises, relying on star actors, a mixture of comedy and melodrama, spiced up by occasional scandal and much well-engineered gossip, independent theatres – small in scale and serious in purpose – articulated a specific aesthetic concept, an intellectual repertoire, often a critical or visionary world-view, and profiled the stage director as a new theatre profession and as the key artistic personality, firmly in charge of the creative process. When W. B.Yeats and Lady Gregory established the Abbey Theatre in Dublin in 1904, they fused the idea of an avant-garde theatre, promoting dramatic symbolism, with the idea of national theatre, preparing the Irish for independence.

The ensemble model

The far-reaching aspirations of the independent theatre movement were most fully realised at the end of the nineteenth century by two Russian innovators: the dramaturg and critic Vladimir Nemirovich-Danchenko and the amateur actor and director Konstantin Stanislavski. In setting up the Moscow Artistic Academic Theatre (MXAT) in 1898, this tandem drew up a set of norms, mutual agreements and common aspirations, which they successfully implemented in the following years, creating a coherent ensemble with a rich repertoire, backed by some regular in-house authors, such as Chekhov and Maxim Gorky, and a recognisable stage aesthetic. In just a few years they built up a loyal core audience of students and intellectuals, but also of a growing Russian middle class, whose need for serious and critical self-representation they successfully met. MXAT shaped the culture of an ensemble as a coherent and harmonious artistic collective, where mutual learning and respect took precedence over any individual sense of stardom or stage narcissism. The composition of the repertoire and its persistent aesthetic were determined by the stage directors, working with regular artistic collaborators and a devoted administrative and technical staff in a long and careful rehearsal process.

Both classics and contemporary plays were staged with meticulous illusionism, originally seen in the Meiningen Ensemble, the company of the Duke of Saxe-Meiningen, famous for its scrupulous historical sets and subtly orchestrated mass scenes. Stanislavski, a stickler for detail, took the company to Rome to find inspiration at the Forum for Shakespeare's *Julius Caesar* and to Cyprus to prepare for *Othello*. No wonder, then, that MXAT's first season inevitably ended with a considerable deficit, gallantly covered by some rich Russian merchants. Nemirovich-Danchenko staged some productions in a symbolist key, and the decision to invite Edward Gordon Craig to stage *Hamlet* in 1908 in Moscow confirms the founders' willingness to broaden the psychological realism for which MXAT became famous, with some more abstract aesthetics. The company reached a level of professionalism that became first an inspiration, and then the norm for many similar companies elsewhere in Europe. Stanislavski's written reflections on the creative process became the source of a comprehensive theatre pedagogy and systematic theory of acting, based on self-restraint, respect for the partner and affective memory, demanding that the actor recall his or her own emotional experiences and invest them in the building of the character, endowing it with maximum plausibility and psychological verisimilitude (Slonim 1962).

With the outbreak of World War I, MXAT fell into cultural isolation from the rest of Europe and after the October Revolution it was forced into a difficult accommodation with the Soviet regime and its cultural policies. Before acquiescing to the Soviet authorities' demand for a revision – under duress – of its aesthetics to fit the proscriptive norms of communist ideologues, the MXAT ensemble spent many months on extensive tours around Europe, extending its influence; some of its members decided not to return to Soviet Russia at all. The stream of theatre émigrés from Russia until 1924 further aided the spreading of MXAT principles and practices, the appreciation of an acting ensemble and the dominant position of the director as the decisive conceptual maker of the production, the creator of its aesthetic universe. Subsequently, a number of German, French, Scandinavian, Polish and Czech directors shaped their own ensembles on the MXAT model between the two world wars and marked them with their own staging style. The theatre director emerged as the dominant figure, an arbiter between the dramatic text and the actors, the invisible inventor of the stage action, derived from the play and offered for the enjoyment of the audience. A following generation of more experimental theatre directors, some of whom were Stanislavski's students, could profit from the recognised dominance of this profession, even if they rejected the illusionism and psychological realism of their master.

Public subsidies ensure cultural respectability

All the diversity of theatre conditions across Europe notwithstanding, much of the artistic dynamics throughout the twentieth century was created by respected ensembles, led by prominent directors, staging a diverse repertoire in a recognisable stylistic key. They were loyally supported by an audience of regular subscribers, recruited from the culturally ambitious middle classes and later even some segments of the working class. As these ensembles acquired prestige and respectability, they were sooner or later challenged by small groups of experimental bent with pronounced avant-garde programmes, which were led by rebellious directors, many of whom in due course joined the establishment and took over mainstream companies. In this way both the repertoire of plays and its rendering on stage could go through modification and innovations. Any artistically and intellectually ambitious theatre enterprise remained, however, a precarious business proposition as long as it was dependent on subscription sales before the beginning of the season and solid cash flow at the box office, generated by a rotating repertoire of productions in the following months. The income generated in such a way often remained below the level of expenditure, creating debt and opening up the prospect of bankruptcy – unless a wealthy donor intervened as a white knight.

MXAT was relieved of financial risk by the generous patronage of rich Russian merchants and then of the new Soviet state, but it had to pay a high price for state funding by conforming to Soviet ideological doctrines, working under the constant shadow of Stalinist censorship and adjusting its repertoire accordingly. After 1945, wherever Soviet military advances and political influence imposed a socialist order across Eastern and Central Europe, the MXAT model was postulated as an aesthetic ideal and repertory theatre practice was upheld and promulgated by state ownership, funding and control, under a strict ideological regime. In parallel, in Western Europe, the welfare state and the post-World War II belief in the immanent goodness of culture and its emancipatory promise created a growing flow of municipal and state subsidies for the established companies, and directed public investment into the rebuilding of the playhouses destroyed in the war. A steady expansion of companies and venues – a growing infrastructure of subsidised theatre, founded on a diverse repertoire, core ensemble and directors' dominance, even when originally shaped by the ideology of nationalism and an ideal of a national theatre as the pinnacle of the system – was now deployed in the huge task of democratising culture. Subsidised companies were expected to address a broad potential audience, beyond the traditional middle-class public, sometimes with special subscription schemes, sometimes with the mediation of the unions. Public subsidies were justified by artistic excellence, aesthetic innovation, the intellectual vigour of the repertoire and a playhouse's contribution to social cohesion and cultural emancipation.

> In taking the leadership of the Théâtre National Populaire in 1951, Jean Vilar wanted to embrace a large Parisian audience, especially the working class, in the huge auditorium of the Palais de Chaillot (2900 seats), offering a classical French repertoire and well-known actors. Roger Planchon was driven by the same ambition in setting up his company in Villeurbanne, a working-class suburb of Lyon in 1957, acquiring the title of Théâtre National Populaire in 1972. After World War II the Volksbühne, which had traditionally been oriented towards a wider audience, was re-established in communist East Berlin and, in response, the West Berlin authorities set up the Freie Volksbühne as its counterpart. Iceland obtained its independence from Norway in 1944 and crowned it in 1950 with a venue for its National Theatre.

For the first time in history, regular public subsidies made theatre accessible and popular but also brought respectability, stability and continuity to the performing arts, which had previously been a habitually risky *show business*, dependent on the appeal of extravagant stars, publicity stunts by managers and impresarios, inflated promotion, hired *claque* and the seductive atmosphere of a morally dubious enterprise, as well as a supposedly permissive professional culture. Commercial theatre remained part of the performing arts in Europe even after the spread of non-commercial theatre, continuing to combine big actor names with well-known titles, popular genres and an easily accessible offer, taking considerable risks, making and losing the money of managers and investors, but lacking the cultural status with which the publicly funded theatre companies and venues were endowed. Gradually, public subsidies also inadvertently created routine, complacency and institutional fatigue among the recipient companies, which in turn fed into the grudge held by small innovative groups on the cultural fringe, who were envious of the established subsidy allocations to the mainstream companies and claimed that they were themselves more entitled to some of this public money than the established, regular recipients.

> Commercial and non-commercial theatres have coexisted as parallel worlds in many cities, with the occasional transfer of titles, productions and talent, but without any direct clashes. In the 1960s, it was rather between the experimental theatre groups and established subsidised companies that animosity grew. In the Netherlands, it culminated in Action Tomato in 1969, when some radical competitors threw tomatoes at the actors of the Nederlandse Comedie, performing *The Tempest* in the Amsterdam Municipal Theatre. The

system of six subsidised companies, linked to the major Dutch cities, subsequently collapsed and was replaced by small public grants distributed to a growing number of innovative groups that changed the image of public theatre and its prevailing aesthetics (Meyer 1994).

The proliferation of repertory theatre companies from the 1950s progressed in parallel with the small-theatre movement. Intimate spaces were filled with small-scale productions, mounted either as commercial enterprises or, more often, with local support, the aid of associations, universities and other non-profit initiatives, offering the public an intensive stage experience and a sense of belonging to a cultural group, or to the acolytes of a specific artistic vision. Large repertory companies countered the growing popularity of the small theatres by creating their own small performing spaces, often by converting rehearsal halls, stage-set warehouses or set-painting rooms, in the hope that they could better employ their ensemble members and offer a more diversified repertoire in an intimate setting.

Autonomous theatre groups, often without their own performing space, proliferated from the early 1960s, fed by the student theatre movement and various alternative and subcultural streams. These were united in most cases by an experimental drift and sometimes by the artistic vision of a charismatic leader that could ensure continuity – despite their poverty, lack of initial recognition and the aesthetic or moralistic irritation their productions provoked. Many such groups disappeared quite quickly, but quite a few survived numerous crises, reached international recognition on an expanding festival circuit and ultimately secured some form of regular public support; these included Ariane Mnouchkine's Théâtre du Soleil in Paris (est. 1964) and Eugenio Barba's Odin Teatret (est. 1964 in Norway, since 1968 in Holstebro, Denmark). Other groups, formed by several generations of ambitious theatre innovators, survived at least for a while, only thanks to incidental, small project subsidies, offered by the public authorities as some sort of appeasement, or rationalised as a necessary investment in artistic renewal, but amounting to only a small fraction of what the established repertory companies received.

Crisis – a permanent condition or a discursive image?

Parallel to the stabilising impact of public subsidies and in spite of it, across Europe throughout the entire twentieth century, theatre was often declared an artistic realm *in crisis*, in the first instance by intellectual observers, critics and cultural analysts (Delgado and Svich 2002). Such a diagnosis related at different times to the organisational model and aesthetic impasse, competition with new media and leisure alternatives, the audience's stubborn refusal to grow in accordance with expectations, and especially to the insufficient public funding of an increasing number of ensembles claiming such support, as against rising artistic ambitions and rising costs, especially in the maintenance of large playhouses. In time, theatre professionals got used to this crisis discourse and even internalised it. The more comfortable among them usually claimed that everything would be fine if the public subsidies were a little more generous and the production and touring system left as it was. Those theatre professionals who felt short-changed by the existing distribution system of public subsidy kept calling for sweeping reforms and overall change. Politicians and civil servants usually sought to stay out of these discussions, find excuses in budgetary restraints and postpone or avoid in-depth change by commissioning more committee reports and research studies, scheduling another public debate or more professional conferences. Especially in times of budgetary restrictions, politicians are reluctant to consider any systemic reforms that require additional resources.

Despite a crisis discourse and a widely shared feeling of structural vulnerability among the practitioners, the performing arts thrive in Europe in a dizzying multitude of arrangements, production and distribution models, public funding schemes and sources, playhouses, festivals, studios, professional associations, sector institutes and voicing organisations. At the same time, unemployment remains pervasive among performing arts professionals, a great majority doomed to modest earnings and chequered, discontinuous career patterns. Despite dim employment prospects, professional training programmes for theatre and dance on the higher education level experience no shortage of talented applicants – even if their vision of success and stardom is most probably nowadays shaped more by television and film than by theatre alone. Theatre and dance studies have become a recognised academic discipline, with their own departments, degree programmes, institutes, archives, specialised libraries and museums, as well as international organisations with their gatherings and publications. But they also entail a gloomy sense that non-commercial theatre has become a minority niche in comparison with the expanding entertainment industry.

A thriving commercial theatre

The line running through the performing arts landscape of Europe, delineating the division between commercial and non-commercial theatre, is not always clearly visible. This book is about the purpose and sustainability of public, that is, non-commercial theatre, but the strengths of commercial theatre need to be duly addressed since they shape the cultural context and consumers' preferences.

Commercial theatre exists in order to make money, which it sometimes does. It is a risky enterprise, where losses are common, but profitability can be achieved with a strong product, finely tuned marketing and a long run of the same production, followed eventually by a long tour and subsequent productions elsewhere. Various spin-offs – a television version, a film, a DVD, a CD with popular songs from the production – and merchandising can increase the profit. A successful product can be multiplied and exploited simultaneously in several places, with the original authors and producers contractually obliging local producers and casts to reproduce in utmost detail the same staging, lighting and choreography, even precisely-set communication tools (posters and playbills with a fixed logo and letter-type). The Lion King and Chicago are staged in the same way everywhere, as copies of the original Broadway productions. Auditions are held to find a cast that will be the best approximation of the original. Buying the rights, mounting the show in a large and well-known venue, as well as launching the publicity campaign, require considerable upfront investment, but offer the high probability of profit-making if a sufficient volume of ticket sales is generated quickly enough on the strength of name-recognition, since *The Lion King* and *Chicago* function as global brands. If the ticket sales sustain a long run, the initial investment will be recovered and the local staging will become profitable. The owners of the original rights will also earn money. A product that has proven its profitability in one place will in all probability be profitable elsewhere, if competently copied, barring some sensitive cultural issues that might not transfer well from the original environment to another, culturally different market.

Even though commercial theatre in Europe has a long history dating from the emergence in the sixteenth century of the first itinerant companies that had to earn their own meagre living, it is New York's Broadway district that today constitutes the epicentre of contemporary show business, run as a large, successful cultural industry. In Europe, commercial theatre has become much more than a mere reproduction of successful Broadway musicals. Of course, these are commonly and successfully produced in the big cities of Europe, repeating the original Broadway formula, but European commercial theatre churns out a wide range of its own original products: new musicals, comedies, farces, melodramas, whodunnits, revues, ice-skating extravaganzas, poetic circuses, equestrian shows, etc. There is a considerable diversification of genres, a great deal of professionalism in staging and marketing, large budgets allowing dazzling spectacles, and reliance on film and television stars to attract a large audience and secure its emotional attachment. All those genres rest on some firm conventions and handle their content without much complexity in order to make it easily accessible. The goal is to please, to entertain, to make the audience laugh, enjoy themselves and shed an occasional tear, have a good night out and recommend the show to others. Producing a completely new show for the very first time, untested elsewhere, requires considerable investment and carries a large risk of failure. Therefore, commercial producers snoop around for successful and potentially profitable shows, produced originally in the non-commercial theatre. They retool, recast and re-stage them with some changes in the big cities and in big venues, hoping for a long run that will generate a large volume of tickets sold and ultimately show a profit.

From the contemporary commercial theatre repertoire: *Crazy Shopping*, a musical; *Gone with the Wind*, a musical; *Slava's Snow Show*, a clown show with artificial snow; *Cavalia, Cavallomania, Magnifico, Theatre Zingaro*, all equestrian productions; *Afrika-Afrika*, an African circus show; *Rudolph, Affaire Mayerling*, a "new Habsburg musical"; *Troja*, a new spectacular show, which "stages the myth of the antique city with music, dance and special effects"; *Ben Hur*, a spectacular tribute to the film and its chariot race.

The closest European counterpart to Broadway is London's West End, where several productions are copies of Broadway hits, but some were originally created in subsidised theatre, where they did well and were then brought into the logic of commercial exploitation on a larger scale. The National Theatre (NT) in London (www.nationaltheatre.org.uk) quite often transfers its most successful productions from its South Bank home complex to the West End, where they can run for months, performed six times a week in a large auditorium and with higher ticket prices, part of the profit going back into the budget of the NT, a non-commercial, subsidised organisation. The Donmar Warehouse (www.donmarwarehouse. com) moves its successful shows from a 250-seat venue to a 750-seat West-End theatre (Grandage 2008). Some of these successful productions might undergo one more transfer, from the West End to Broadway, with extra investment, recast, made more dazzling and relaunched with a new marketing campaign, adjusted to US tastes. That London remains the centre of commercial theatre in Europe and the place with the strongest connection to the Broadway entertainment industry has much to do with tourism. All London theatres benefit from the wide spread of the English language and sell many tickets to foreign visitors, a rather significant privilege that cannot be reproduced in most other big European cities. London is a prime tourist destination and many package tours include tickets for West End shows.

Several other large European cities have seen a boom in commercial theatre in the last 10–15 years. The musical *Chicago* does well in Moscow, a city of 15 million inhabitants and thus a huge potential market. Paris has a vibrant tradition of boulevard theatre, commercially run large houses that feature popular comedies, farces and revues. After the reunification of Germany, Berlin (population 3.4 million) became a market for commercial theatre despite strong competition from numerous public companies with their own venues. Madrid and Barcelona, Hamburg and many other cities with more than one million inhabitants, and even some smaller ones, such as Amsterdam or Copenhagen, have at least one large commercially exploited theatre venue. Athens, a city of almost four million inhabitants, has dozens of small venues that are run commercially in the expectation of making some profit, although they often fail to do so; the risk, however, rests with private producers and their backers. After the end of communism, commercial theatre has become a regular feature of the larger cities of Central and Eastern Europe, where previously only subsidised repertory companies existed. What all these cities, with the exception of London, still lack is a clear spatial concentration of commercial venues in one district, together with the integration of the commercial theatre offer into the hub of hotels, restaurants, bars, garages, taxi fleets and ticketing agencies. These factors all together make Broadway the world capital of showbiz and enable many adjacent and related commercial activities to prosper and profit from the commercial success of a stage production.

Despite the rising costs, some commercial productions go on extended tours across Europe and visit even smaller cities, performing in venues that can be booked for one performance, or for a few nights. Usually the risk of not filling them with large enough audiences rests chiefly with the local venue operator, while the tour management takes a fixed fee, but there are variations in these arrangements. Commercial theatre with its genres, repertoire, hits, marketing and merchandise appears all over Europe and competes successfully with publicly supported theatre. If there is a temporary shortage of hits, or if their rights are too expensive to buy, commercial producers can always rely on the hits of the past, bringing them back in nostalgia and "retro" packaging and assuming that what worked well in the past will work again. Commercial theatre is very good at nourishing its own mythology and repackaging it in new nostalgia-inducing merchandise, in repeated recycling of its own successes, by making a stage production become a film and then bringing the film back to the stage, as in the popular show *The Producers*.

With its pronounced formulaic approach, commercial theatre reflects the cultural facets of globalisation, the standardisation and uniformity of a creative process, product and its exploitation mode. The product is highly mobile and reproducible across the globe, wherever there is enough potential audience to buy tickets. By standardisation of the process and the product and its open-ended run (as long as enough tickets are being sold), commercial theatre reduces the risks and increases the potential profitability of the endeavour. The key function in this context is that of the producer, who gathers the capital with the project idea and makes the most significant business decisions, as well as the artistic ones, in order to protect the investment and ensure its profitability. Artists working in commercial theatre – writers, actors, composers, directors, designers and musicians – are expected to respect this ultimate authority of the producer, who has chosen them and contracted them. Behind individual contracts – except those of the leading artists – are collective tariffs and rules, fixed in negotiations of venue owners and producers with various unions of performing arts professionals. Producers work within an elaborate corporate structure that often includes subsidiaries and incorporated partnerships, relying much on the know-how of lawyers specialising in authors' rights. Today cross-media exploitation of those rights connects commercial theatre corporations and business units with the advertising, music, film and television industries, various digital spin-offs and an array of subcontractors involved in merchandising various products related to a branded and copyrighted stage production.

Joop van den Ende is not a famous European, and many performing arts professionals have never heard of him. Yet he is one of the major figures in commercial theatre in Europe. His Stage Entertainment (www.stage-entertainment.com), a conglomerate of 35 companies, owns 25 large venues in Moscow, Berlin, Hamburg, Milan, Paris, Barcelona, Madrid, London and other European cities and a complex of five venues on Broadway. The holding's original productions and Broadway remakes enjoy long runs in several European cities and subsequent tours, and subsidiary businesses are involved in casting services, events management, ticket-selling systems, real-estate development around the venues, and digital recycling of successful stage productions. From very humble beginnings running a store in Amsterdam with paper hats, funny masks and other party articles, Van den Ende went into small-scale productions and simple tours in the 1960s, made money on television with entertainment shows, sold his TV interest in the 1990s at a huge profit and then concentrated on the commercial theatre. The Netherlands was too small a market for him, even though he pioneered bringing groups of German spectators to his venues in Utrecht and Scheveningen by bus. He then took over more than a dozen venues in Germany, often acquiring them for just one euro from despairing municipalities saddled with their debts, investing millions in their refurbishment and relaunching them as commercial theatres for long runs of his own productions. He also set up his own Van den Ende Foundation, which gives grants to young talents for advanced schooling and supports the professionalisation of marketing operations in non-commercial performing arts organisations. The foundation is the main investor in a new venue in the very centre of Amsterdam called DeLaMar (www.delamar.nl). Stage Entertainment systematically develops its own products, tests them in various markets and duplicates them if successful. Among its major successes is *Mamma Mia*, based on the music of the pop group Abba; it has enjoyed long runs in several cities and has at least four touring ensembles on the road. With 14 million visitors and a turnover of €550m, Stage Entertainment is among the biggest live entertainment businesses in Europe.

The specific merits of public theatre

In itself, there is nothing wrong with the overwhelming success of commercial theatre, run as a legitimate business, providing employment for many and satisfying millions of spectators. Upon entering a theatre lobby, an audience may often not know whether they are coming to a commercial or publicly subsidised venue and show, although they perhaps expect a rather steeper ticket price to give them a hint. During the last two decades, public theatre often imitates the commercial theatre in its repertoire and style of publicity, hoping to boost box-office income, with the result that these two realms of the performing arts might not appear so very different at first glance. Many subsidised programmed venues offer a mix of commercially produced and subsidised shows. Aesthetically and intellectually speaking, commercial theatre can be criticised for its clichés and formulas, for its sentimentality and escapist fantasies, for its fascination with stardom, success and instant glory that shun complexity and eliminate critical stances. Its products belong to the cultural industry that has become one of the most propulsive branches of contemporary capitalism, dealing with ideas, images and heroes that produce and globally distribute experience opportunities in a variety of interlocking media with considerable profitability.

Nevertheless, from the point of view of politics, and especially of cultural policy, the success of commercial theatre undermines public theatre and makes the need for public subsidies less self-evident.

Why does one company or venue depend on public subsidy if a private producer in the same city can successfully make theatre without any subsidy and even make a profit? The answer to this question is not only complex and convoluted but it also invokes the priority of artistic impulse over the money-making drive. It rests on innovation and artistic renewal rather than the perpetuation of standard products. It reiterates the value of artistic risk-taking, of diversity of artistic expression against the uniforming pressures of a commercial cultural industry that imposes fixed templates and formats. It invokes the need to discover and nurture young talents, who are given the privilege of playing alongside experienced peers and learning from them, rather than foregrounding only stars and treating everyone else on the stage as part of the set.

In addition, there are arguments of an intellectual and civic order. Without absolute dependence on the box office, public theatre can deal with obscure and not very appealing topics, unlike the commercial theatre, which must focus on typical situations and narratives and rehash stereotypical plots. Public theatre articulates critical stances towards reality rather than offering escapist fantasy. It can advocate unpopular views, break taboos, engage in historical revisionism and debunk mythologies, stir up controversy and initiate a public debate; the commercial theatre stays away from any controversial matter and reduces the twists and challenges of human existence to a few predictable patterns, to common denominators, to a schmaltzy, self-serving triumph of the good guys over the bad ones, of love conquering jealousy and hatred, of justice affirmed over evil and wrongdoing.

While commercial theatre gathers a large auditorium of people willing and able to pay good money for their own entertainment, public theatre brings together a diverse micro-society of individuals, groups and constituencies, who might be aware of their substantial differences and discords but come to the public theatre to have them sharply articulated and challenged. Public theatre can group and even mobilise the partisans of a cause, but needs to take into account the adversaries and the dissenters in the complex arena of public opinion. Public theatre is about free enquiry in a democracy; commercial theatre is about making money in a mass leisure market. An audience in a subsidised theatre is a micro-community of citizens, engaged in deliberative democracy, whereas in commercial theatre it is a group of consumers paying to be amused. Commercial theatre inflates hits to boost the box office; public theatre addresses various interests and tastes in a local community and allows for specific artistic niches to be set up and made sustainable.

All these distinctions of principle and all the arguments for public theatre and its qualifications for public subsidy are well-known and often reiterate the contrast with commercial theatre in a sharp, clear-cut manner. For performing arts professionals and all others who put them forward, these arguments reflect a conviction, a self-evident truth, but also vested interest on the part of all those who work in public theatre or depend on it. The most important question is: *Do all these arguments persuade politicians to sustain public subsidies for theatre? And if yes, for how long?*

Those who work in commercial theatre do not have much interest in this argument. They might point out that their sort of theatre is also familiar with unexpected shifts and turns, takes occasionally less popular themes and stances, affirms new values and norms, caters to a varied audience, finds evidence of its own essential humanity in its capacity to provoke popular enthusiasm for *The Lion King* and similar shows in a variety of cultures and sociopolitical circumstances on different continents. But ultimately, the professionals of commercial theatre know that they need public theatre as their own research and development department, a nursery for upcoming talent and a source of innovation from which they ultimately benefit. Yes, public theatre with its subsidised ticket prices is certainly a competitor as well, drawing away some of the potential audience they could otherwise perhaps recruit, but there are enough other potential spectators to engage. When all is said and done, commercial theatre operators know that they are allied with a powerful cultural industry complex of entertainment and they derive their strength and propensities from it, not from government support. If the government keeps taxes down and does not embark on additional regulation of the showbiz industry, of its labour relations and especially of public and occupational safety in their venues, everything is hunky-dory. They prefer to depend on the fickle and risky market rather than on a judgemental government.

Since culture in Europe is heavily influenced by the cultural industry of the United States, analogies between the performing arts systems on the two continents are often too easily drawn. The traditions and contexts are markedly different, however. In the United States, theatre has traditionally been considered a matter of private entertainment for which the public needs to pay the full price, without expecting any government support. On this premise the performing arts have blossomed as show business of success, fame and wealth at hand. From the early nineteenth century celebrated European actors embarked on strenuous US tours in order to earn a great deal of money on commercial terms. Only in the 1930s did President Roosevelt's administration decide to support the performing arts with taxpayers' money, in a broader government effort to pull the country out of the Great Depression by boosting the public employment of all professions, including the arts. After only three years, the remarkably successful Federal Theatre was de-funded and dismantled by the US Senate, which saw it as a source of communist indoctrination (Mathews 1967). More than 30 years later, the US government reconnected with the performing arts as a beneficiary of President Johnson's Great Society effort, through a very modest grant programme, offered to non-profit arts organisations and individual artists by the new National Endowment for the Arts (NEA, www.nea.gov), state arts agencies and the grant programmes of a few enlightened cities. Non-commercial theatre spread across the United States and profited from this government support, especially under President Nixon, when the NEA budget was at its peak. Since these government grants have been very modest and difficult to obtain, non-commercial theatre has remained dependent on the box office, corporate sponsorship and especially on the donations of individuals and private foundations, encouraged by generous tax write-off laws (Martel 2006).

In Europe, however, a markedly different tradition prevails. Reliance of theatre on public subsidies goes further back to aristocratic patronage, extended since the Renaissance, embodied in the Comédie-Française (1680) and Vienna Burgtheater (1741) as court and state theatres, continued through the investment of the emancipated middle classes and some municipal authorities since the eighteenth century and reaffirmed by the ideology of nationalism and the national theatre movement of the nineteenth century. The provisions created after World War II saw theatre as a legitimate beneficiary of the welfare state and an instrument of cultural democratisation in Western Europe. Behind the Iron Curtain, in the communist countries of Central and Eastern Europe, theatre thrived as a powerful medium of the ideological indoctrination of the masses. Since the end of the Cold War and the victory of belief in the free market with its accompanying predominance of neo-liberal ideology, public theatre everywhere across Europe has been feeling vulnerable and menaced, and the public support it has been enjoying for decades has come to appear as a less self-evident privilege than before. The success of commercial theatre is increasingly perceived as destabilising and delegitimising; hence the steady flow of arguments propounding public theatre's merits, some of which have already been invoked above.

Starting from these arguments in the belief that most of them make sense in principle – or are valid under some specific circumstances – the following chapters examine the structural weaknesses of public theatre in Europe and seek to identify systemic solutions and specific strategies that could make it more vital, vibrant and appealing, whilst at the same time recognisably distinct from the commercial stage. Public subsidy can be neither an entitlement nor a renewable privilege; it should rather be a support extended in recognition of clear public benefit delivered by non-commercial theatre, conscious of its core responsibilities and specific remit.

Chapter 2

Public Theatre: Challenges and Responses

While commercial theatre thrives in Europe, public theatre struggles with some persistent frustrations and difficulties. The audience volume is stagnating in most European countries and in many of them the greying hair of the audience is quite visible – spectators are on average getting older, not only because the huge "baby boomer" generation (those born between 1945 and 1955) is turning into senior citizens but also because fewer younger citizens become theatregoers. Marketing specialists are signalling that audience loyalty is also on the wane. People are shifting their interests, passions and patterns of how they spend their leisure time, and if they go to the theatre at all, they go less often and do not have a clear, stable set of preferences, neither for a venue nor for a company, genre or theme. Instead, they behave as fickle, unpredictable consumers. European national statistics are difficult to extrapolate and compare since theatre, musical theatre and even concert attendance get lumped together, and public and commercial theatre are often not differentiated (Eurostat yearbook 2010). Nevertheless, the trend towards a shrinking or stagnating audience as against an increased offer is clearly visible. This is also happening in the United States, where the number of non-profit theatres doubled in the 15 years from 1992 to 2007, but the adult audience for non-music performances shrank from 25 to 21 million spectators (NEA 2008).

Rising costs, limited compensation

Every theatre manager will be quick to complain about the rising costs of making theatre and presenting it to the audience. Communication costs especially are rocketing because audience interest needs to be stimulated in various ways. Theatres are obliged to invest in digital communication but they cannot terminate (yet!) paper publicity, such as newspaper advertising, leaflets, programmes and posters. As competition grows on the cultural market of larger cities, with many presenters of cultural events competing for the potential audience's leisure time, communication is becoming more persistent and intense, thus also more expensive.

As a process, theatre has become dependent on technology in all its aspects and phases, in big and in small venues. This dependence brings with it the pressure to invest continuously in upgrading the technology – not only the stage equipment but also process-management and ticket-sales systems, especially in big venues that keep a large number of productions in the repertoire, each with its own cast, sets, costumes, props, lighting schemes, build-and-strike times, as well as touring costs, all contained in complex databases, used to deliver work schedules and assignments. Complex technology in turn requires the engagement of an expert labour force. On average, both communication and technology specialists stand higher than artists in the labour market and thus can command higher salaries. Politicians pressurise public theatre to attract a young audience through various educational activities and programmes, which in practice means adding education staff members to the payroll. The public expects higher standards of comfort in the venue, which in turn requires further investment in the renovation and upgrading of playhouse facilities.

Through its European Agency for Safety and Health at Work, the European Union has imposed rather strict standards of public and occupational safety in public spaces, which include theatres as well as clubs, congress centres and sports facilities. Fire prevention, air quality and reduction of noise pollution are regulated according to strict norms and there are work standards for theatre employees, especially stage crews, which are intended to reduce their risk of injury in the workplace (osha.europa.eu/en/front-page). While these binding regulations are gradually being integrated into the national legislation of the member states, theatre venues are given limited time to adjust, acquire the technical competence required and implement solutions that generate high additional costs. In order to reduce professional hazards, the technical crews of a venue and of touring groups are allowed only limited overtime hours, which in practice often means the imperative engagement of extra crew capacity and higher labour costs. EU norms also demand easy access and placing for wheelchair-users, which necessarily entails some rebuilding in older venues. There has also been a strong demand to make theatres offer special provisions to visually or hearing-impaired people, although only in the United Kingdom have sign-language interpretation of the performance and special earphones for hearing-impaired spectators become a matter of routine.

This dynamic of cost-escalation acquires dramatic dimensions when set against the leveling-off, or even shrinking of public subsidies. As practically all European governments seek to curb public expenditure, reduce budgetary deficits and meet the strict norms of indebtedness proscribed by the euro monetary system, cultural budgets are shrinking or at least stagnating while at the same time there is a constant growth of the number of prospective subsidy recipients. These cultural organisations and initiatives, big and small, old and new, demand some sort of public support, but in practice most of them are turned down or funded with less than they expected. A small number of performing arts organisations has a steady, yearly renewable subsidy, while all the others apply for incidental project subsidies. Only in a few countries in Europe is there a system of two-, three- and four-year grants from public authorities, as in The Netherlands and the Flemish part of Belgium. Until the 2008–2009 recession, the tight culture budgets of national governments were partially compensated for by the rising culture expenditure of regions and cities, but not in all countries. As a relatively expensive form of artistic practice, the performing arts suffer more than other artistic domains from the growing gap between operating costs and public subsidies, especially as subsidised theatres are expected to do more for less: to sustain artistic quality and the volume of output (the number of premieres and performances per season), increase seat-occupancy rate, achieve a better cultural and generational mix in the audience, run educational programmes and go on tours within the country and abroad.

Increasing own income

Public authorities seek to reduce dependence on subsidies by requiring theatre organisations to increase their own income. Most public theatres have only a limited range of opportunities to do so. Productivity increases are practically impossible in their complex artistic processes, as noted decades ago by Baumol and Bowen (Baumol and Bowen 1966). In more comfortable cultural systems in Europe, public performing arts organisations still receive around 80 per cent of their budget from subsidies; in the most austere ones, only 45–50 per cent, which is quite visible in the programming choices, limited runs, "downcasting" and rather eye-catching publicity material, generously spiced-up with the excessive usage of adjectives. In the former communist countries of Central and Eastern Europe, where repertory theatres used to get 95–97 per cent of their budgets in subsidies, the situation has become more chequered: some are still close to the Dutch standard (up to 83 per cent of the company budget subsidised), while in the Baltic countries some have come close to the British norms (c. 50 per cent of the budget subsidised). Subsidised theatres seek to boost box-office revenue with productions one would expect to see in commercial venues, or they rent their halls for conferences, congresses, business promotion events, fashion shows and political party rallies. When the renowned Lithuanian director Eimuntas Nekrosius wants to perform with his own company Menofortas (www.menofortas.lt) in Vilnius for a larger audience than his studio offers, he needs to pay a great deal of money to hire the venue of the Lithuanian National Drama Theatre (www.teatras.lt). Proud of its exemplary and protected status, this National Theatre nevertheless seeks to supplement ample public subsidies with its own income, thus in fact exploiting its own prominent colleagues.

Sponsorship has been invoked as a miraculous solution to decreasing income, but in practice it works in a very restricted manner: only larger performing arts organisations with a name, tradition and prestige, large audience volume and a conventional programme can expect to attract some sponsorship. Even if they are very successful, the sponsorship rarely brings in more than 3–6 per cent of the operating budget. Finding, keeping and entertaining a sponsor takes up a lot of time, thus also money. Smaller performing arts organisations, with lower name-recognition and prestige, but a more adventurous and experimental programme, risk wasting considerable time in seeking a sponsor without result. In the best case, they might find in-kind sponsorship – goods and services offered by regular business partners, such as hotels, restaurants and caterers, taxi companies, printers, external accountants – a valuable relationship but with very modest financial effect.

Forms of sponsorship that directly benefit theatre audiences are quite rare. The National Theatre in London is able to offer £10 (€12) tickets for each performance thanks to the sponsorship of Travelex. The scheme has dramatically increased the seat-occupancy rate in all three NT venues and visibly diversified its audience. In some German cities a spectator with a theatre ticket in hand can enjoy free public transport for two hours before the performance and for some hours afterwards. This concept is ecologically sound, reduces inner-city congestion, to some extent relieves the theatre of the worry of providing adequate parking facilities for visitors and popularises the usage of public transport – but it makes sense only in areas where there is a good and well-integrated public transport system that does not stop at 9pm. In the 1980s some German city theatres organised taxi-sharing routes during the intermission to ensure that for a nominal fee senior citizens could count on a safe and low-cost door-to-door return home after the performance. Theatregoers in no rush to go home after the performance might expect some discount in nearby bars and restaurants, but other alliances and cross-marketing deals between performing arts organisations and providers of other cultural goods and services, such as bookshops and museums, remain rare.

There are few other opportunities for performing arts organisations to generate their own income. Programmes, DVDs and some merchandising are of promotional rather than financial value. Venues with a larger audience-capacity might expect to make some money with drinks and ice cream, a safe selection that has a long shelf life and can be sold at a considerable profit. But the moment theatres go into the sale of food, even if only sandwiches and cakes, they incur the risk of unsold, spoiled merchandise, the business complexity increases and well-trained staff need to be hired to organise and supervise the logistics, as well as respond to health protection requirements. As a result, many larger venues prefer to sublet their catering operation to specialised corporations and take only a part of the profit.

Larger venues have an additional cash-generating resource – extra square metres. Built in the decades after World War Two, many theatres across Europe have spacious foyers and, with the pressure to generate extra income, these venues have started subletting some of this extra space to small entrepreneurs selling books, postcards, videos and CDs, various trinkets and even souvenirs from an improvised desk. In Central and Eastern Europe this trend became visible with the surge in small-scale private retail business after 1989. Desks became stores, modest coffee shops in theatre venues were converted into bars and fully-fledged restaurants, while in some theatres in Moscow – a paragon city of capitalist excess and fast profit-making – entire floors of theatre venue lobbies were filled with gambling machines (until the total government ban on gambling in 2009); one theatre even housed a car dealership! The consequence was the rapid criminalisation of performing arts organisations engaged in such income-generating practices, because not all the profit was transacted legally. In Moscow and elsewhere, some money was passed under the table to the artistic and business managers, who supplemented their modest incomes by favouring this or that sublet business, but also created private slush funds to supplement the modest salaries of the artists whom they were especially eager to keep in the ensemble and prevent from transferring to a competing company.

Tinkering with the box-office income to increase revenue is a delicate matter. Prices of tickets for comparable theatre programmes in various European countries and cities vary a great deal, from roughly €5 to €45, not counting opera, where the upper price range goes above €300 per ticket. In general, theatre tickets are more expensive in the northern and western parts of Europe than in the South and East, and more expensive in big cities than in smaller towns. Various discount schemes for young and student audiences, for senior citizens and the unemployed extend this range even more. These discrepancies reflect not only variations in the local cost of living but also differences in the capacity of public subsidy systems to make theatre broadly accessible. The elasticity of the ticket prices is quite limited, however. Companies and venues fear that they will lose their most loyal audience if they raise the ticket prices too much. They know that students, teachers, the retired and humanist intelligentsia in general – all commonly the most frequent theatregoers – have a modest disposable income. With restraint in ticket pricing, public theatre hopes to lure an audience and stimulate it to come back a few times during the season. Commercial theatre, in contrast, permits itself rather high ticket prices because it appeals chiefly to people who go to the theatre once or twice a year, and favours group sales with large discounts.

There are repertory theatres that sell tickets for recent productions for a higher price than for productions that have been in the programme for several seasons. A production that is more in demand can command higher prices than another one in the same theatre, in a similar way to the variation in the price of opera tickets, which can rise significantly for the guest appearance of an international star. It seems that neither commercial nor public theatres have yet started pricing by demand, as practised by airline companies, which first sell a few seats on a flight at a low price and then raise the price as demand grows.

Traditional subscription schemes that used to raise advance cash for theatre organisations before the beginning of the season still exist in a surprising number of public venues, especially in Germany, but many subsidised theatres have developed loyalty-rewarding schemes instead, seeking to encourage people to come back and see at least four productions in a season, with a high discount and flexibility in the concrete choice and dates. Pinning someone down to see a play every third Thursday in the month is not an appealing proposition any longer, even with a discount. Theatregoers with busy professional and social lives refuse to be put in this straitjacket of binding advance commitment, so theatres seek to please them with more options and customised choice, hoping they will be rewarded with audience loyalty.

Performing arts organisations seek to reduce operating costs by trimming the budgets of new productions (sets, costumes, fees, royalties), but margins are small and very quickly affect the essential artistic choices and determine the programming: productions with a smaller cast are imposed, titles with a certain name-recognition are favoured and those without it marginalised; adaptations of literary bestsellers and of well-known film scripts are prompted. In many countries, repertory companies have replaced the *rotating repertory* (where several productions are performed in the same month) with a *sequential repertory* (one or two productions have a limited run before a new premiere takes their place in the schedule) and subsequently seek to replace longer artistic contracts with short-term ones. Some efficiency savings are also sought in shared production capacities and workshop operations, as practised, for instance, by the Vienna theatre organisations subsidised by the federal government (www.artforart.at).

Opera companies increasingly pull budgets to co-finance a new production, or seek to recover some of the investment by selling the most successful productions as a concept, set and costumes to other opera houses. The English National Opera (www.eno.org) transfers its productions to some 25 opera houses, and its *Madam Butterfly*, directed by the film director Anthony Minghella, was a co-production with the New York Metropolitan Opera (www.metoperafamily.org). Product placement, as pioneered in film, is also becoming a tacit theatre practice. Following the habits of the corporate world, already tested in commercial theatre, public theatre executives are also considering steps beyond partnerships, such as franchising and even hostile takeovers, which would mean that a successful public theatre appeals to the authorities to take over the management and programming of an unsuccessful public company or venue. In practice, public authorities arbitrate in imposing mergers and reassigning the responsibility for venues (Greater Copenhagen Theatre Board 2006). A financially strained public company tends to poach the commercial-theatre type of repertoire, or yields its stage to a commercial producer for a limited run in order to make some easy money.

A minority leisure option

All these interventions to close the subsidy versus cost gap in public theatre cannot remove some externally imposed structural factors, which modify the position of public theatre today. Theatre has become only one option in an immense range that consumers have at their disposal to fill their leisure time. Any public theatre performance competes with other public theatre offers, with commercial theatre, with concerts of all sorts of music and with all the other forms of entertainment, live and digital. During the twentieth century neither film nor radio, nor even television, could kill theatre as a medium, but they did lure away some of its potential audience.

Considered in a historical perspective, theatre is evidently no longer the main public pastime it was in the big West European cities of the seventeenth, eighteenth and nineteenth centuries. It has become a minority option, one of many, among which are consumption of high-quality digital cultural goods, chiefly at home but increasingly on the move: on notebooks, MP3 players or smartphones, in one's own time and at one's own pace. All this is available for a fraction of the cost or none at all, and without the hassle of advance reservation, journey time to and from the theatre venue and the pressure of theatre rules to come half an hour before curtain-up to pick up the reserved tickets. In addition, today's leisure options include sports activities and gym exercises, social dance (tango, salsa, capoeira clubs), volunteering in a variety of civic associations and popular civic movements (human rights, ecology, solidarity with refugees, migrants or indigenous people …), amateur practice of singing and music, not to mention a mesmerising choice of indoor and outdoor hobbies. On top of this, employed and self-employed people are expected, even pressured, to acquire new skills, get advance degrees, attend seminars and workshops.

Despite all the fashionable talk about the 24-hour economy, most of all these activities take place in the evening hours, when theatres usually offer their performances. Consequently, the competition for the allocation of those evening hours is enormous, and only a small part of an urban population can be counted among theatregoers, that is, among people who go to the theatre more than once a year. There is no reason to expect that their number will ever increase, even in cities with a growing population. Owing to language barriers, even a local tourist boom does not induce an increase in theatre audiences, except in London, although a tourist public is increasingly important for opera houses and concert halls in cities such as Vienna, Berlin, Madrid, Budapest and Amsterdam.

The social, economic and cultural stratification of European societies makes it more difficult for theatres to identify, capture and bind a specific audience, which they could then consider their own. The process of individualisation among Europeans has resulted in a vast scale of preferences, interests and sensibilities that cannot any longer be captured with standard demographic parameters, such as gender, age, education level and income. The traditional middle-class education that, until a few decades ago, created a predictable group of theatregoers with a secondary school diploma no longer exists, at least not among urban populations. And although people with more education are still more likely to go to the theatre than people with less education, those with a high-school diploma and a university degree do not automatically become ready-made theatre audiences. Even many people who read books, go to concerts and to museums, in other words people who could be considered legitimate and regular cultural consumers, never go to the theatre, giving a variety of excuses: too complicated, too expensive, burdened with a high risk of disappointment, boring, too slow, too long, too far, etc.

There is no clear-cut method of proven effectiveness to turn theatregoing into a habit. Being taken as a child to the theatre by parents or school, acting in school productions, going to theatre or ballet school, being given a theatre subscription as a gift as a teenager – none of these can induce with certainty a long-lasting habit of theatregoing. If anything, social motivation seems to count the most, perhaps even more than a cultural interest: people go to the theatre because people with whom they like to spend time go to the theatre. Only rare die-hard theatre lovers go to the theatre alone. Most people go as couples or in small groups of family members and friends. Theatre is a profoundly social experience: before the curtain, as anticipation, going with someone to see the production on the basis of available information and shared or induced interest; during the performance, sharing the experience with one or more known people and many unknown spectators by observing, joining or countering the reactions of others; meeting friends and acquaintances in the theatre lobby by chance before and after the show and in the intermission; reflecting on the experience afterwards with those who shared it and those who did not. As a social experience, theatre might enhance status consciousness, a sense of belonging to a group, whether social, cultural or political (Bourdieu 1984). To be a theatregoer means being a person of some social exposure and dynamic social life – and socially isolated individuals, increasingly numerous in modern cities, tend to stay at home and away from theatre venues. Theatre venues that are capable of creating an atmosphere conducive to sociability might expect to attract a larger audience than drab, shabby and unappealing playhouses.

> Several schemes have been launched to stimulate youngsters to go to the theatre. Arts Council England (www.artscouncil.org.uk) announced a scheme to make one million free tickets available to anyone younger than 26 in 95 venues between March 2009 and March 2011 at a cost of £2.5 m (€3 m). The Italian government developed a similar scheme to stimulate a young audience for artistic festivals. And in 1999 the Dutch State Secretary of Culture Van der Ploeg introduced €50 vouchers for all secondary school students, redeemable for any cultural outing, including the theatre. These sorts of scheme seek to create a theatregoing habit by removing financial obstacles (the price of a ticket) and expecting to make it entrenched and lasting. They ignore other logistical, spatial and social factors that impede theatregoing and do not control frequent shifts of leisure time allocation by young people, caused by study, work, sociability and mobility.

Along with sociability, theatre can exert an exclusionary and segregating impact. Historically, theatre has reflected social hierarchies and boundaries. In the fifth century BC, theatre performances were given in honour of the god Dionysus, but also celebrated Athens as the prime Greek city state and the cultural unity of the Greek world. They accommodated women and slaves in the audience while reserving performance for men only. Medieval religious theatre was inclusive, but hierarchical in assigning special places and roles to the clergy. Renaissance theatre was partially a court affair, set up for the entertainment of courtiers and only occasionally accessible to the masses. From the appearance of the first public theatre venues, in London and Madrid at the end of the sixteenth century, theatre followed strict hierarchies of social class by its space configuration and separate zones for distinct categories of audience. In early Spanish playhouses, women and clergy had their own separate and secluded viewing spaces, while in the Elizabethan theatres on the outskirts of London, aristocrats were seated separately. Those spatially marked social boundaries were further reinforced through entry-price differentiation. For the last 100 years, newly built and renovated theatre venues have provided more spatial unity to avoid this rigid reflection of class hierarchies, but they have kept galleries while usually eliminating boxes (except for opera). Yet the social stratification of the audience through price differentiation survives in otherwise democratic, even egalitarian societies, rationalised by different degrees of comfort and quality of view. To reinforce the coherence of the audience, smaller venues frequently opt for a one-price ticket policy and even for unreserved seating. The difference between the cheapest and the most expensive tickets is bigger in larger venues where viewing lines and proximity to the stage can vary considerably so that the audience is divided into various categories of comfort and prestige.

As long as theatre was an institution for aristocratic amusement or middle-class emancipation, it emanated an exclusionary effect on people from the other classes. Even if they were interested in going in, could afford it and would be let in, they would probably feel awkward and out-of-place, as social intruders. Today, with a high degree of informality in public behaviour and interaction, a relaxed or non-existent dress code, and airports and shopping centres as emblematic pseudo-public places where people of all sorts of background mix, most theatre venues would not be perceived any longer as intimidating or exclusionary. People who stay away from them do so on the strength of their cultural affinities and idiosyncrasies rather than because of the financial cost or assumed social barriers, especially since so many public theatres guarantee reduced tariffs for the young, old and unemployed. And yet, in most European cities – whose demography has been radically altered by immigration from other countries and continents – theatre audiences are predominantly white and middle-class.

Altered urban demography

This constitutes a serious shortcoming in public theatre that undermines its claim on public subsidies, based on its own supposed inclusiveness. The failure of public theatre to attract a local audience from an immigrant background beyond tokenism is pervasive and stubborn, difficult to resolve and politically compromising. No claims to and proofs of artistic excellence and intellectual vigour can neutralise or cover up this shortcoming. Without cultural diversity of audience, the public character of theatre lacks legitimacy. And yet, admittedly, theatres cannot solve this issue alone as it reflects a broader failure of cultural adjustment (or "integration," as politicians like to call it), especially on the part of non-European immigrants and the juncture in the notion of citizenship as a cultural practice. The failure is systemic and permeates a range of cultural and educational organisations, government agencies and business corporations, but because of the nature of theatre as a public, collective event, it becomes especially visible precisely there.

It is easy to offer reasons why immigrants and even their offspring do not attend the theatre much. A rather standard and predictable list of excuses is usually recited: immigrants have poor language skills, lack education that would prompt them into theatregoing, feel financially too vulnerable to spend money on theatre and lack free time, because they seek to work as much as possible in order to become more established or support their family members left behind. The explanations that invoke cultural background are more complex: they point to the fact that most non-European immigrants come from cultures that lack organised performing arts activity in the manner of European professional companies and playhouses and their programme offer. Rural and tribal cultures incorporate performing arts elements in their own traditions of ritual and celebration, and not as a pastime to be paid for, offered by professional players every evening. Some immigrants do have moral objections to the theatre experience, which keeps them away because they seek to avoid foul language, nudity and the public display of intimacy between men and women, all of which are not condoned by their original culture. Those immigrants who come from authoritarian and repressive societies where free debate is not allowed find intellectual confrontation and challenge to the authorities and social norms – a regular feature of the stage action in Europe – quite unsettling. Fearing the moral and cultural contamination of their children, immigrant parents ban or discourage theatregoing.

All these explanations undoubtedly contain much truth, but, taken separately or all together, they are today inadequate and cannot be accepted. With second-, third- and even fourth-generation immigrants growing up in European cities and in some of them forming half of the elementary school population, any theatre that claims to have a public character and expects public subsidy cannot hide behind these explanations that were perhaps more convincing 25 years ago than today. No public theatre needs to hire expensive cultural-diversity consultants to come to a rather simple conclusion: people of immigrant background and especially their offspring do not come to public theatre because they feel it is not *about* them and thus also not *for* them. No increase in the cultural diversity of the public can be achieved without a deliberate policy of active recruitment of culturally diverse personnel: stage artists, backstage and front-of-house staff. But the real interest of this specific potential audience group could be attracted only with changes in the repertoire and the insertion of themes, issues, characters, language and other cultural markers in the stage action that immigrants and their descendants will recognise as their own, or related to their own cultural and social experience.

This shift could be achieved with classical works and modern ones and should be supplemented whenever possible by the commission of new work from authors and artists who have themselves issued from immigration. Various strategies, developed and tested to implement such a lasting commitment, will be further discussed in Chapter 7. Here it suffices to stress that the credibility of public theatre and the legitimacy of its public subsidy claim cannot be taken seriously with less than such commitment. It must involve artistic and human resources, educational and marketing departments and be championed by the leadership and the board of theatre organisations; lip-service to cultural diversity and some superficial adjustments in the marketing will not be enough. Only a comprehensive effort counts, sometimes described as a "4P approach" covering programming, partnership, personnel and public outreach. Theatre needs to engage with organisations of migrants or inhabitants of migrant origin and make them feel not just an intermediary, but also a partner. Insensitive, paternalistic personnel will not be able to create such a feeling. Much depends on the programme, which in itself needs to contain cultural markers that make it clear it does not just address the mainstream audience. And public outreach must contain a series of engaging gestures that convey the seriousness of purpose and continuity of effort, making it clear that it is not merely a short-term campaign.

Insufficient coping solutions

Public theatre professionals talk most willingly about the subsidy versus cost gap and various solutions for closing it, but they rarely want to question the institutional model and the patterns of production and distribution that perpetuate the gap. Globalisation has imposed the dominance of the financial perspective in debates on contemporary culture – hence the focus on the cost versus revenue issue and at the same time a reluctance of theatre people to acknowledge the fact that public theatre has become a minority option, one among many, in the deployment of people's leisure time. The harsh competition between public theatre and the cultural industry with its enormous output of digital products has caused some confusion, even bitterness among practitioners.

The paradox is that public theatre in Europe suffers from the cultural consequences of globalisation, visible chiefly in uniforming tendencies in cultural production and the forceful imposition of hits, fads and bestsellers; but, at the same time, public theatre suffers from the individualisation of taste and sensibilities, an emancipation process to which theatre has been catering since the Renaissance and that now works against it by making any envisaged audience opaque and diffused. In addition, migration has made the urban demography more heterogeneous and thus it is more difficult for public theatre to count on one coherent and discernible core audience. Both cultural uniformity and cultural diversity challenge the public theatre and force it to define its own specific cultural position more sharply than before, as well as delineating its field of action in terms of what other cultural producers and intermediaries cannot and will not do.

Instead, one sees often half-hearted coping approaches that in themselves cannot match the far-reaching challenges public theatre encounters, nor substantially consolidate its position. Several of these options can be quickly discussed in their limited effectiveness and inherent self-defeating outcomes:

- *Do nothing.* This is quite easy, especially for theatre companies and groups that are usually preoccupied with the next premiere, next tour and the next season. Mid-term future prospects thus remain neglected and continuity with the past is seen as a guarantee for a secure future. Marginalisation is internalised, re-framed as something inevitable, or blamed on incompetent politicians and civil servants who do not come to the rescue with more subsidy. The outcome is an internal culture of complaint and embitterment that negatively affects the creative process.
- *Hide behind the artistic process.* Making artistic works is of course the core business of a theatre. But if this focus on artistry leads to the neglect or suspension of contextual

analysis, if political, social, economic and cultural issues in the physical environment of the theatre organisation are not addressed, the theatre risks self-ghettoisation and institutional autism. Preoccupied with artistic matters only, the company or group risks neglecting their own audience and allowing a public perception of itself as a closed, self-centred enclave. Sooner or later, accusations of elitism will be raised and the subsidy flow will be jeopardised.

- *Imitate the commercial theatre.* This is the most common approach, undertaken in order to boost box-office revenue, quickly recognisable if one scans the repertoire offered, full of light comedies and musicals, or if one looks at the aggressive publicity material and at the production photos that show a trivial, if not vulgar acting style, borrowed from television sitcoms. On a short run, this approach might improve the box-office revenue, but the more indistinguishable from the commercial theatre the company or the venue becomes, the faster it loses any legitimacy in its expectation of continuing public subsidies.

- *Affiliate public theatre with a political or social movement or group.* This is what theatre in Europe did in the nineteenth century by jumping on the bandwagon of national ideologies and profiting through their promotion to a national theatre as a key institution of the nation. Today, nationalist politics – clearly on the rise to profit from the widespread anxieties caused by globalisation, EU integration, migration and the economic crisis – do not need theatre for promotion but seek to spread influence through the mass media. Nationalism in its predominant populist variant today lashes out at the non-commercial theatre as a playground of elites. Feminism, gay emancipation, environmentalism, human rights, solidarity with the unemployed, refugees, battered women, indigenous people – all worthy causes that mobilise the resources of civil society, could profit from some alliance with theatre and theatres could benefit from such association as well. Venues that are clearly focused on the cultural production in a migration context – such as Ballhaus Naunynstrasse in the Kreuzberg district of Berlin (www.ballhausnaunynstrasse.de) – have a clear audience pull. A starting theatre group could expect to profile itself with such an alliance and a sustained thematic focus of its own work, but later on this could become a limitation – artistically, politically and intellectually. For a larger theatre company such persistent political involvement in one cause would be interpreted as one-sided, excessively partisan and exclusive, and thus risks losing further public subsidies from culture and arts budgets. Besides, artists are not the most disciplined ideological foot soldiers and they would sooner or later experience politics, any issue-driven politics, as a restrictive rather than inspiring and sustaining force.

The inadequacy of these coping strategies becomes obvious when weighed against the changed expectations of the subsidy givers. As a condition for subsidy, public theatre faces, or will soon face, a more radical demand to demonstrate its relevance to the entire society, to prove that it has become more complex and diversified, and to address and involve various social and cultural groups, interconnect them and accommodate their preferences and agendas. It is quite probable that in the years to come artistic merit will not be enough to secure public funding and that theatres will be subsidised on the basis of their capacity to connect artistic exploration with societal issues and enhance a public debate on them. By expanding and strengthening the participatory basis of a deliberative democracy, public theatre could be rewarded for building social capital and enhancing social cohesion. This is obviously a tall order that goes beyond mere partial coping approaches and requires some alternation of prevailing production and distribution models, consideration of the prevailing output forms and rethinking of programming templates, a sort of systemic change. It is therefore necessary to examine these essential models and probe their transforming potential.

Chapter 3

Production Models: Reps, Groups and Production Houses

I n this chapter repertory theatres and autonomous theatre groups are considered as two distinct models of theatre production made possible by public funding. Numerous variants and in-between options are taken into account, as the analysis seeks to point out their mutual influences, emerging trends and transformation options.

Repertory theatre: Limitations and adjustments

The model of a repertory theatre company as established and affirmed by MXAT, the Moscow Art Theatre, since 1898 marked many artistic theatre developments throughout the twentieth century and has been replicated with small variations in hundreds of companies. The idea of a theatre company with a strong artistic leader shaping a recognisable aesthetic profile, working with a fixed ensemble of actors, as well as administrative and technical staff, in their own building with one or more stages, with their own workshops and production facilities, and counting on a regular, diverse audience – that idea dominates the theatre landscape of German-speaking countries and much of Central, Eastern and Northern Europe even today. With some modifications and specific features, it also appears in Western and Southern Europe, but less often and not as the main model. This type of company is called a repertory theatre because the same group of artists and other collaborators produces a number of premieres in a season and presents them in a rotating or sequential schedule.

The model is based on the assumption that the company can sustain a permanent ensemble of actors, belonging to various generations, and that those actors will stay with the company for several seasons, if not for most of their working life, learning from each other and growing artistically from small roles to larger responsibilities in the repertoire. A specific and recognisable stage style blends individual talents into a strong collective aesthetic profile, reinforced by one director, or a few regular ones. The productions are expected to be so successful that they create a strong demand and remain in the repertoire for several seasons, some to be performed a hundred times or more.

In practice, most actors today have a rather dynamic and mobile idea of their own careers. They seek to work in various settings and with diverse partners and directors, as well as jumping from stage work into film and television engagements. Many feel a need to break away from permanent immersion in an ensemble, which could be experienced not only as familiar and comforting, but also as too hierarchical, predictable, stifling, too busy with planning and logistics and not sufficiently inspiring in the artistic sense. Especially actors from bigger cities feel that they have more options and need to pursue them.

Public demand for individual productions, however, has diminished in the past decades hence the productions increasingly tend to stay on the repertoire for just one season, perhaps two, but are then removed to make free slots in the schedule for new productions. Most companies now lack the means to sustain a large permanent ensemble of 20, 40 or even 60 actors that producing and keeping a large complex repertoire would require. In the companies that still offer permanent employment there are employed, salaried actors who hardly ever appear on the stage – the bigger the company, the higher the percentage of such "dead souls." It is difficult in larger companies to use all ensemble members optimally and keep them all busy with old and new roles from one month to the next. If the company creates not just five or eight productions in a season but 15 or even 25 on its own stages (as some larger German companies do), a long run for a successful production is an exception. Such a theatre inevitably becomes a production factory in which a strict planning regime overwhelms the creative process and alienates some actors, so that they are inclined to seek more concentration and fewer logistical pressures elsewhere.

Many companies are financially unable to sustain even a small ensemble throughout the entire season. They sign up only a core group of a few actors for the season and then cast them in several new productions, supplementing them with actors engaged for a single role in a specific production. In this case, a repertoire is more a season's packaged offer than a panoply of productions – older and more recent – sustained from one season to another.

The *rotating* repertoire, in which one can see a different production every evening, is a luxury that is becoming a rarity. It means building and striking a production set and rearranging stage lights every day, or at least several times a week if the same production stays for a few evenings and then comes back for a few more evenings the next month or later in the season. A *sequential* repertoire has become more common, with one or perhaps two productions replaced with new work after running for a few weeks.

Those repertory companies that guarantee a subscription system are even more restricted in their work because they make a commitment before the start of the season to put on several productions, with performances specified by date, announced and sold to subscribers in advance. Consequently, a theatre has to maintain a schedule of performances regardless of their success and the demand they generate, with little opportunity to add extra performances of the most successful productions to the monthly programme, and practically no possibility of withdrawing the less successful productions from the rep schedule or reducing the number of performances. In this sense, repertory companies are rigid and slow-motion systems that find it hard to shift course, since it is set far in advance through a commitment of human and material resources and detailed planning of the usage of available capacities, both on the stage and in the production workshops. And yet, the ultimate product – a production – is always volatile and unpredictable in its outcome, quality and audience appeal. The option available to the National Theatre in London, to move a successful production out of its repertory schedule and relaunch it on commercial terms in the West End for an open-ended run, is not feasible for other repertory companies elsewhere in Europe. The best thing they can do with a successful production is to move it for the next season from a small stage to a bigger one, where it can be seen by a larger audience and increase box-office income.

A repertory theatre company needs to synchronise several simultaneous processes within the same organisation: rehearsals of new productions, the making of costumes and sets for productions that will premiere in a few months, the run of already-premiered productions in a pre-set schedule at the home venue and on tour, and preparations for the forthcoming season. Technical, logistical and creative processes are interdependent and sometimes at odds with each other, while in parallel the externally focused process of communication and marketing operation seeks to create interest among a potential audience for both the productions that are still in preparation (and thus uncertain in outcome) as well as for the productions that are already running. Capacity bottlenecks are difficult to avoid and certain employees or departments and work units end up being busier and more in demand than others. Under these conditions, sending one of the company productions on tour, to a foreign festival, for instance, could be appealing in terms of the prestige and professional satisfaction the trip offers – it may even be financially attractive – but it cannot fail to disrupt the entire planning process at home. Those who go abroad to present a production just twice and stay away for four days disrupt ongoing rehearsals of new productions and make other productions impossible to run at home.

One would think that the theatre would perhaps be happy under such circumstances to host another company – local, regional, national or foreign – for a few evenings, but this rarely happens. Repertory companies are not especially hospitable and do not like to mix their own repertoire offer with the productions of others. They are also struggling to meet their own targets of performances played, tickets sold and income generated; moreover, hosting another company incurs higher expenses than box-office receipts would bring in. Consequently, repertory companies rarely travel and take little account of travel when conceptualising new productions in terms of technical complexity and the volume of the stage set. If they are invited to a festival, they expect the public authorities to come up with additional subsidy to pick up the bill.

A German repertory theatre company is always ready to attend the Theatertreffen in Berlin (www.theatertreffen.com), if selected for this prestigious review of the best German-speaking drama productions, because it determines prestige and advances institutional and individual reputations. If the company goes abroad, to a foreign festival, it usually expects the hosts to pay a fee and the travel costs or, if this is impossible, the Goethe-Institut (www.goethe.de) is called upon to cover the tour budget because the company is thought to be representing German culture abroad. In the past, the British Council (www.britishcouncil.org) supported long international tours of UK repertory companies, with productions of Shakespeare specially adjusted for touring perceived as an ideal vehicle for enhancing the prestige of the UK through its theatre culture. This is a disappearing practice, however, since governments seek cheaper and more effective means of implementing their "cultural diplomacy" objectives.

Repertory companies outlive communism

Repertory companies were practically the sole model of professional performing arts in the communist countries of Central and Eastern Europe before 1989. They had to submit their repertoire plans for advance approval to the ministries of culture, and for every premiere they were subjected to preventive government and Communist Party censorship that often imposed changes to both the dialogue and the stage action; in more dramatic cases premieres were postponed and further substantial revisions of the production were ordered, or an outright ban pronounced. On some occasions censorship intervened even after the premiere, judging the audience reactions to some scenes and dialogue inappropriate and subversive. In return for this regime of close scrutiny, repertory theatre companies not only offered permanent employment to actors, administrative and technical staff, kept directors, designers and dramaturgs on a salary, and engaged others as well-paid freelancers, but also commissioned new plays and translations of foreign works, assured of a steady flow of public subsidy. There was hardly any competition and no commercial theatre (Klaic 2009).

> Agnieszka Holland's feature film *Provincial Actors* (*Aktorzy prowincjonalni*, 1979) offers a satirical view of a Polish rep company in the provinces, seeking to attract metropolitan attention and praise through the staging of a national classic and the engagement of a young director from Warsaw. The limitations of the provincial environment seem insurmountable, the actors are weak and insecure, the director is pretentious but inexperienced, and the technicians totter about in a constant drunken stupor. The artistic ambitions get lost in clouds of cigarette smoke, among more and more empty vodka bottles, and the fiasco at the premiere is shown as the inevitable product of provincial culture. Today the film is a powerful testimony of the provincial theatre culture under communism.

An unofficial alternative emerged in the 1960s in Poland, Czechoslovakia, Hungary and Yugoslavia, in some non-professional or semi-professional groups, often composed of university students. They combined artistic experimentation with a disguised, allusive critique of the political system and of social hypocrisy, seeking to expand the standardised repertoire and create their own production material. More radical than the repertory companies, these groups had a limited outreach and less visibility, but enjoyed a small, loyal following and found some material support in amateur cultural associations and university cultural centres. When assaulted or even closed down by the repressive mechanisms of the regime, their idiosyncratic, critical energy was quickly resurrected in another group, or re-emerged in the next generation.

After the collapse of communism, the theatre system changed little but the subsidy flow was sharply reduced. The repertory theatres sought to work in the old manner, now happily free of censorship interference, and to survive with much less public funding, so increasingly they relied on extra money earned by subletting space and with more commercial elements in their offer, as described in the previous chapter. In the meantime, their cultural context was sharply altered by an avalanche of commercial cultural industry products; radical alternatives for family budgets represented by newly available travel opportunities and new consumer passions; and the socio-economic stratification of previously rather homogeneous societies. Autonomous theatre groups and commercial theatre endeavours appeared as direct competitors (Stefanova 2000; Popescu 2000). In the mid-1990s there were over 600 subsidised repertory companies in Central and Eastern Europe and more than 450 in the former USSR, each producing between 1 and 16 new productions per year and keeping 100,000 to 150,000 people in permanent employment (Klaic 1997). Some of these companies, especially in the newly independent countries that had once been parts of the USSR, such as Moldavia and Ukraine, but also in Albania, became practically dysfunctional owing to the fact that dramatically reduced and often delayed subsidies meant the quality and quantity of the output dwindled down to almost nothing. But at the same time, exceptionally, some repertory companies achieved a substantial improvement in overall management, logistical support and planning as well as in communication and marketing, acquiring fund-raising skills and joining international theatre networks such as the European Theatre Convention (ETC) and European Theatre Union (ETU), even starting to run their own international festivals at the beginning or the end of the theatre season. The theatre in Sibiu, Romania (www.sibfest.ro), acquired international acclaim with productions directed by Andrei Serban and Silviu Purcarete, while in Warsaw, Poland, Krzysztof Warlikowski and Grzegorz Jarzyna took the Theatre Rozmaitosci, now better known as TR (www.trwarszawa.pl), on frequent international tours, with both directors being invited as guests by other European companies and opera houses. Slovensko Mladinsko Gledališče in Ljubljana, Slovenia, originally an ensemble for children's theatre, transformed itself into a rep for adults in the 1980s, and has frequently toured Latin America.

Hardly any rep companies have disbanded in the 20 years since the end of communism, even though some – those beyond redemption – actually deserved such a fate. That this inefficient, oversized and by and large dysfunctional system of repertory companies has continued to stagger along indicates the strong failure of political will in the new democracies to innovate their cultural policies and tackle the inherited performing arts system. Instead, they have accepted dispensing public subsidies, much reduced by inflation and budgetary and monetary reforms, to the regular recipients, on the basis of habit and routine or historical record, and without any re-assessment. Much of the public money available is inevitably wasted on moribund institutions instead of supporting new, promising initiatives and organisations. Aggressive protests come from the repertory theatre sector whenever the authorities signal an intention to undertake even a tepid reform. The repertory theatre leaders appear as gatekeepers seeking to preserve their privileged positions in relation to other less institutionalised colleagues and initiatives, and together with unions and professional associations, actively seek to block reform processes, usually meeting with success. Very quickly the minister of culture is changed and the reformist ideas and plans are put aside. Peter Inkei's analysis of cultural policies in post-communist countries reveals more continuity than discontinuity, more effort to sustain the inherited infrastructure than to make it more effective through institutional and systemic reform (Inkei 2009).

In public and professional debates, the systematic and structural problems of the repertory companies have been misinterpreted as down to *personnel* ("Give us a good manager who can run the theatre properly and knows how to find much needed extra cash!"), or as a *budgetary* issue ("All is well but could be even better with some extra subsidy."). A *legislative fallacy* appeared with the widespread belief among theatre professionals that if politicians would come up with a comprehensive theatre law, the entire performing arts system would be automatically revitalised and transformed, as if with a magic wand, into a state of prosperity and artistic excellence. In reality, drafting theatre laws is used to secure existing privileges for the future and exclude or weaken possible competitors. Where ministries of culture have pushed such laws through the legislative process, ministries of finance have withheld most of the subsidies needed to enact the legal provisions.

Paradoxically, politicians who have shut down hundreds of factories and laid off hundreds of thousands of workers have displayed a strange reluctance to act on repertory companies, fearing they will be attacked as cultural barbarians and pronounced traitors of national culture. As an appeasement gesture, political elites have made funds available for refurbishment, technological upgrading and renovation projects, which have brought some of the venues up to the level of EU safety norms and increased the comfort of the audience – but also provided ample opportunities for graft and pilfering. Many venues have turned out to be too big for the shrunken interest in theatre, so that impoverished companies have difficulties sustaining them through the winter and paying heating and electricity costs. Regional and national tours by repertory companies, once especially subsidised by the communist authorities, have become practically impossible because of the prohibitive costs. Smaller towns have suffered from dramatically reduced and discontinuous theatre programming, dependent on external supply, usually an occasional tour of small-scale commercial programmes.

> The renovation of the opera house in Odessa (opera.odessa.ua) took 12 years and returned historic glory to the venerable building, but left the artistic product unchanged, mediocre and rather old-fashioned. The thorough restoration of the Bolshoi Theatre (www.bolshoi. ru) in Moscow started in 2005 and finished in 2011, costing 16 times the amount originally budgeted. This has pitted the City of Moscow and the Ministry of Culture against each other over the control of the renovation process, caused parliamentary inquiries and a barrage of accusations of graft and embezzlement, a prolonged drama comparable to the rebuilding of La Fenice Opera in Venice (www.teatrolafenice.it) destroyed by arson in 1996 all the way up to its reopening in 2003.

The study of the prospects for repertory companies in the post-communist transition in Eastern and Central Europe (Klaic 1997) concluded that the inherited one-model system is unsustainable and that it will be diversified in due time, more by default and through decay than by focused policy intervention and artistic innovation. Several future scenarios, which were sketched out have by and large been fulfilled. Few repertory theatre companies have maintained or acquired excellence and reputation on a par with the Katona Jozsef

Theatre (katonajozsefszinhaz.hu) in Budapest or the New Riga Theatre (www.jrt.lv) of Alvis Hermanis. Far more companies have slid into commercialisation, while still officially maintaining a non-profit status and (inadequate) public subsidies. Some have embarked on illegal activities, such as money laundering for dubious sponsors, and created black funds for a variety of private purposes. Radical transformation from a rep ensemble into an open venue has proved the exception rather than the rule. The Archa Theatre in Prague (www. archatheatre.cz) let the entire ensemble of the former Burian Divadlo go in order to become a presenter and producer – an almost unique evolutionary move.

Some production houses have emerged outside the repertory infrastructure, such as Trafó in Budapest (www.trafo.hu) and the Arts Printing House in Vilnius (www.menuspaustuve.lt), or Praktika in Moscow (www.praktikatheatre.ru). The logic of being a production house is still poorly understood and practical examples are few, so this model will receive additional attention later in this chapter.

If national authorities withdrew subsidies from some decaying repertory companies, municipal authorities most commonly failed to prop them up, claiming lack of revenue. This was the case in Bulgaria in the 1990s, where several ensembles were disbanded and their venues, with only a skeleton staff left, became spaces to hire for any kind of event, thus weakening or eliminating their previous cultural purpose.

Many directors, musicians, singers and dancers have moved abroad, mainly westward, especially from Bulgaria, Romania, Albania, Moldavia and the former Yugoslavia. New autonomous groups have proliferated and enlivened the artistic constellation – only in Poland there are more than 500 of them. Their rapid growth has forced public authorities to create project subsidy schemes, and some of these groups have initiated and mobilised alternative performance venues and created their own circuits for touring and cooperation, often working with international festivals.

What was postulated in 1997 as a set of possible future scenarios for the state of the performing arts after the fall of communism can be interpreted today as a set of ongoing trends, and even applied selectively to the condition of repertory theatre in the rest of Europe. The difficulties experienced by the repertory theatre model in Central and Eastern Europe have little to do with the painful inheritance of communism, or with the turbulence of the post-communist transition; they are more related to the contradictions in cultural productions in globalised capitalism expanding across Europe. Moreover, these difficulties signal in a sharp, dramatic manner the structural problems of public theatre in Europe as discussed in the previous chapter, and more specifically of the repertory theatre model. Extreme poverty, collective demoralisation and political neglect make the decay of a provincial repertory company in Ukraine or Albania appear as specific, yet it is only different *in degree* but not *in kind* from the problems of repertory companies in Finland, Spain, Greece or some other wealthier countries in other regions of Europe that do not share the communist past. Owing to multiple pressures and restrictions, the repertory theatre model is in the process of transition and adjustment in many countries, with quite common instances of decay and impasse. In some places this indicates a systemic erosion; this is true in Italy, for instance, where the municipal and regional authorities, in partnership with the local banking foundations, have not managed to compensate for the meltdown in national art subsidies.

Groups: An ethos of innovation

In contrast to the dense institutionalised infrastructure of repertory theatre companies and of presenting and producing venues in Europe, there is a dispersed archipelago of thousands of theatre groups, semi-professional and professional, some quite informal, others set up as associations or non-profit organisations, many with decades of remarkable history. Most groups were established by determined artistic pioneers and innovators with a strong vision, who recruited followers and believers and developed and implemented a specific aesthetic from one production to another. Other groups have been set up by friends, colleagues and peers who shared a common analysis of the prevailing state of theatre in their immediate environment and a certain frustration with it to which they wanted to respond with an alternative theatre idea and practice based on experimentation. Groups emerged from a feeling of resentment towards both commercial and public institutional theatre, the former because of its commercial purpose, the latter because it has been perceived as a conventional, mainstream and apparently bureaucratised Moloch. The truth is that some mainstream performing arts organisations are in fact former rebellious groups that have grown and undergone institutionalisation – thanks to public acceptance and the access they gained to public subsidies.

From the end of the nineteenth century, experimental theatre groups relied on the fostering and elementary support of various avant-garde movements and coteries, interacting with poets, artists and musicians, as well as with small publishers and magazines. After World War II, groups proliferated in Western Europe, which fed on the chamber theatre movement, and later on the cultural revolution of the 1960s and 1970s, the countercultural streams and subcultural constellations. Some were inspired by experimental US groups that toured Europe because they could not secure their survival at home, such as the Living Theatre, Open Theater, The Performance Group and Bread and Puppet. Many European groups disbanded rather quickly, or faded away once their generational support-circle declined, but many achieved longevity and went through multiple transformations. Across the decades, theatre groups have not only been a platform for innovative practices, but also a lab that shaped, equipped and propelled many artists, who later found their vocation in other performing arts models and embarked on their own long march through the institutions, to become ultimately prominent leaders of larger companies, venues and festivals.

Since the mid-1960s one stream of groups has come from European universities, capturing students' passion for theatre experimentation but also articulating generational social criticism and the politics of anti-authoritarian protest. Another stream emerged from the theatre experiments of political and economic migrants and their offspring, displaced across Western Europe by decolonisation, seeking to articulate their identity, pursuits and dilemmas on stage. Further theatre groups emerged from the feminist and gay liberation movements, setting themselves up in the struggle for emancipation and against discrimination. A significant aspect of theatre groups has been an insistence on the development of their own specific theatre language in opposition to the traditional and dominant textuality and the practice of scrupulous play staging. Physical theatre, movement theatre, the search for ritual effects and, later, the obsession with new-media applications created a series of aesthetic waves, theatre families, clans and tribes, studios and laboratories, inspired by Antonin Artaud and Bertolt Brecht, by Herbert Marcuse, Frantz Fanon and Guy Debord, but also by Germaine Greer, Edward Said and Jacques Lacan (Schino 2009). Those with the most influence were theatre innovators themselves, such as Jerzy Grotowski, followed by his friend Eugenio Barba of the Odin Theatre and the Nordic Theatre Laboratory in Holstebro (DK), not to mention Peter Brook, who in 1971 switched from a successful career in the British theatre mainstream to international and intercultural experimentation in his International Centre for Theatre Research in Paris (Kustow 2005, www.bouffesdunord.com).

Successful groups were able to cope with poverty, marginalisation, public indifference and critical incomprehension, chiefly because they were nurtured by the strength of their own theatre ideas and aspirations. They could live with the discontinuity of public appearance as long as they could sustain a continuity of research, reflection and experimentation, as well as recruit new members and supporters. Their audience has always been small but has contained enthusiasts, friends, proselytisers and an occasional donor. Since the 1960s a parallel "alternative," "off" infrastructure has emerged across Europe to sustain and empower this movement, starting with venues that presented these groups regularly in an informal setting, festivals, workshops, seminars and occasional publications. Starting in the 1980s, networks and support and development organisations also grew up to make the theatre groups an international phenomenon, with many mutual connections, kinship and cooperative ventures. Gradually, the acceptance and acknowledgement of public authorities came along and created access to public subsidies, even if they remained meagre and incidental in most cases, disproportionately small when compared with the steady flow of much larger amounts going to the institutionalised repertory companies.

After the Soviet military intervention in Budapest in 1956, the Dutch Communist Party could not repair its damaged reputation nor sustain its formidable building on Amsterdam Keizersgracht 324. Lower floors were sublet to groups of experimental artists. That is how in the 1960s the Shaffy theatre emerged as a podium "where everything is possible" – at least until the venue went bankrupt in 1986 and the Communist Party disbanded itself (Gompes 2007). Similar experimental niches emerged in other European cities, as a sublet or squat, in abandoned or neglected spaces. The inhabitants sought each other out and connected mutually, establishing a growing international touring circuit, reinforced by the international student theatre festivals in Nancy, Erlangen, Wroclaw and Zagreb, which effectively broke the obstacles of the Iron Curtain. Belgrade International Theatre

Festival (BITEF) (www.bitef.rs) was set up in 1967 in Belgrade as a municipality-supported festival of new theatre trends. The Informal European Theatre Meeting (IETM) network of autonomous groups, venues and festivals (www.ietm.org) emerged in 1981 from the informal gatherings of their leaders, followed by many similar cooperative initiatives, such as Junge Hunde (bora-bora.dk/en/about-junge-hunde) and EON – European Off Network (www.freietheater.at).

Theatre groups have turned their poverty and small scale into an advantage by being very mobile and eager to travel in order to ensure proper working conditions and access to the audience. Today, however, their numbers have grown so much that every group inevitably competes for subsidy and exposure with many similar groups, on local, regional, national and international level. They remain dependent on the interest and good will of producers, presenters and festival programmers and approach the same public authorities, private foundations and international funds for financial support. Those that have realised a long standing desire to have their own studio, lab or a small venue, discover afterwards that a piece of real estate offers some comfort and flexibility but also imposes a heavy financial burden, and that by presenting only their own work they cannot always attract enough audience. Incidental subsidies do not assure continuity, do not even cover the basic overheads, and regular application rounds are experienced as a major hassle and distraction from the core artistic pursuits. In the vital matter of artistic growth, many groups experience difficulties as well, especially to avoid repetition, routine and the degradation of their own artistic language and style in a predictable set of clichés. The common danger of theatre groups is that they become self-centred, closely knit collectives that ultimately consume all the combined energy of their members and then collapse because they failed to absorb new impulses, ideas and talents from their surroundings. And yet, rare are those artists who are capable of making a radical gesture to disband, part ways or liquidate their primary artistic and social niche for the sake of a risky new beginning.

Post-communist Hungarian theatre produced very few new theatre groups outside the solid network of state-supported repertory companies in Budapest and major cities. Two such groups reached international recognition rather quickly, started intensive touring, made new productions with the backing of European co-producers and then both disappeared rather abruptly as a result of the frustration of their leaders, who experienced continuity as a burden and routine, and yet could not articulate plausible alternatives. Mozgó Ház/Moving House (www.mozgohaz.hu), led by the director László Hudi and manager Zoltan Imelyi, rested on the harmonious relationship between these two and was gone once that relationship soured. Krétakör Szinház/ Chalk Circle Theatre (www.kretakor.blog.hu), led by the director Arpad Schilling and manager Mate Gaspar, attempted to transform itself around 2008 into a community-based artistic initiative, working with high-school students and staging installations and happenings outside theatre spaces but effectively put its continuity at stake with the loss of visibility.

Some long-standing groups struggle with succession issues, since their founders and long-standing leaders have passed the usual retirement age and have not, even in their seventies, found heirs and successors to take their organisation to the next generation of artists and audiences, nor decided to terminate the enterprise after leading it for decades. This creates a dilemma for their funders, mainly public authorities: the veterans do not project a strong and sharp vision of their future development any longer, but at the same time they are too important, well-known and meritorious to be simply de-funded. The dilemma of funding agencies is aggravated by the growing pressure of newly established groups, competing for the same minuscule subsidy funds, and the pervasive cultural obsession with artistic innovation and emerging talent, which automatically puts at a disadvantage those groups that are still rhetorically committed to innovation and experimentation but are, at the same time, burdened with decades of experience. Many individual artists, who emerged in the group movement, such as Peter Stein or Peter Sellars, transcended this setting and found their place in the opposing infrastructure of large companies, venues and festivals, pursuing an international career from one production to another, shifting organisational contexts, empowered by considerable budgets and often working with a cohort of regular or reoccurring collaborators.

Pina Bausch died abruptly after a short illness in 2009 without any succession scenario for her Tanztheater Wupperthal (www.pina-bausch.de), in contrast to Merce Cunningham (www.mercecunningham.org/newwebsite/), who at the end of his long and productive life (1919–2009) came up with a clear legacy plan: a foundation to keep the copyright of his choreographies and supervise their staging, while his company was to be disbanded after one last farewell world tour. John Fox and Sue Gill wrapped up the Welfare State Company (1968–2006) (www.welfare-state.org) and created a new venture to stage contemporary civic spectacles and rituals (www.deadgoodguides.com). Odin Theatre (www.odinteatret.dk), Théâtre du Soleil (www.theatre-du-soleil.fr), Theater a.d Ruhr (www.theater-an-der-ruhr.de), identified since their inception with their leaders, have not announced succession plans.

There has always been a great divergence in the structure, organisation, working dynamics and temperament of theatre groups, their inner coherence and the interdependence of their members. With artistic growth come new aspirations, opportunities and predilections of some members, which cannot any longer be contained by the group's identity and working process. Factions emerge, fight, split, restructure on their own terms or disband. Groups change name, place, associates, members and leaders. Their evolution is more frequently a tumultuous, convulsive succession of distinctive phases, shifts, breaks and jumps rather than a straight line of consistent artistic process under more or less steady conditions and leadership. In some cases, the group moves into the background, serves as a shared facility for various activities of its members, a common and well-known brand to invoke in autonomous projects, a convenient legal entity and subsidy applicant and recipient.

The Catalan group La Fura dels Baus (www.lafura.com) emerged from street performances in the 1970s, rose to prominence when it opened the Barcelona

Olympics in 1992, developed and toured a great number of spectacular productions, which became increasingly more violent and deceptive, often staged in hangars and warehouses. Today it operates in several branches and teams, offering courses and seminars, producing mega-spectacles, staging corporate promotional events, and working for major European opera houses, such as the Paris Bastille (www.operadeparis.fr) and English National Opera (www.eno.org) in London (Purcell 2009). Within a much shorter period, three graduates of "applied theatre studies" (Institut für Angewandte Theaterwissenschaft) at the University of Giessen (www.uni-giessen.de/theater), Helgard Haug, Stefan Kaegi and Daniel Wetzel, created Rimini Protokoll (www.rimini-protokoll.de) in 2000 and, after working together on a series of social reality projects, nowadays often work solo or in duo under the same name, collaborating with festivals, production houses and groups. Footsbarn Theatre (footsbarn.com), a nomadic group originally from Cornwall, eventually settled in rural Auvergne in central France and created a training and documentation centre there in 1991. They undertook long expeditions across Europe and other continents, performing in a portable tent, but in 2010 appeared for weeks in large commercial venues in European cities, between such shows as *Crazy Shopping, Ben Bril Boxing Gala, Vienna Operetta Gala* and *Spamalot*.

Transformation dynamics

Repertory theatre companies and autonomous groups appear to belong to two opposing, quite different worlds. In practice, those differences are less striking, especially as both models have been influencing each other for quite a long time. Artists have been crossing over from one realm to another and both have been under pressure to re-examine and modify their initial features and ideological postulates in order to strengthen their sustainability. The most obvious difference between them is one of scale and degree of institutionalisation; the number of employees or collaborators engaged in a production; and the degree of labour specialisation and functional hierarchy that size brings with it. The intensive serial production model of the reps stands against the slow emergence of a single production in a group, where the next production might follow only in a year, after the previous one has been performed as many times as possible.

Both models operate with a structural dependence on public subsidy (albeit of different scales) and find it increasingly difficult to lock a specific audience group into their specific aesthetics. Professionals working in both models are discovering that their commitment to artistic purpose no longer automatically assures sufficient legitimacy and social acceptance, and both types are being weakened and marginalised by the overwhelming assault of commercial cultural goods, both digital and industrial, whose consumption takes up most of people's available leisure time and with which they can hardly compete. Both the repertory companies and the autonomous groups, as well as all the transitional variants between them, struggle with the risk of institutional and artistic fatigue whilst seeking, each in its own way, to articulate and convey to the public their distinctive artistic features. Inevitably, this is a frustrating effort because artistic ambitions always surpass the public funds available and the audience remains amorphous, unstable, quite unpredictable and fickle in its own predilections and idiosyncrasies.

Repertory theatres tend to care more about tradition, basking in their own institutional mythology, while groups tend in principle to take a more experimental approach, although their inherent vulnerability leads them quite easily into opportunistic entrapment. The mutual influence of these two models leads to a further hybridisation. Between the model of a large repertory company, doing 15 productions a season for a big and a small stage, and a group that brings out a new production once a year, there are of course numerous organisational and production variants and subtypes articulated in practice. They connect these two models more than their affiliate artists are often willing to admit, and unify them in a shared anxiety about the inroads made by all sorts of commercial theatre. Within a national theatre system, both models tend to snub and belittle each other, the dominance of one making the existence of the other difficult, if not impossible.

When the Dutch system of several municipal rep companies collapsed after Action Tomato in 1969, the Dutch theatre landscape was resettled by a growing number of small theatre initiatives, collectives and groups that secured small, incidental government subsidies. After 1989 the most established and appreciated among them could receive subsidies in a four-year cycle, while the other groups depended on incidental, one-year and two-year grants. Such a group makes two to six productions a year, engaging actors for a few weeks of rehearsals and usually a two-month run, in the course of which the productions are performed around 40 times in different venues. The Netherlands now have no repertory companies or ensemble culture, but many short-lived productions, made possible by small, efficient production core teams, led by a theatre director as the artistic leader and a business manager counterpart, who engage all the other collaborators and ensure post-premiere touring in a dense network of venues, subsidised by the municipalities. A highly productive system of huge output and great mobility, fitting a small, densely populated country with good infrastructure and communications. Productions are made to travel easily and appear in different venues from day to day but because of this intensive mobility some groups cannot build stronger ties with the audience and reinforce their name recognition.[1] In contrast, Germany has some 300 repertory theatre companies operating with the support of cities and regional governments, and 84 opera companies, which are autonomous organisations or part of the municipal or regional theatre structure, with a chorus, an orchestra and singers engaged for the entire season. Very few of these companies have less than 100 permanent employees and some have more than 800. The system employs some 45,000 people and costs €2bn, a quarter of public subsidies for culture (Walter 2010). Each season sees a large number of productions made. Against this impressive system are ranged numerous free groups (Freie Gruppen), which can only occasionally count on some very meagre municipal subsidy. They are structurally condemned to stagnation in poverty and dilettantism, because the rep system attracts almost all the money and media attention, all the top talent and a large majority of the public.

One example: Hessisches Staatstheater in Wiesbaden (www.staatstheater-wiesbaden.de), the capital of the federal state of Hessen with a population of 275,000, but definitely not a metropolis like Berlin, Hamburg or Munich, is quite close to the mighty theatre centre of Frankfurt and to Mainz and Darmstadt with their own rep companies. This Wiesbaden theatre has produced 30 new productions in the 2008–2009 season, gave 40 concerts, performed 41 productions from previous seasons, and counted over 322,000 visitors at 950 performances in 11 different performing spaces in the town. The average seat-occupancy was 76.8 per cent, including 31 performances given abroad. Additionally, 4,000 visitors attended free events, such as discussions and lectures, and 13,000 took part in school programmes and other educational activities. Each year the theatre organises a May festival that in 2009 included 40 performances from 14 countries and had 22,000 visitors. In addition, every second year the theatre organises a well-loved Neue Stücke international festival (the next one in June 2012) (www.newplays.de). After such an intensive season, over 600 employees take six weeks' summer holiday, but the formal opening of the season occurs at the beginning of September and several premieres follow in that month alone.

In Romania, a much poorer country than Germany, the National Theatre in Bucharest (www.tnb.ro) keeps over 50 different productions in its repertoire played in 4 halls, with the number of seats ranging from 75 to 1114, using an ensemble of 115 permanent actors and 32 guest actors. It produces 12 premieres in a season, offers over 600 performances, sells over 207,000 tickets, and plays 20 performances on tour in the country and abroad. This is without doubt a huge enterprise, whose overheads are covered mainly by state subsidies since the ticket prices vary between RON 10 and RON 50 (€2.35–€11.75), so that the box-office income is a small fraction of the budget.

One could look at these statistics with admiration and respect, even envy; or resent them as examples of the industrialisation of public cultural production pressured by the subsidy flow to produce more and more and thus turn theatre into a "culture factory." A rep company is a finely calibrated operation, all geared to specific outputs in precisely determined time-slots. Consequently, the artistic process risks being overwhelmed by the planning and logistics details of enormous complexity, which cannot tolerate improvisation, spontaneity, changes of mind or a crisis that would redraw the project, give it more time to mature or cause it to be abandoned altogether. In any case, "free" groups have little chance against such giants with huge output and audience pull. While Germany will in all probability remain a country with a dominant repertory theatre model – because it is anchored in tradition and the regions and the cities can still afford it for a while – the prospects are quite different in the rest of Europe where the erosion of this model is more advanced and where various hybrid forms of making and presenting stage work are emerging.

Mutual influences and the emergence of hybrid models are most evident in the Flemish theatre in Belgium. Here the traditional repertory theatre companies, set up after World War II as instruments of Flemish cultural and political emancipation and further strengthened by the federalisation of the country that empowered the Flemish community with cultural autonomy, have all been taken over and transformed by artists coming from the group movements that exploded in the 1970s and 1980s. In the 1990s, Koninklijke Nederlandse Schouwburg in Antwerp merged with the Blauwe Maandag group, led by Luk Perceval, who took over the new organisation. After his departure for Germany, Guy Cassiers created a consortium of several associate artists, each pursuing their own projects without a permanent ensemble, operating under the name Het Toneelhuis (www.toneelhuis.be). A protracted venue renovation destabilised and weakened Koninklijke Vlaamse Schouwburg (KVS) (www.kvs.be) in Brussels, but once it was taken over in 1999 by Jan Goossens, a one-time collaborator of Peter Sellars, this former bastion of Flemish culture and Dutch language in predominantly francophone Brussels became a centre for intercultural exploration, where several associate artists produce and co-produce a variety of work in Dutch, French, English, Turkish and Arabic, all with multilingual subtitling, causing some dissatisfaction among Flemish nationalist and cultural conservatives (Goossens et al. 2005). Nederlands Toneel Gent (www.ntgent.be) was taken over in 2005 by the director Johan Simons and his collaborators from the disbanded Dutch group ZT Hollandia and turned into a mixture of repertory company and production house that regularly co-produces with major foreign festivals and companies as well as hosts Wunderbaum (www.wunderbaum. nl), a group of younger artists. Following the departure of Simons to Munich to take on the leadership of the Kammerspiele repertory theatre (www.muenchner-kammerspiele. de) in 2010 Nederlands Toneel Gent got a new artistic leader, Wim Opbrouck.

On the basis of these developments, some ongoing trends can be tentatively delineated:

- Rep = Rep: The best and most successful repertory companies will probably remain repertory companies, with some flexibility added in season schedules and in the rotation and clustering of specific productions. It is difficult to imagine that some repertory companies with a long history and tradition-enhanced status, such as the Comédie-Française or the Burgtheater in Vienna or their counterparts in other capitals, which constitute the principal national theatres of their countries, could be significantly altered. Smaller ensembles put together for a single season with more reliance on guest actors, hired only for a specific production, are to be expected, as has been the practice of the National Theatre in London and the Royal Shakespeare Company. Besides the multitude of repertory companies in Germany, sustainable for some time at least and especially strong in large cities, there will be at least one repertory company with reasonable life insurance in the capitals of other Northern, Central and Eastern European countries, vacillating between mediocrity and excellence, but assured of continuous public funding.

- Rep → Booking House: Financially and quality-wise impoverished repertory theatre companies will stick to the existing model through fear of any alternatives and ultimately lose both the company and the repertoire. More able members will abandon them and so will the audience since their production output will dwindle to insignificance. Especially in smaller places, repertory companies are very vulnerable and practically unsustainable. When they go out of business, that is, get de-funded and disbanded, what remains is the playhouse that will in the worst-case scenario remain dark or become a booking venue – a hall anyone can hire for an evening or longer, for whatever purpose, with some skeleton technical and administration staff, and quite uncertain cultural purpose and function.
- Spin-off/Adoption: Some repertory companies will spin off autonomous groups that will detach themselves and seek more diverse production and performing conditions elsewhere, perhaps treating the original rep company as a safe home base to which they will sometimes return. Other repertory companies will adopt outside groups – as NTGent has adopted Wunderbaum – or occasionally bring other groups in for shorter cooperative projects and special niche productions in order to diversify their own programming offer and appeal to specific target groups in the audience, as the Vienna Burgtheater, with 140 permanently employed actors (www.burgtheater.at), brought Jan Lauwers and his Needcompany (www.needcompany.org) from Brussels as artists-in-residence in the 2010–2011 season. The Burgtheater's Intendant (i.e. General Manager) Matthias Hartmann voiced an expectation that the Needcompany will help his ensemble chart a new artistic course as he has incorporated the Needcompany productions into the regular programme. As a debut, Jan Lauwers and the ensemble presented Needlab 16, which includes a foretaste of the feature film-to-be, *Dead Deer Don't Dance* (Needcompany 2009).
- Programmed Venue: Audiences prefer to see a diversified programme offer in a venue they like and trust, so the repertory companies that control and jealously guard their own venue and reserve it exclusively for their own productions might face more competition from more diversely programmed venues. In such a public facility an artistic presenter equipped with taste, programming concepts, a good network and a programming budget can bring in a diverse mix of companies, genres, styles and forms inviting both domestic and foreign productions for one or a few evenings. Such venues are quite numerous in Europe and also function as facilities created in the widespread network of cultural centres that provide other cultural programmes and services (such as exhibitions, debates and lectures, film screenings, a library, etc.) and might become even more widespread because they are in a better state to create a programming mix for a heterogeneous public than a repertory company, as well as being able to successfully vary programming templates and formats.
- Production House: Some successful and well-subsidised presenters of programmed venues are deciding to go one step further and produce and co-produce new work rather than just shop around and bring in what they like for an evening or two. They

seek to establish a more intensive association with artists they like and trust, enabling them to make new productions or work with other artists with whom they feel an aesthetic kinship. These could be individuals, asked to compose their own team and cast around a project, or groups brought in for a residence to perform some older work and make a new production at the same time. Another way for the production house to emerge is from the transformation of a repertory company, as at KVS Brussels, where there is no ensemble any longer but the artistic leader chooses several artists with whom to develop one or more productions in the course of two to four years, each of them engaging another team of collaborators. The artistic leader of a production house also works to ensure that productions made in his house go on tour elsewhere, after or during the run. English theatres outside London – in Sheffield, Liverpool, Bristol, Plymouth and elsewhere – no longer operate as ensembles but have opted for a mixed model, where they create their own productions, invite groups in residence, co-produce with groups and festivals and host touring productions. Hebbel am Ufer in Berlin (www.hebbel-am-ufer.de) with its three stages (HAU 1, HAU 2, HAU 3) sees its role chiefly as presenter of international work but occasionally appears as a producer of young talent, as a co-producer, an organiser of concerts, debates and lectures, and even as a partner of the Komische Oper (www.komische-oper-berlin.de). In France, organisations designated as national drama centres do not have the means to operate as repertory companies with a permanent ensemble but produce a series of productions in cooperation with other similar organisations in other cities and regions, pulling budgets and talent and intensifying touring. Festivals are increasingly resembling production houses because they are initiating and (co)producing their own new stage work in association with selected artists and groups, other festivals, production houses and programmed venues.

- Groups: These benefit from the growth of programmed venues and production houses but suffer from stronger competition from other groups. Fewer groups will be able to sustain themselves in a small venue that they control, and will come under mounting pressure to travel more and further in order to secure enough performances and production support for new work in association with production houses and festivals. Some less tightly knit groups already function as a pool, a consortium or a loose association, whose members engage in diverse individual projects with other artists elsewhere, as La Fura dels Baus and Rimini Protokoll do.

This ongoing transformative dynamic shapes a more complex landscape of producing and performing opportunities and affects the position of actors and other artists who are less able to count on continuous engagement, either in a repertory ensemble or in a group. Many performing artists are already shifting their professional circumstances by working for the stage and for film and television, collaborating with commercial producers, working in advertising, taking part in educational projects, developing their own solo work, teaming up with different colleagues and groups. Theatre directors, playwrights, set-, costume- and lighting designers, composers and even dramaturgs operate increasingly as freelancers, gravitating perhaps to some producing organisations and having some privileged associations with a few others. Actors, designers, composers and dramaturgs are quite dependent on theatre directors, who repeatedly invite them to collaborate on a new project carried out in some other place. They seek to reduce this dependence by creating and developing their own projects and taking director's prerogatives on themselves.

Since the second half of the twentieth century, when in many parts of Europe the notion of the actor harmoniously integrated into the permanent ensemble of a repertory theatre was more or less the norm, another career pattern has prevailed, as a study of the Vlaams Theater Instituut (VTI) (www.vti.be) notes (VTI 2007): the actor has become a theatre-maker, appearing in various working associations, reconnecting with a small group of close peers, changing media outlets and occasionally passing the boundary between subsidised and commercial arts, cultural production and education, art and business. The notion of a fixed, small autonomous group, united around a founder-leader and led by his or her aesthetic programme, is also under increased pressure.

There is a growing individualisation of artistic identity observable across all performing arts professions, with their working relationship becoming multiple and of a temporary nature, facilitated by a growing number of production houses, presenting venues and festivals, which themselves often cooperate and co-produce. These changes indicate a commodification of performing artists and their work on a globalised market that encompasses both commercial and non-profit organisations. Despite enhanced mobility and opportunity to work beyond national borders, competition is increasing since the work opportunities remain limited. Permanent contracts for actors and other artistic professions are being phased out across Europe and a patchwork of temporary contracts and engagements cannot hide the frequent discontinuity of career development, periods of unemployment, income drop and loss, and a general precariousness, characteristic for artists in other domains as well. Not all national social security systems are equipped to deal with these gaps and discontinuities, and for the artists working in several national systems, inconsistencies and differences among the systems and their provisions create additional socio-economic problems and act as obstacles to artistic mobility (Polacek 2007; Staines 2007).

Note

1   At the time of writing, it could not be foreseen that drastic budget cuts becoming effective in 2013 would fundamentally upset the current arts subsidy system in The Netherlands, both on the national and the municipal level.

Chapter 4

The Specific Offer of Public Theatre

P roduction and distribution models as discussed in the previous chapter provide only a framework for public theatre to fulfil its specific mandate. What types of spectacle, what genres and what impacts are the primary remit of non-commercial theatre? Non-commercial theatre must delineate its mandate in contrast to commercial theatre and thus accent the features the latter leaves aside in order to focus on profit-making entertainment: experimentation, innovation and stimulation of public debate. In a programming sense, this means that public theatre covers dramatic theatre, based on both classic and contemporary plays; post-dramatic theatre that is not driven by dramatic literature; opera and contemporary forms of musical theatre; classical ballet and contemporary dance; theatre for children and young people; and other idiosyncratic forms. These categories are examined in this chapter for their strengths and weaknesses and for the specific issues they invoke, not with the intention of outlining the major aesthetic trends but in order to postulate the key features of public theatre output.

The emergence of the theatre director as the crucial artistic profession in dramatic theatre, with a decisive role in shaping a spectacle, reinforced the autonomy of theatre as art and weakened its connection with literature. Directorial artistic strategies affirmed the staging of a play as an autonomous, collective act in which the subtle artistic decisions of the director, actors and all collaborators shape a complex work of art, open to multiple interpretations. The question of the fidelity of a theatre production to a play on which it is based, as traditionalists like to put it, is in fact disparaging for both drama and theatre. It assumes that the play has only one meaning and thus only one possible and legitimate mode of staging, thus reducing the idea of a stage creation to a prescribed, supposedly proper transaction from the text to the stage, as if it were a matter of mechanical, linear transposition. Every dramatic text implies a range of staging strategies rather than prescribing only one. With the dominance of a director as a separate profession throughout the twentieth century, the friction between the play as a staging material and the director's concrete solutions became a structural feature of the contemporary stage.

Making sense of classical drama

In staging an older play the theatre director appears, together with all artistic collaborators, not just as a media intermediary (leading the process from the dramatic text to the performance) but also as an intermediary among different time frames: the one in which the play was created, the one in which the action is set, and the present one of the staging. Directing is also a transcultural operation that seeks to make the dramatic situation and the issues of the play comprehensible to a contemporary audience, and at the same time challenging and confrontational, beyond cultural or geographical differences. Creating a theatre production inspired by a play by Euripides, Shakespeare, Goldoni, Musset or Ostrovsky can engage an audience only if it is driven by an elaborate concept of thematisation, localisation, and some language updating. If the production is in the original language, this tinkering with the language is difficult to undertake and condone – even though much of the meaning of Shakespeare's English nowadays escapes many native speakers, and Racine's Alexandrian verses might strike many in a French-speaking audience as too effete and excessively formal. A production in another language can always rely on a new translation of an old play or adapt the existing ones, inserting contemporary vocabulary, pronunciations, accents and rhythms in the language spoken on the stage.

Critics of conceptual directing raise their voices as self-appointed defenders of dead or living authors and of the assumed integrity of their work. Such criticism makes sense only if it dissects the inner contradictions of the directing concept or exposes its superficiality, revealing it as not much more than a gimmick, which is sometimes the case. Public theatre has at its disposal an enormous treasure trove of plays written between the fifth century BC and now, which it can translate and adapt, inserting new meaning in the staging. A production prompts our contemporaries to read the play and re-read it as a text for its literary merit, cultural heritage value and theatrical potential. As a live art form, theatre does not work on museological premises of scrupulous preservation and remote presentation in the name of a presumed authenticity. Textual scholarship, disseminated by academic publishers, can be of some help in contemporary staging but cannot dictate its course. Productions that seek to stage plays in the same manner as they were supposedly once staged in the past can easily baffle and put off a modern audience by obsolete stage conventions, as well as outdated social behaviour and cultural norms, in addition to an obscure, anachronistic language. This accumulation of anachronisms can give the play a grotesque character and make it more difficult to consider seriously on its own merits. However radical the transmission of a play into a performance might become, the integrity of dramatic text itself remains preserved in its original form, hopefully printed and available in a separate edition, in the theatre programme booklet, or increasingly on the Internet. What else, who else will keep this huge dramatic corpus from Euripides to Pinter accessible, read, discussed and made to come alive on the stage in some idiosyncratic manner if not public theatre? But public theatre can fulfil this task only if its professionals look at plays of the past as a resource, rough material and a provocation, and not as a cultural heritage embedded in a fixed staging mode.

Repertory theatre is capable in principle of keeping a production alive for several seasons, but in many cases the signs of wear and tear appear after 50 performances or even fewer, with routine creeping in and the stylistic coherence disappearing. One must admire the sense of discipline that has kept Gosch's *Macbeth* at the Düsseldorfer Schauspielhaus (www.duesseldorfer-schauspielhaus.de) or Tamas Ascher's production of Chekhov's *Ivanov* in Budapest's Katona theatre sharp and of undiminished stylistic brilliance for years since the premiere. By the same token, once splendid productions of the Moscow Art Theatre, MXAT (www.mxat.ru), the Piccolo Teatro in Milan (www.piccoloteatro. org) or the Berliner Ensemble (www.berliner-ensemble.de), meticulously preserved and untouched for decades, today appear like ghosts of their former selves, as a preserved remnant of their past glory, as a mechanical imitation of what was once a subtle organism, and is now less than a plausible documentary trace. Forced longevity is incompatible with live arts and therefore celebrations of the 350th or 500th performance of a production, quite common in a dramatic theatre, especially among the repertory companies of Central and Eastern Europe, come across more as perverse occasions rather than festive ones. Commercial theatre, by way of contrast, with six or eight performances a week, needs a long run to maximise the profit and, since it consumes performers' spontaneity and passion rather quickly, it replaces them mercilessly with new casts. If the tickets keep selling, a show goes on for years.

Stimulating new playwriting

Subsidised dramatic theatre has another essential task: to stimulate, nurture, develop and produce new plays, even if this often turns out to be a rather risky endeavour. In some countries theatre dramaturgs complain that they receive hundreds of plays a year from unknown aspiring authors. Most of these texts are put aside, however, after a quick glance at first few pages of dialogue. Programmes, universities and art schools train playwrights as well as scriptwriters for film and television, and some are remarkably successful such as, for instance, the playwriting programme at the Faculty of Dramatic Arts in Belgrade (www.fdu. edu.rs), which over the last 45 years has produced several generations of highly successful dramatic authors, many of them women. Subsidised theatres commission new drama from established authors or organise competitions in order to tap new unknown talent. London's Royal Court (www.royalcourttheatre.com) has implemented a complete development method to help new authors improve their plays in intensive engagement with the company dramaturgs, through careful redrafting and feedback, public readings with discussions, tentative studio-staging of some scenes and early versions, all in the expectation that these intermediary trials will help the text mature and reach an advanced level for full successful staging. Such an approach has been adapted by some other companies in Europe.

Theatre companies and venues build their identity on their commitment to new plays, as the small Praktika theatre in Moscow does by stubbornly presenting new Russian plays, in contrast to the dominance of classical drama or contemporary foreign plays on the repertoire of numerous Moscow reps. In some theatre cultures, new playwriting is stimulated by specialised festivals, such as Mülheimer Stücke (www.stuecke.de), which has brought recognition to three different generations of German-language authors in the last 30 years.

The founders of the Neue Stücke festival, originally located in Bonn in the early 1990s and then moved to Wiesbaden, have sought out new European plays with unprecedented interest and commitment, translating those plays, and bringing their productions into a rich festival programme, attended by authors, critics, dramaturgs, translators and journalists, engaged in daily debates and panels and much informal discussion. Thanks to this festival, several authors from smaller language areas have become better known and more recognised in Europe, with their plays translated and produced elsewhere. Some European networks, such as ETC (European Theatre Convention, www.etc-cte.org) and UTE (Union des Théâtres de l'Europe, www.ute-net.org), together with international consortia, have also been working in a systematic manner to stimulate new playwriting and to make it better known across the boundaries of theatre systems, cultures and languages.

In some countries, complaints are often voiced that there are no new dramatic authors of value. No one since Koltès, exclaim French colleagues frequently with some resignation, and this dictum becomes an excuse for not trying harder to discover and support emerging authors. In the meantime, Yasmina Reza, who writes in French, has become a favourite of both subsidised and commercial theatre across Europe, although admittedly she is a skilful entertainer, not an author with her own vision like Koltès. Elsewhere, there is more than indifference, even a prejudice of theatre professionals and audiences against new plays. In Romania, where classics regularly re-appear in the repertoire, contemporary Romanian plays still suffer from a bad reputation originating in the Ceausescu era before 1989, owing to the ideologically driven, sycophantic drama his regime prescribed. Meanwhile, new Romanian authors, such as Saviana Stanescu, are more appreciated in Germany and the United States than at home.

Some observers argue that there is a tentative European new drama movement or at least a cohort of authors, advancing since the 1990s, inspired by Sarah Kane's angry radical plays and numbering many authors in their thirties and forties of divergent aesthetic orientations, dramatic strategies and genre preferences but with a rather consistent critical stance towards reality and eagerness to provoke, even outrage the spectator. Therefore the movement has been baptised by the British critics *In-Yer-Face Theatre*. Each author named as part of this movement would probably insist on their own uniqueness and many would deny having anything in common while some others might feel strengthened by such an association.

Belarus: Viktar Jyboul, Pavel Prajko, Pavel Rassolko, Nikolaï Roudkovski. *Belgium* (Flanders): Arne Sierens. *Bosnia and Herzegovina*: Almir Bašović, Almir Imširević. *Croatia*: Ivana Sajko, Asja Srnec-Todorović, Filip Šovagović, Tena Štivičić, Milko Valent, Ivan Vidić. *Czech Republic*: Jiří Pokorný, Roman Sikora, Petr Zelenka. *France*: Xavier Durringer, Laurent Gaudé, Jean-Daniel Magnin, Fabrice Melquiot. *Germany*: Fritz Kater, Dea Loher, Marius von Mayenburg, Armin Petras, René Pollesch, Falk Richter, Moritz Rinke, Roland Schimmelpfennig. *Great Britain*: Samuel Adamson, Richard Bean, Simon Block, Moira Buffini, Jez Butterworth, Martin Crimp, David Eldridge, Harry Gibson,

David Greig, Nick Grosso, David Harrower, Sarah Kane, Gary Mitchell, Anthony Nellson, Joe Penhall, Rebecca Prichard, Mark Ravenhill, Philip Ridley, Shelagh Stephenson, Judy Upton, Roy Williams, Che Walker, Richard Zajdlic. *Hungary*: István Tasnádi, Gyorgy Szpiro. *Ireland*: Sebastian Barry, Martin McDonagh, Conor McPherson, Enda Walsh. *Italy*: Fausto Paravidino, Antonio Tarantino. *Lithuania*: Sigitas Parulskis. *Macedonia*: Dejan Dukovski, Žanina Mirčevska. *Moldavia*: Nicoleta Esinencu. *Norway*: Jon Fosse. *Poland*: Krzysztof Bizio, Magda Fertacz, Monika Povalisz, Marek Pruchniewski, Pawel Sala, Andrzej Stasiuk, Ingmar Vilquist, Michał Walczak, Szymon Wroblewski. *Portugal*: João Carlos dos Santos Lopez. *Romania*: Calin Blaga, Gianina Carbunariu, Vera Ion, Stefan Peca, Saviana Stănescu. *Russia*: Yevgeni Grichkovets, Oleg and Vladimir Presniakov, Vasilyi Sigariov, Ivan Viripaev. *Serbia*: Milena Bogavac, Milena Marković, Maja Pelević, Biljana Srbljanović. *Slovakia*: Pavol Janík, Miloš Karásek, Viliam Klimáček, Silvester Lavrík. *Slovenia*: Saša Pavček, Matjaž Zupančič. *Spain*: Rodrigo Garcia, Juan Mayorga. *Sweden*: Lars Norén. *Switzerland*: Lukas Bärfuss ...

This long but rather arbitrary list of contemporary authors, offered by an erudite colleague (Lazin 2008) to challenge and arouse interest, signals how difficult it is to grasp the multitude of artistic movements in the European dramatic theatre. Even well-informed theatre professionals would admit that they are unfamiliar with most foreign names on the list, but will certainly recognise a few that have enjoyed numerous productions of their plays abroad: besides the British authors – Sarah Kane, Martin Crimp and Mark Ravenhill – who are seen as the instigators of the *In-Yer-Face* wave, and the veteran Swedish author Lars Norén, other names, such as Jon Fosse, Dea Loher, Marius van Mayenburg, René Pollesch and Biljana Srbljanovic, often appear on theatre posters across Europe. It is worthy of note that Bulgarian, Estonian, Finnish, Greek, Latvian, Dutch, Turkish and Ukrainian authors are missing here, even though some of these countries have a vibrant contemporary drama production scene. Although playwrights emerge from very specific milieus, which they capture in their plays, globalisation propels them across national borders while festivals, conferences, specialised magazines and websites, workshops and seminars make them better known across an emerging European cultural space. Those who write in bigger languages enjoy an automatic advantage: they are more easily noticed, read, written about and ultimately produced abroad than those authors who write in smaller European languages and have more difficulties breaking through the constraints, usually by having their work translated first into English or German.

Public theatre embraces contemporary drama as it reflects current life, its paradoxes and obsessions, and responds to volatile pressing issues, social upheavals, political crises, the madness of war (Hristo Boychev, *Colonel Bird*), colonialism and postcolonialism (Wole Soyinka), whenever it challenges patriarchy as the most protracted form of hegemony and rebels against the cultural corsets of gender (Elfriede Jelinek), probes the vagaries of globalisation, invokes the economic crisis (Rupert Gold's *Enron*, again Jelinek, *Die Kontrakte des Kaufmanns*), recalls the brutality of history (Ronald Harwood, *Collaboration*), grapples with scientific breakthroughs (Michael Frayn's *Copenhagen*) and their political appropriation, sometimes in documentary form, sometimes metaphorically. Most of these plays would not find an outlet to be staged for the first time were it not for subsidised theatre. In the vast realm of public theatre, they are staged in multiple productions, in different ways, so as to probe the critical consciousness of the audience, instigate and frame the public debate and advance it further, beyond the easy punditry of television's talk shows and newspaper columnists and the vacuity of the blogosphere.

Not all public theatre systems in Europe are equally open to contemporary foreign drama. For years German theatres have been most diligent in the production of contemporary foreign plays, both as a percentage of their entire output and in the absolute numbers of productions. This attentiveness and interest are certainly linked to the generosity of public subsidies in Germany, as well as to the production model of the repertory company, each delivering 15–30 productions every season and employing several well-trained multilingual dramaturgs who watch what is happening in theatres and festivals across Europe. The French stage is much less outward looking and perhaps culturally more self-centred but Maison Antoine Vitez (www.maisonantoinevitez.fr) and Maison d'Europe et d'Orient (www.sildav. org), as well as a few other organisations have used public subsidies to systematically translate foreign plays and read them in public during the Avignon Festival (www.festival-avignon. com). Yet most producing organisations and theatre directors – who ultimately decide! – have remained reluctant to consider them for full-size productions. Despite its tremendous cultural diversity, the United Kingdom is a difficult realm to penetrate with non-English plays – the valiant efforts of the Royal Court, The Gate Theatre (www.gatetheatre.co.uk) and a few other places that regularly produce new foreign drama are the exception. There is a huge supply of British work, of American and Irish plays, and even of works of foreign authors who write in English. Translations into English of foreign language plays are available thanks to the effort and investment of their authors, but most producers feel financial constraints and fear that a foreign play by an unknown author will not do well at the box office.

Post-dramatic theatre

Today some leading performing artists and collectives operate outside the dramatic theatre, indifferent to both classics and contemporary plays, developing productions in which they may use various types of text, but where the text is not the driver and not the starting point of the production. An authorial concept, an aesthetic notion, a thematic interest and a metaphor or a situation are the starting points for these artists who see themselves not as theatre directors in the traditional sense but as theatre-makers. Their productions are autonomous works, inspired perhaps by other works of arts but not constructed as an extension of them. Jan Lauwers' Needcompany, Jan Fabre's Troubleyn (www.troubleyn.be), La Fura dels Baus (www.lafura.com), Romeo Castellucci's Raffaello Sanzio (www. raffaellosanzio.org), Kirsten Dehlholm's Hotel Pro Forma (www.hotelproforma.dk) and many others embody the trend, which the theatre scholar Hans-Thies Lehmann called the *post-dramatic theatre* (Lehmann 1999, 2006). It radicalises the notion of performing arts as an autonomous durational and spatial structure, disconnecting it from the tradition of literature and especially of drama, as well as a panoply of inherited genres, shaping performance as a hybrid. It is itself a broad aesthetic phenomenon that relies on digital technology in Eric Joris' Crew (www.crewonline.org); on music and singing in numerous Christoph Marthaler productions; on the combination of mini-objects and mini-cameras in Hotel Modern (www.hotelmodern.nl); or on movement, the recycling of documentary material and other strategies and resources. For some, like Emergency Exit (www.eea.org. uk), each production has its own starting point and focus while others display more continuity and consistency or shift from theatre to performance, like the Norwegian Baktruppen[1] and Derevo (www.derevo.org), an exceptional exiled transplant from Soviet Leningrad to Dresden in Germany. While the work may invoke a set of references, contemporary or historical, it does not seek to represent objective reality but rather to create its own stage reality on the ruins of representational edifices of the traditional humanist imagination. Contradictory, fragmented, elusive and unpredictable, instances of post-dramatic theatre challenge the audience, its patience, concentration and associative imagination and alter its usual perceptive patterns – just as the visual arts or contemporary music often do. Post-dramatic theatre deserves its place within the realm of public theatre because of its explorative and experimental orientation, its intermedial and interdisciplinary striving. With its conceptual complexity and demanding performativity, post-dramatic theatre remains almost by default a small-scale phenomenon, sustained by festivals, experimentally oriented arts centres and small venues. Its key perspective is in the critical deployment and demystification of digital technology, applied to perception, collective imagination and sociability and the shaping of performance as an event that engulfs, surprises and destabilises its participants.

Opera and music theatre: Confronting elitism

Opera is a remarkable survivor among all forms of performing arts, with a tradition stretching back 400 years, a strong canonical repertoire and millions of affectionate followers. Tradition has a dual impact: it turns away those who consider opera as dead musical theatre, hopelessly entangled in its own conventions and performing habits, pretentious, even silly and irritatingly elitist; while others admire it precisely for maintaining its own traditions and vehemently protest whenever they feel that a contemporary staging undermines their favourite opera with some outrageous innovation. Between these two poles, opera arouses a tremendous amount of passion, enjoyment and anger, dismissal and devotion. At the curtain call, there is often some hissing and booing from the auditorium rising above all the applause and cheering – a protest from outraged opera-lovers who feel that the staging took impermissible liberties with the sacred piece of musical theatre. Today's opera directors take such protests for granted, as a professional risk, if not a badge of honour, but they encounter very real and more substantial opposition from those conservative conductors who defend tradition and resent the staging concept of the director, or from singers who sabotage it with their stiff posture, limited movement and vacuous gestures. Opera remains a cultural battlefield, in rehearsal and in public performance.

Accusations of opera's traditionalism make a strong case: anyone undertaking a tour of hundreds of opera houses across Europe would tire quickly of productions that stubbornly reproduce old staging clichés, inherited from nineteenth-century practice, made even more absurd by sophisticated modern lighting and sound technology. Mediocrity – visual, conceptual and often also musical – makes this traditionalism even more difficult to bear. But even the most severe critics of opera have to admit that the form itself has strong public appeal, reinforced by those opera houses of excellence where the foremost theatre directors bring to musical theatre innovative strategies developed in other forms of performing arts, working with their team of dramaturgs and set designers of stage sets, costumes and lighting, and on fortunate occasions with open-minded musicians and singers who are willing to trust them and collaborate with enthusiasm. Combined with musical excellence, when accomplished, such productions cause much excitement and overwhelm the audience with their great bravura, imagination and wit. After Peter Sellars' stagings of Mozart's and Handel's operas, Kentridge's versions of Monteverdi, Willy Dekker's work with a highly diverse repertoire, the recent stagings of Peter Konwitschny and other directors, no one can write off opera as dead theatre or a cultural graveyard. Ambitious opera directors seek lesser known and forgotten operas of past centuries and integrate works of twentieth-century modernism (Schoenberg, Janaček, Korngold, Bartok…) in the repertoire in order to stretch that canonical selection of no more than 30 or 40 operas performed every season in dozens of opera houses again and again, often in a totally predictable fashion.

The common charge of opera's elitism needs to be addressed seriously, however. Indeed, opera is a very expensive form of cultural production and part of the costs incurred are reflected in high ticket prices, even with the ample public subsidies that European opera houses are, practically without exception, fortunate enough to enjoy. Short seasons, the limited number of performances per production, large auditoria that have to be sold out, well-pampered sponsors and high ticket prices are the means by which opera houses cope with their structurally high expenditure. Many are finding ways to release a limited contingent of low price tickets in order to diversify their audience and facilitate access to a less affluent and younger public. Increasingly, opera houses address the high costs by engaging in bilateral and multilateral co-productions whereby they pull resources to create an ambitious and quite costly production with several series of performances in the venues of all partners, with their home orchestras and different conductors, even with different casts, but with the same *mise-en-scène* and with the same sets, costumes and lighting design. Another popular option is that opera houses buy entire productions (concept, sets and costumes) that have been successful elsewhere and integrate them into their own offer, especially if they work with the *stagione* model of successive productions performed five to ten times within a few weeks rather than with a rotating repertoire of some 20–40 titles available throughout the entire season.

The elitism of opera is not only financial but cultural and social as well, since the form has traditionally catered to the social elites of the rich, educated and powerful, followed their taste and nurtured their patronage, while providing occasions for elitist socialising among the champagne-sipping, gossip-obsessed, elegantly dressed *beau monde*, interspersed with stars, celebrities and connoisseurs. The traditionally configured auditorium of older houses has always many less glamorous seats in the upper galleries and on the sides with a restricted view, which need to be sold. These cheaper tickets are snapped up by less wealthy music lovers willing to put up with non-carpeted vestibules, less glorious lighting in their lobby, less comfortable seats or even standing room only, in order to enjoy an evening at the opera. Consequently, a popular and even a populist sentiment is also part of opera tradition as much as the elitism, which has been a steady marker since opera's origins at the Italian courts of the beginning of the seventeenth century. The most staunch traditionalism and defence of old-fashioned staging practices come more from the opera fanatics in the third and fourth galleries than from the wealthy audience in the stalls and the first gallery boxes, routinely more at ease with the dynamics of cultural innovation. Teatro di San Carlo in Naples (www.teatrosancarlo.it), La Scala in Milan (www.teatroallascala.org) and the Liceu in Barcelona (www.liceubarcelona.cat) dread protest from the traditionalist part of the audience.

The architecture of opera venues stresses the elitism and the prestige of the form and resists innovation. While La Scala was being thoroughly renovated in 2002–2004, the temporary Arcimboldo venue was erected on the outskirts of Milan in an ex-industrial area, near the Bicocca University. Simple and functional, with 1,800 good seats, all with an excellent view, decent acoustics and the choice of three languages for subtitles in front of each seat, it was a most impressive structure, connected with the centre of the city by a free shuttle bus and minibuses picking up passengers from the nearest metro station. But when the renovation of La Scala's eighteenth-century building was completed, opera returned there and Arcimboldo was sacrificed to sporadic and mostly commercial programming. The Liceu in Barcelona and La Fenice in Venice were successfully rebuilt after devastating fires, "and they were where they were," following the promises of politicians. The former was extended with an impressive technical block, finished after more than a decade of foot-dragging and criminal embezzlement. In contrast, the new opera house in Copenhagen (2005) is a €320m gift from a shipping-container tycoon who put pressure on the architect and insisted on a location directly opposite the royal palace, in a spot completely surrounded by water and deprived of any urban context, making the venue an isolated edifice, and condemning those visitors who arrive too early to wait around in a windy car park. The new Oslo Opera (2008) celebrates a century of Norwegian independence and appears to be rising out of the sea, creating a popular promenade cum playground day and night.

It is not surprising that accusations of elitism still hound opera at the outset of the twenty-first century, when many middle-aged and even older people have never come to terms with classical music, when rock-music veterans are turning into senior citizens, when pop music remains the core business of cultural industry and when some grandparents perpetuate the 1960s Woodstock mythology when putting their grandchildren to bed. Indeed, opera remains a minority affinity even among the rather marginalised performing arts, especially as the dictum that people turn to classical music after they reach a certain age seems to be no longer valid. Opera houses rarely seek to convert middle-aged and older people with other tastes in music into opera lovers; rather they invest their limited resources into arousing the interest of the young, involving them in educational activities and making them feel at ease when they come. In the summer months, opera producers hope to recruit a new audience with the aid of a seductive ambience, such as the sunset picnics at Glyndebourne (www.glyndebourne.com), or Bregenz Festival performances (www.bregenzerfestspiele.com) on the huge floating stage on Lake Konstanz, in the historical ambience of Orange and Aix-en-Provence and elsewhere. Musical theatre blends with a fascinating setting and opera is appreciated as a force that can boost the tourist industry – as long as the weather stays fine.

> This is nowhere so true as in the Verona Arena (www.arena.it), where operas have been staged since 1913 for up to 16,000 spectators a night. With such a huge capacity, most of the marketing effort today goes into targeting groups of spectators in the tourist camps around nearby Lake Garda, the majority of whom come to attend an opera event for the first time. Consequently, opera productions, chiefly works by Verdi and Puccini, and an ancient Zeffirelli rendering of Bizet's *Carmen*, are kept alive for more than 20 years, suffering from inevitable routine and shabbiness. On over 50 evenings during the summer months, visitors to the Arena are accosted by sellers of programmes, cushions, ice cream, sandwiches and drinks, all confirming that selling is more important than artistic quality. The Foundation that runs the Arena receives over €16m from public authorities – even though the national government contribution is in steady decline. Local banking foundations and Volkswagen as sponsors are supposed to make good the rest of the budget but deficits have plagued the Foundation and led to the replacement of its board by an extraordinary commissary, appointed by the government to consolidate the enterprise. The Foundation's self-congratulatory claim that the Arena generates €500m in tourist income for the city and its surroundings must be taken with a great deal of scepticism. While the Arena summer season certainly benefits Verona tourism, it is not clear why a public subsidy is needed at all for an operation that could, in principle, sell over 800,000 tickets (price range €18–€198) in a summer season and thus generate over €25m at the box office. And why should a programme of rundown old productions, kept alive beyond any artistic endurance, deserve public subsidy at all?

The hardest test of value for a subsidised opera is its attitude towards the commissioning and production of new opera. Most of the opera repertoire consists of works composed over a range of 350 years, from Monteverdi to Stravinsky and Britten, with new operas appearing very rarely. Just as the audience attitude towards contemporary music remains apprehensive and sceptical, if not downright hostile, so regular operagoers are reserved about new opera. Very few of the new opera works premiered in the last 30 years have entered the standard repertoire and experienced subsequent productions after the first one. And this is not just a matter of taste and a prejudice shared between audience and opera professionals, of cowardice and cultural conservatism. It is also a practical matter. Opera is a complex and expensive product, developed under formidable time pressures, and only a production of a work from the standard opera repertoire, more or less known to all in the opera professions, can be mastered within such time constraints. A new opera requires much more preparation and production time, much more trial and error, and most opera houses simply cannot afford the extra time, intense concentration and extensive deployment of capacities required. With any new opera, the outcome is somewhat risky and the reactions unpredictable. The huge capacity of most opera houses – almost always more than 1,500 seats – is eminently unsuitable for innovation, experiment and risk-taking, all for a minority interest in the development of the form, which can perhaps bring only 300–400 spectators together for a performance. And, of course, most opera houses do not have a smaller hall or studio.

Today, with considerably altered staging standards, it is difficult to imagine that a new opera production can smoothly emerge from the traditional creative chain: writer writes libretto – composer composes opera – General Manager takes brave decision to produce it and engages director – director and conductor lead rehearsal process of five to six weeks and bring new work to premiere. A more intricate development method brings together the librettist, composer, producer, director and a dramaturg, later also joined by designers and singers, to work from the beginning in several phases, with some work done at home in the meantime, in a process that might take two to three years. Opera houses are eminently incapable of engineering and implementing such a delicate and protracted process from its inception to the premiere. The best they can do is allocate an additional week of rehearsals to the production of a new opera, which, in most cases, is not enough.

It is for these reasons that new opera or musical theatre today is often produced not by opera houses but by small, specialised, non-profit-making organisations. They are able to initiate and chaperone the long process required, perform in smaller venues, and cooperate with the co-producers and festivals, which are becoming key instigators and co-producers of such work. Muziektheater Transaparant in Antwerp (www.transparant.be), Lod in Ghent (www.lod.be), Cryptic in Glasgow (www.cryptic.org.uk) and some others have built up an international track record and broadened their range of partners. Münchener Biennale für Neues Musiktheater commissions and produces four new works for each festival (www.muenchener-biennale.de). It was founded and initially run by Hans Werner Henze, whose several operas have found their way into major opera houses, as have *Rosas* and *Letter to Vermeer* by Louis Andriessen, directed by Peter Greenaway, and Kaija Saariaho operas, written by Amin Maalouf and directed by Peter Sellars. Successful film directors such as Anthony Minghella and bestseller-author Ian McEwan have also turned to libretto-writing and yet many initiatives in this international field never move past the early stages, and newly created work gets stuck after the premiere and just a few performances afterwards. Jonathan Dove and Arthur Japin (*Kwasi & Kwame* 2007), Alberto Garcia Demestres and Cristina Pavarotti (*El secuestro* 2009), David Blake and Keith Warner (*Scoring a Century* 2010) and Klaas de Vries and David Mitchell (*Wake* 2010) have at least succeeded as composer/librettist duos to move projects through to the premiere. The crucial relationships between the librettist and the composer, as well as between the composer and the director, require some fine-tuning and special attention extended by the producer. Most of the works developed in a long serial workshop-based process are small-scale pieces, with just a few performers, counting on a small ensemble of musicians, not on a fully-fledged orchestra.

Public opera subsidies are often contested on populist grounds, as an extravaganza that benefits the wealthy. A counter-argument could be offered that opera houses deserve public subsidy if they go beyond the standard repertoire of classical works, invest in innovative stagings, commission and absorb new musical theatre work, run the gamut of educational activities to recruit new audiences and eliminate the leftovers of elitism from their buildings and events. They deserve to be rewarded from public funds if they engage in co-productions, run an efficient, lean organisation with a substantial output, avoid huge payrolls, invest in digital communications and take the initiative to produce and market their own CDs and DVDs in order to reduce dependence on a decaying recording industry. Most importantly, they deserve subsidies if they do not rush to imitate commercial theatre by (re)producing well-known musicals, which the commercial producers do successfully without any subsidy.

Varieties of dance

Despite a long tradition and accumulated prestige, dance remains a vulnerable part of the performing arts spectrum, with a rather limited audience and thus a noticeable reluctance on the part of programmers to feature it in programmed venues. Classical ballet might still enjoy the reputation of a noble art form and assure its sustainability by incorporating classical ballet ensembles in opera houses where they stage their own productions of a very narrow standard repertoire (*Swan Lake, Giselle, Coppélia, Romeo and Juliet,* and the mandatory *Nutcracker* for the Christmas season), using choreographies derived from the nineteenth century. Classical ballet ensembles, some consisting of 60–80 dancers, tend to be quite expensive to maintain but also hierarchical, based on demanding drilling and extreme pressure on the dancers to stay slim and fit; they are often rather jealous, gossipy environments, locked into a narrow lifestyle and daily routine of exercise and self-sacrifice, internalised by practitioners. Today, classical ballet could be seen as a poetic, de-eroticised, middle-class entertainment, obsessed with technical excellence and formal beauty but insulated from innovation. It appeals primarily to young girls and boys who themselves take ballet lessons and to those who once took them. Otherwise classical ballet draws an older, artistically rather conservative and non-adventurous audience willing to re-immerse itself in the repetition of well-known subject matter, themes and sequences from the classical works.

Modern ballet, instigated by European expressionism, postulated by Balanchine in the New York City Ballet and made quite popular in Europe in the 1960s by Maurice Béjart, provides a way out of the constraints of rigidly defined movements and a narrow range repertoire, but as a form and aesthetics it was quickly surpassed by the liberating drive and unrestrained energy of the contemporary dance movement, which exploded in the 1960s with a baffling diversity of styles and approaches and which today dominates the field. Some of the larger companies, especially those residing in venues and integrated into opera organisations, seek to strike a balance between classical and modern ballet but the latter has never achieved a convincing, popular and highly appreciated body of contemporary work and successful collaborative relationships between choreographers and composers remain rare.

Contemporary dance, in contrast, originally fed by energies and rhythms from the United States and the aesthetic concepts of postmodernist performance and visual arts, boasts a rich cohort of formidable choreographers and outstanding groups and performers, an ability to integrate classical music and instigate productive relationships with contemporary composers. It transcends narration and approaches the non-representational nature of visual arts as articulated throughout the twentieth century. It numbers a few stable, larger ensembles and many smaller ones, with most ad hoc productions initiated by freelance artists wherever the opportunity arises. Not being language-bound, contemporary dance has become remarkably internationalised, both in the creative process and in frequent touring, a tiresome and expensive chasing after more audience and income, as well as additional exposure. A dozen contemporary dance festivals across Europe are of crucial importance for the form, since they affirm new styles, promote groups and artistic personalities and facilitate their touring and cooperation, advance professional discourse, generate extra publicity and seek to win a new audience, in addition to offering advanced professional training in workshops and master classes.

As is the case in classical and modern ballet, the choreographers of contemporary dance are usually former dancers. While professional training opportunities for dancers on higher education level have spread to many conservatoriums, arts academies and universities, accomplished choreography training remains scarce, constricted to a few master's programmes. All forms of dance have also benefited from the development of dance studies as a scholarly discipline, on a par with more established theatre studies. Dancers – classical, modern and contemporary – survive on dedication to their *métier*, despite rather precarious economic conditions, with systemic self-exploitation accompanied by anxiety about how their professional career will develop in the short span of years available, possibly even shortened by injury, and the uncertainties of life and work prospects after dance. Only in a handful of European countries are there programmes to offer professional retraining to dancers after the end of their career and enable them to start a new one, often in a field unrelated to dance, enjoying another 30 years of productive life. It is rare for a dancer to stretch their dancing career beyond the age of 35 in a manner that is appropriate to their reduced physical abilities, but still artistically satisfying. In the 1990s, Jiří Kilian established NDT 3 as a small unit of the foremost seniors within the Netherlands Dans Theater in The Hague (www.ndt.nl), but after his departure as Artistic Director the experiment was discontinued, despite some remarkable productions.

There is a paradox in the fact that contemporary society, obsessed as it is with movement and speed, focused on the human body and its glamorisation and commodification through advertising, caught up in a media-enforced cult of youth, displays so much indifference to contemporary dance. Why does contemporary dance as an art form appeal to a very small audience group, consisting to a great extent of current and former dance professionals, while so many youngsters spend hours dancing in discos? Anyone who thinks that the reason could be the dominance of non-narrative structures and the lack of plots in contemporary dance has only to remember Woody Allen's hilarious "A Guide to Some of the Lesser Ballets" (Allen 1975) to conclude that contemporary dance would not be better off if choreographers sought to tell a story as in classical ballet. With a bewildering variety – which does not, however, exclude sameness, similarity and tiresome repetition – contemporary dance explores in the first place the vagaries of the human body, its frailty, decay, wear and tear, its iconic expressive capacity to focus on the pain and stress of existence, to fall short of fantasies and aspirations. Movement, that is, the body set in motion, and the shifting relationship with space and other bodies of other dancers is a form of considerable abstraction, rather demanding on an audience, presented with touching minimalism, directness and informality or, at the other extreme, with considerable "staginess" and theatrical framing.

Choreographers seek to enhance interest in their work by investing in its visual quality, through exquisite lighting, stage sets and costumes. They deploy digital technology, working with multiple screens, interactive floors and walls, and establishing online connections with other parallel performances elsewhere (Berg and Hansen 2009). Or they create their pieces outside dance venues, in a found environment, in cultural heritage sites, in former industrial plants, in natural settings, counting on the fact that the attractiveness of these ambiences will generate additional public interest. Others work with live music, with musicians on the stage. Pina Bausch and Mats Ek, and to some extent Sasha Waltz (www.sashawaltz.de), sought to narrow the gap between dance and theatre, to theatricalise dance and endow it with a strong thematic core or base it on dramatic material. Alain Platel (www.lesballetscdela. be) derives his pieces from a strongly determined social milieu and foregrounds the lot of marginalised outcasts. Anne Teresa De Keersmaeker and her Rosas ensemble (www. rosas.be) excel in complex conceptual work, driven by serial music, becoming increasingly minimalist. Looking for alternative traditions as an inspiration source, contemporary dance has turned to Japanese *butoh* or, with Akram Khan (www.akramkhancompany.net), has invoked the Indian *katak* tradition. Some choreographers have ventured into film, hence a whole stream of dance films, sustained by the availability of sophisticated video techniques, creating digital versions of live work and specific made-for-camera pieces and yet lacking adequate distribution models and channels for them.

Oddly, contemporary dance has failed to benefit from the explosive popularity of recreational dance, especially tango and salsa, which brings thousands of people of all ages to workshops, classes and dance sessions. Nor was it lifted on the wave of breakdance and hip-hop that penetrated the mainstream of popular and industrial culture from marginal urban communities, shaped by migration. In order to affirm their own artistic identity, dance professionals insist on securing their own provisions, setting up dance facilities where they will not be marginalised by other kinds of performing arts. The result is a number of smaller venues, studios and dance houses that programme and produce only contemporary dance work, especially in the Nordic countries, France and Germany, but the consequence is that dance is less programmed in other venues, among other performing arts forms, and thus becomes even more segregated and isolated, its core audience not replenished by other performing arts audiences.

Just how vulnerable contemporary dance is can be seen in the whimsical decision of the City of Frankfurt to disband Ballet Frankfurt, led for 20 years by William Forsythe, one of the most distinguished choreographers today. If Forsythe could lose his funding overnight, on the pretext that the city preferred to invest in a resident classical ballet ensemble (which costs much more and takes several years to establish), then what kind of security could any other choreographer count on? After international outrage caused much embarrassment to the Frankfurt City Council, Forsythe's company (www.theforsythecompany.com) survived in a scaled-down form, stretched between Hellerau Festspielhaus in Dresden (www.hellerau.org) and Bockenheimer Depot in Frankfurt (www.bockenheimer-depot.de). The sudden death of Pina Bausch in the summer of 2009 makes the prospects for her Tanztheater Wuppertal (www.pina-bausch.de) quite uncertain although the company claims to preserve continuity in the years to come. Rosas experienced a boost when it became the resident company of the Brussels Opera De Munt/La Monnaie (www.demunt.be), but was in turn weakened when the new opera management terminated this arrangement, forcing De Keersmaeker to reduce her permanent ensemble from 15 to 8 dancers.

Contemporary dance could seek some consolidation of its marginal position in more instances of community dance, whereby choreographers and professional dancers work with large groups of laypeople through a rather lengthy process, which is expressive, empowering and mobilising, rather than being just recreational, and which offers an opportunity to link dance to the infrastructure of civil society, to concrete neighbourhoods and social groups and nourish it with specific collective experiences, memories and frustrations. Many of the difficulties of contemporary dance come from the fact that it is locked into venues and made dependent on them and their programmers, consequently losing exposure under the competition of other forms that do better at the box office. Therefore, all efforts at the expansion of dance to other public spaces – accidental, appropriated or invaded – to zones of sociability and human movement, are most welcome:

to plazas and streets, shopping centres and railway stations, office buildings and hospital lobbies, including parades and processions, such as the Holland Dance Festival in The Hague (www.hollanddancefestival.com), introduced in 2007. One should not be afraid that these occurrences will become cheap entertainment but rather hope they will engage a new incidental audience, which would otherwise never come on its own to a dance performance in a venue.

Another aspect to reconsider is the common templates in which dance is routinely programmed. There are few choreographers who have the artistic capacity to make a full-size dance piece, filling an entire evening of 60–90 minutes, or at least half of it, before or after the intermission, lasting 35–45 minutes. Too often going to a dance programme means watching four or five short pieces by different choreographers, lasting perhaps even less than ten minutes each, or going on for up to 20 minutes, with frequent and annoying intermissions for set and lighting changes. While such enforced "grazing" could perhaps appeal to the interest of a professional spectator, for many others the evening loses its coherence and destroys concentration, inhibiting any deeper engagement. A mixed programme of different choreographers, without necessarily any real connection among them, an arbitrary grouping to fill the available evening slots, results in an imposed hodgepodge, in tedium. Unfortunately, to avoid such enforced combinations choreographers come under pressure to develop longer pieces – even if they do not have the imagination and conceptual richness to fill 30–45 minutes, failing to cut and throw away enough of the material developed in the studio, or sliding into repetition.

As an alternative, it is still a rarity to commission and create several dance pieces, joined by some musical affinities shared between several choreographers, or within more complex thematic templates. Not slogans or arbitrarily chosen common titles, but a common reference framework, jointly developed, to reflect the multiple interests of a few artists, a shared theme, reinforced through the collaboration and contribution of others, would give dance programmes more visibility and perhaps appeal to audience groups that are now indifferent to dance.

Encapsulating thematisation requires from the choreographers to take a stance, articulate and convey a sense of the world, to engage in the social, cultural and anthropological exploration of reality. Not through those bland, fashionable thematic shortcuts such as "identity" and "globalisation," used as buzzwords and arbitrarily attached to the work, nor is anyone waiting for more opportunistic jumps on the AIDS, Darfur or Guantanamo bandwagons, but thematic frameworks evolved with some patience, research and reflection. Choreographers need to be equipped for such a search, and have to develop their own research tools, borrowed from other disciplines, before they cast, choose music and enter a studio to start rehearsing. That means taking notice of the world outside the dance studio, following social debates and polemics, defining oneself towards the world and building up a coherent world view, as is always recognisable in the pieces of Mats Ek but suspiciously absent in the work of many other well-known choreographers, who make one wonder whether they ever read a newspaper.

To shape such an attitude to the world and make it intelligible, most choreographers would benefit from a loyal sparring partner – a dramaturg, capable of articulation of the theme and its receptive context. Choreographers still rarely deploy a dramaturg, missing a chance to ensure intellectual and conceptual reinforcement. Dance dramaturgs, a tiny emerging speciality, hardly ever write about their experiences and the tensions of working with the choreographers, or about how they function as keepers of conceptual clarity and consistency in the intense relationship between the choreographer and the dancers in a studio.

Increasingly, dancers are also choreographers, and choreographers dancers. Since ensembles are difficult to sustain, fluid, multiple working relationships emerge, often in crossing borders and international associations, making the field quite nomadic, endowing it with a sense of community, with shared passions and structural weakness, a precarious existence and career uncertainty. Such a fragmented community reconvenes in facilities created to further contemporary dance in some 30 European cities, studios, small venues, labs, production houses and professional development institutions, from the minuscule studios converted from private apartments in the Beyoglu quarter of Istanbul to Trafó in Budapest, where dance is enmeshed with music and visual arts, Tanzquartier Wien (www.tqw.at), a complex multi-functional support base, to German Tanzhäuser, French centres nationales de choréographie, The Place in London (www.theplace.org.uk), Dutch and Flemish production units with two- or four-year subsidy guarantees,[2] dance houses in Copenhagen, Oslo and Stockholm, the Arts Printing House in Vilnius, Kanuti Gildi Saal in Tallinn (www.saal.ee) and many other modest or even impoverished places that provide shelter for a fragile art form and its practitioners, their friends and core audience.

Choreographers tend to lead the working process with a strong hand in the rehearsal studio, but most of them avoid appearing in public and are reluctant to talk about anything but their own work. In this sense, the dance community lacks artistic leadership as a public role with a strong strategic vision and convincing public appearance. Seeking to surpass the overwhelming structural weakness of dance, the Bundeskulturstiftung launched a Tanzplan Deutschland (www.tanzplan-deutschland.de) with an investment of €12.5 m for 2005–2010, to be used mainly as a seed and matching money, complemented by other, predominantly regional, local sources. This intensive and well-orchestrated developmental strategy seeks to firmly anchor dance in local communities, secure the funding commitment of local authorities, spread dance education in schools, elevate the competence and the status of its teachers, enhance co-productions and collaborations from the local to the international level, intensify touring, seed artists-in-residence schemes, consolidate the fragmented collective memory of dance in interconnected archives and collections, set a transition scheme for retiring dancers, such as has been effectively applied in the Netherlands for over two decades. All these measures and improvements should reduce the gap in funding, opportunities and exposure between dramatic and music theatre with their solid institutionalised infrastructure on the one hand, and dance on the other.

Similar consolidation initiatives have been undertaken elsewhere. The Vlaams Theater Instituut launched a Masterplan dans in 2007, on the basis of serious field research on the dynamics of dance development after the famous Flemish wave of choreographers profiled the cultural landscape of Flanders in the 1980s. Their work, groups, festivals, subsidies and Rosas' P.A.R.T.S. school attracted new generations and many foreign dancers to Brussels, Antwerp, Ghent and Leuven, creating a regional dance constellation that is international in its protagonists, patterns of mobility across Europe and material used. Several Nordic and Baltic dance organisations, very different among themselves in typology, size and orientation, set up Kedja (www.kedja.net), a consortium to foster mobility, touring and co-production in the region, with a three-year grant (2007–2010) from the EU culture programme and support from the Nordic Council. Kedja sought to expand and intensify the Northern European dance realm and to boost the position of contemporary dance in the Baltic neighbour states, where, as in all communist countries, contemporary dance did not have any standing before 1989. Other regional initiatives, such as Dance Bassin Méditerranée and Balkan Express, had difficulty sustaining their impetus because of a weak infrastructure, low regional subsidy level and lack of external solidarity in the field.

Unlike many popular dance forms that are easily integrated into the offer of commercial producers, contemporary dance cannot be made and shown without public support. Even when such support is extended, contemporary dance organisations and professionals feel vulnerable and tend to withdraw into their own territory, where they feel safe and indiscriminated against. Inadvertently, they reinforce their own self-ghettoisation and marginal position within the performing arts. Investment in educational activities and community dance, cooperation with other performing arts organisations and artists from various disciplines can affirm contemporary dance and strengthen its artistic, cultural and intellectual context, thus expanding its social base as well.

Theatre for children and young people

Another form of performing arts that suffers from benign neglect and marginalisation is theatre for children and young people. This marginalisation is two-fold: firstly, it originates from the dominance of theatre for adults, which always enjoys more exposure, prestige and support; secondly, innovative and unorthodox theatre for children and young people has until recently been pushed aside by the growth in commercial theatre for children, young people and "the entire family," monopolising the attention of children, parents and educators with its professional marketing acumen, large-size venues and conventional topics and style. In facing the competition of specialised commercial theatre, subsidised theatre for children and young people shares the fragility of the entire *public*, non-commercial theatre, being often insufficiently assertive when it comes to the promotion of its own values and societal benefits beyond the entertainment function, as promulgated by commercial theatre and other products of the cultural industry.

One could argue that the quality of theatre for children and youth is an indicator of the maturity and sophistication of a theatre culture in any given country, its sense of vision and responsibility, its deliberate investment in the future theatre audience. It is so easy to belittle and ignore this segment of performing arts just because it addresses children, who are supposedly easy to please. Hence in many places those who perform for children enjoy lower professional status than their colleagues who play for the adult audience. In some instances, theatre for children is indeed bad or mediocre, caught in the endless reproduction of staged fairy tales and showing condescension towards the youth audience. What keeps this segment so constrained is also the widespread paternalism of those conservative teachers who oppose any critical, emotional or dramatic confrontation of the young audience with the unpleasant, menacing and disgusting aspects of reality and who quickly jump to intervene, censor the performers and protect their pupils. Performers who defend their sense of autonomy by insisting with some arrogance on their own status as artists, leaving educational concerns to educators, reinforce the bias of teachers and miss the opportunity to create allies and ambassadors.

The best features of theatre for children and young people today can be traced back to a cultural revolution that occurred in West European societies in the late 1960s and early 1970s. A radical shift in values, social ideas, political orientation and aesthetic notions, generated among students and urban youth, was anti-authoritarian and anti-hierarchical in its inspiration. In the performing arts, it instigated the proliferation of small groups and collectives that resented the established theatre system and sought to stimulate and enlighten a theatre audience of students and other underprivileged social groups. Some of these theatre artists understood that educational theatre, inspired by Brecht's didactic dramaturgy, as well as the sit-ins and teach-ins of political protests, can hope to initiate a significant transformation in social values and social behaviour only if it starts from the youngest spectators and thus proceeds to develop an unconventional theatre for children.

Radical politics and confrontational performing styles found further inspiration in the new pedagogical and psychological ideas that aimed to break away from traditional paternalism and authoritarianism in the treatment of children and affirm their sense of freedom and a respect for their imagination. In the choice of subject matter and its treatment on the stage, practically all taboos were gradually peeled away. Parental divorce, incest, child abuse, death and murder, mental retardation, teenage motherhood, bullying in school, street violence, ongoing conflicts in the world, juvenile crime and drugs – all these issues became the topics of new plays and productions for young audiences. By treating children with respect and trust, as future fully-fledged fellow citizens, theatre transcends and subverts the traditional fairy-tale repertoire with its conventional socialisation messages, but also implements artistic and attitudinal, value-driven and civic-minded changes through all the genres and types, including dance and opera/musical theatre for children.

Several theatre-makers have created remarkable theatre for children in the Netherlands, with over 250 professional premieres each year, and found ways of bringing the idea of disturbed, threatened and endangered childhood elsewhere in the world to the relative comfort and safety in which Dutch children grow up. The playwright and director Ad de Bont wrote and produced *Mirad, A Boy from Bosnia* at the height of the Bosnian War 1993–1994 in order to explain its violence and the flow of refugees it instigated to Dutch children aged eight and over. He also wrote and staged plays about the cruelty of slavery in the former Dutch colony of Suriname, about a Romanian orphan who becomes a loyal Ceausescu guard and then his murderer, and also about children's perception of mafia encroachment on society in South America. In his play *Anne en Zef* (2009), Anne Frank meets her counterpart in some other world, a boy killed in a revived wave of blood revenge in post-communist Albania. Liesbeth Coltof in her company Huis aan de Amstel (www.huisaandeamstel.nl) developed productions about a child killed in the first Palestinian Intifada, and on the generation rifts slowing down post-war healing and reintegration in the divided Herzegovinian city of Mostar. Roel Twijnstra of the Rotterdam company Het Waterhuis (now called Theatergroep Siberia; www.theatergroepsiberia.nl) made productions about child prostitution in India, and about two boys from Guinea who froze to death in the cargo hold of a jumbo jet, seeking to smuggle themselves into Belgium.

The major challenges for theatre for children and young people take shape in the context of globalisation, technological innovation and migration. Theatre-makers look at the altered nature of childhood and children's sociability under the influence of a weakened traditional nuclear family structure and the intercultural, inter-ethnic, inter-linguistic and inter-religious contexts in which children grow up in schools and on the street. Especially the impact of digitalisation and digital culture on children, their use of time and their patterns of communication re-frame the values and unique benefits a theatre performance can offer. If computers and the Internet make children more lonely and isolated, pushing them into virtual realms of childhood, they also enable them to communicate beyond their immediate surroundings, with their peers elsewhere. How can this global perspective enter the theatre and how can the stage action acquire the intensity of an Internet or SMS chat? The legal or illegal downloading of music and its processing and re-arrangement, something that many children do as a matter of routine, could be seen as a cultural practice capable of inspiring an open dramaturgy in children's theatre, based on interactivity, debate and the reshaping of traditional and contemporary stories, myths, legends, literary material and personal experiences.

Among the theatre companies specialised for children and young people, there is a visible uneasiness about future direction and modes of engagement. The intercultural dimension is only one point on the emerging agenda that also includes the inclusion of elements of digital culture in performance and interdisciplinary creation, which overcomes the boundaries between drama, dance and musical theatre. The size of the audience and the capacity to communicate in large theatre venues rather than preferably in small spaces for 60–120 spectators, as well as the inter-generational mix in the audience are all connected to the perennial question of how to make children come to a performance and how to avoid losing them later, when they become moody, restless teenagers. Some companies are resolute in touring schools because they can reach children of all socio-economic standings, even those whom parents will never take to a theatre venue. Others prefer the venue for its advanced facilities and comfort, debating whether specialised venues for children work better than programming performances for children in venues that also offer programmes for adults. The answers are certainly not hidden only in the intricacies of marketing, but reach to the essential creative core of the work, to the artistic choices made in the production. In addition, there are some practical issues. More intensive use of gym halls by larger schools makes them less available for theatre performances. Complicated EU labour regulation makes it more complicated and expensive to tour. And even though there is growing competition in non-subsidised productions for children and even in commercial ones, statistics show that many children in Europe do not see a single performance for a whole year, or even two.

One strategy tested by several companies is to create more of participative forms, transforming theatre *for* youngsters into a theatre *with* youngsters by developing a production with 15–20 teenagers that will especially appeal to their friends and other peers. In the effort to please the young audience and reflect a supposedly homogeneous urban youth culture, producers rely on some standard features: an excess of loud music, hard beat, brisk movement, the uniform costumes of T-shirts, baggy pants, sneakers and baseball caps for boys, tight short tops, jeans and high boots for girls, syncopated fast action that imitates MTV video clips, a vague dramatic motif, barely articulated through improvised exercises, no thematic structuring but rather a gaping intellectual void. The rushed tempo and a rather large number of participants leave hardly any time for individualisation, articulation of personal experience, reflection or confrontation of views and stances, as if the professionals behind these productions fear that they will lose the attention of the young spectators the moment they slow down a little and address any content matter. The danger in these productions is that they seek to imitate and compete with MTV and other commercial television channels, a race they cannot expect to win; they pursue the dumbing-down strategies of the entertainment industry and find themselves on the slippery slope of reproducing the facile stereotypes of contemporary youth culture. While these productions might pretend to manifest cultural diversity on the stage and stimulate it in the auditorium just because they rely on hip-hop and rap, they in fact reiterate the uniforming pressure of the cultural industry, without taking a critical stance towards its products. There is too much easy pandering to young taste, shaped by the same cultural industry (including its cult of violence) and its mighty advertising machinery, and too little investment in youngsters in terms of skill, imagination, concentration, intellectual pursuit and verbal articulateness, and a disregard for the development of intercultural competence.

From the perspective of the much-altered demography of most European cities, with a large proportion of young people issuing from immigration, theatre for children and young people deserves public support if it affirms cultural diversity, clarifies cultural differences as dynamic and negotiable concepts and social practices rather than as fixed barriers among population groups. In the heated debate in several European countries about multiculturalism and its supposed failures as a policy and the politics of integration, theatre for children and young people should be seen as a platform that furthers participatory citizenship and affirms cultural diversity as an asset and not as a plague. Politicians concerned about social cohesion could look into the capacities of this specific form of performing arts and support it if it makes a clear and continuous effort to become inclusive, beyond faceless universalism and defensive identity cocoons, making all the youngsters feel that the production addresses them and counts on their response, and if it challenges stereotypes and prejudices and opens up room for debate rather than imposing ready-made integration clichés as quick-fix solutions.

Other theatre forms

While traditional circus with trained animals, acrobats and clowns under a great tent is slowly going out of business, or is at least becoming a rare sight on the outskirts of European cities, the spectacular success of the super-commercial Cirque du Soleil has revived interest in circus as a subtle art form of acrobatics and juggling, enhanced by design, lighting and music. Especially in France, there has been serious public commitment since the 1980s to small-scale experimental circus art, based on acrobatics and juggling, enhanced by humour or poetic flair. Several generations of performers have emerged from L' École Nationale des Arts du Cirque in Rosny-sous-Bois (www.enacr.com) and disseminated their skills beyond French territory. In Paris, in the Parc de la Villette cultural complex, a space is always reserved for various circus performances under a tent. The experimental nature of such circus shows stands in stark contrast to the more conventional, though occasionally breath-taking, acrobatic shows of various travelling Russian, Chinese, Korean and Mongolian circuses, which cannot survive any longer on much reduced state subsidies at home and thus seek to earn money in Europe as an export-oriented art form. In their footsteps the long European tour of *Afrika! Afrika!* by the Austrian André Heller (www.artevent.at) brought together one hundred performers from 15 African countries in an essentially commercial endeavour, counting on African exoticism and marketing it unabashedly.

With European cities increasingly anxious to build their own image, attract tourists and shoppers, and provide some exceptional excitement to local residents, large-scale street-theatre performances, parades, processions and animations have gained popularity. There is a definite market for such companies, much driven by the demand of municipal authorities and the desire to open a sports competition or some other large festive event in a spectacular fashion. Royal de Luxe, established in 1979, is a pioneer of the genre, with giant puppets animated through huge crowds. After tongue-in-cheek, pseudo-didactic shows, such as *La véritable histoire de France*, a spoof on all national myths, subsequent shows have been derived from popular stories, such as *The Sultan's Elephant, Les chasseurs de girafes, Le géant tombé du ciel, The Diver* and *The Little Mermaid*. Royal de Luxe, based in Nantes, always attracts tens of thousands of spectators who follow a skilful crew of puppet animators and accompanying musicians, supported by a regiment of local volunteers needed to move the giant puppets, manage the crowds and make way for the cortège.

Again, public subsidy, primarily French and sometimes from the European Commission and other national and local authorities, has made it possible to sustain a documentary centre for such kinds of performance. HorsLesMurs in Marseille (www.horslesmurs.fr), together with the Circostrada network (www.circostrada.org), provides a range of training courses, research, cooperation and publications (Floch 2008; Gaber 2009; Barghouthi and Floch 2010), driven by the ambition of a growing number of festivals dedicated to street theatre to exchange experience and know-how but also to pull resources in cooperative projects. French authorities also take puppetry seriously. L'Ecole Nationale Supérieure des Arts de la Marionnette in Charleville-Mézières, coupled with the archive and library of the Institut International de la Marionnette (www.marionnette.com), trains puppeteers on an international scale, many of whom create productions for an adult audience.

Other small-scale forms of theatre of movement, as well as visual and object theatre, exist in the realm of public theatre, or rather on its very margins, under-funded and under-structured, and thus under pressure to emphasise their own specific entertainment function. Cabaret performers and stand-up comedians, if successful, easily move into the zone of commercial theatre and perform in large halls with relatively low costs, thus making considerable potential profits.

The range of types, forms and approaches discussed in this chapter can feed and stimulate the successes of commercial theatre but cannot stand on their own without some form of public subsidy. Taken all together, these programming options determine the diverse aesthetic realm of public theatre and its creative and innovative potentials, as well as its capacity to challenge and confront its audiences.

Notes

1   Baktruppen ceased to exist on March 1, 2011.
2   But with the prospect of being closed from 2013 onwards.

PART II

Asserting Own Distinction

Chapter 5

Programming Strategies

Smorgasbord

Main Entry: smor·gas·bord

> Pronunciation: \'smȯr-gəs-ˌbȯrd\
> Function: *noun*
> Etymology: Swedish *smörgåsbord,* from *smörgås* open sandwich + *bord* table
> Date: 1879

1: a luncheon or supper buffet offering a variety of foods and dishes (as hors d'oeuvres, hot and cold meats, smoked and pickled fish, cheeses, salads, and relishes)
2: an often large heterogeneous mixture: mélange

> (*M. Webster Dictionary*)

Theatre programmes announce a huge number of productions with an immense variety of titles and authors, but most of them are unknown to the majority of potential theatregoers today. A programmed venue usually deals with more than 100 different titles each season. A repertory company includes in its schedule some 30–40 titles. What do all those names of playwrights, from Greek classics to Yasmina Reza, mean to younger audiences? They recognise the names of sports and popular music heroes, television and film stars and fashion models, but Goldoni, Goethe, Gorky, Ghelderode, Giraudoux and Gombrowicz would probably elicit a shrug of indifference as much as Marivaux, Mickiewicz, Maeterlinck, Mrozek, Mamet or Terence, Tourneur, Turgenyev, Toller ... Of course, some Italians recognise the name of Goldoni, Germans that of Goethe and French that of Giraudoux, Poles know Mickiewicz and Mrozek, and perhaps vaguely Gombrowicz. Few British know of Tourneur today but have probably heard of Marlowe, Congreve, Sheridan, Oscar Wilde and Noel Coward, of Osborne, Pinter and Sarah Kane. Only perhaps Shakespeare, Ibsen, Chekhov, Brecht and Beckett enjoy some degree of name recognition in most European theatre cultures because they appear quite often on the production posters. Audiences in each European nation are familiar with a few of their own classic dramatists, but these are unknown or forgotten elsewhere (Mádach in Hungary, Držić in Croatia, Caragiale in Romania, Nušić in Serbia, Blaumanis in Latvia, Čašule in Macedonia ...). But theatre – even dramatic theatre – cannot count on the public's familiarity with a *canonical* repertoire, for such a corpus has been lost, unlike in the sphere of opera, where works by Mozart, Verdi, Wagner and Puccini dominate, followed by those of Rossini, Donizetti, Bizet and Richard Strauss. Such a canonical drama repertoire existed as a firm set of cultural references in most European countries until the mid-twentieth century, reinforced by the national curriculum and a subscription system that rested on regular re-staging of some well-tried and much appreciated standard plays.

A disorienting abundance

Intensive artistic developments and the exploding diversity of theatre in the last 50 years have increased and differentiated the offer but high-school graduates and even people with a university degree cannot be counted automatically among theatre connoisseurs, nor can they as a rule name more than five playwrights, if so many. *Bildung*, a corpus of general cultural literacy, once supposedly produced by traditional humanist education in Central and Eastern Europe, with its specific national equivalent in France and Great Britain, probably disintegrated after World War II and became unsustainable with the rapid succession of avant-garde movements that undermined and subverted standard cultural references, at the same time introducing a cascade of new features, styles, genres, names and titles to theatre repertoires.

Without name recognition it is difficult for theatre presenters to attract the attention of a potential audience and to stimulate their curiosity. There is perhaps too much publicity material available, digital and in print, too many photos, blurbs, titles, quotes, statements, interviews and juicy adjectives. The effect is the saturation of a disoriented, almost dizzy public, which cannot make up its mind and cannot sort out what would be of interest for me, you, us. Every season is announced as a formidable feast with a rich *smorgasbord*, displayed to titillate and appeal, but the potential theatregoer tends to remain reluctant, sceptical, hesitant and slightly confused. An appetite-killing abundance, an overflow of consumer options – but is it really necessary? Why do theatres compete with department stores, believing that abundant choices will appeal to all types of potential spectator?

In the repertory companies, the composition of the annual repertoire is a matter of a balancing act among many divergent objectives and interests: affinities of individual directors, eager to stage specific plays; the necessity to employ all members of the ensemble in the best possible way; the needs of individual members of the ensemble who are specially suited to a role, or who need to be appeased and rewarded with a specific prominent role; a mixture of genres and periods; some plays that are in the school curriculum and whose staging is expected to bring school classes to the theatre; a mix of plays that will appeal to various parts of the audience; some smaller, more simple productions to stage and run alongside more complex and more massive productions; productions made in the expectation that they will be invited to festivals or be suitable for touring – the list goes on.

A programmed venue is confronted with an enormous offer from groups and agents, with all sorts of productions available in the next season. Programmers tend to travel, some even internationally, and look out for novelties they would like to invite to their venue. They work with a set-programming budget that includes some subsidy and perhaps even some sponsorship and seek to supplement it with their own box-office income. The resulting programme of the season includes a mix of theatre forms, genres, styles and companies, with a few productions that are expected to be sold out and are supposed to indirectly subsidise those productions that are of high quality and that will enhance the prestige of the venue but will probably appeal only to a limited audience and therefore generate less box-office income. Various constituencies need to be satisfied: dance lovers and comedy fans, world music followers, children, teenagers and more traditional senior citizens. The structure of the season's offer reflects the position of the venue, its appeal, focus and artistic orientation, or its internalised notion of a broad community service. The danger is that the effort to satisfy all affinities results in a broad, varied programme, which may lack some distinct features when compared with the offer of a similar venue elsewhere and fail to cast enough clear cues for each of the imagined target groups.

A production house usually constructs its season with a combination of its own productions, conceived as adding a special flair without being necessarily connected among themselves in any way, and some invited productions expected to accent diversity. Yet the mixture might not be transparent enough for the potential audience, nor facilitate its selection.

Prompting name recognition

There are a variety of standard strategies that venues and companies use to increase the name recognition of their offer. They programme classic works that are well-known to several generations of theatregoers but also risk inducing a certain *classics fatigue syndrome*, when the older audience does not come because they feel there is nothing new to be experienced and the younger audience stays away assuming this is some old stuff of no contemporary interest. Venues bring in or commission adaptations of classic novels or of more recent literary bestsellers whose authors have achieved some notoriety in the media. This has been a method theatres employed even in the nineteenth century in order to ride on the success of popular literature at a time when middle-class reading habits were rapidly growing. Increasingly today, theatres make productions based on the scripts of well-known films, since they have become the dominant art form of popular culture and references to them are widespread and well known. Home-watching on DVDs, film-on-demand cable offers and film downloading from the Internet have made the public less dependent on cinema programming and many people tend to see the same film several times. Since art film houses propel some films to a cultural icon status, setting them apart from the commercial-film mainstream production, the promise of an intense film experience can lead to great public interest in seeing a script staged. At least that is the expectation, and it has prompted numerous stage versions of *Festen* and *Dogville*.

Films that focus on few characters and few locations, so-called conversation films (Bots 2010), can be adapted for the stage without much difficulty. In all other cases, the stage artists follow the script to some extent but cannot hope to match the strong visual impact of the film itself nor evoke the specific atmosphere of a Bergman, Pasolini, Antonioni or Visconti film. The limitations of theatre as a medium, as opposed to film, become quite obvious and that is why the expected audience appeal effect of a well-known film title as a theatre production can backfire.

Some venues succeed in engaging film and television stars to appear on stage live, counting on the fact that celebrities will act as a magnet for audiences. And they often do. There is a visible proliferation of solo shows and two-handers, tailored for well-known performers appearing as a couple. Confessional monodrama, where a single character reveals his or her own life, is a favourite vehicle. Cabaret productions and stand-up comedy have acquired rather a large audience. Made usually without subsidy, they do get programmed in subsidised venues to boost the box office against minimal costs. Narrative forms, where a well-known actor tells a story, are also common. In Italy, where complex theatre productions have become increasingly difficult to produce because of the subsidy meltdown and decaying infrastructure, Roberto Benigni reaches out to a large audience with his solo rendering of Dante's *Divina Comedia*, his cultural-hero status from the Oscar-winning film *La Vita è Bella* (1997) ensuring a huge interest. Marco Baliani, well known but not famous, travels throughout Italy with his solo shows, appearing as a narrator. Both Benigni and Baliani have their own story to tell yet also seek to avoid being entrapped in a dysfunctional system that causes too much inconvenience as a collective endeavour but hopefully still works if reduced to a minimum – one solo performer addressing the audience, supported by one single technician.

Seeking to convey to the audience a sense of business *not* as usual, some theatres stage huge productions that require exceptional concentration, patience and stamina on the part of the public and a huge time commitment. Remarkably, these productions usually do quite well, probably because they distinguish themselves, at least by their exceptional duration, from the steady flow of productions that cannot stir audience imagination. Usually, these mega-productions can be seen in two or three parts or over a weekend, in one long marathon performance, lasting sometimes 12 hours, with several generous breaks. They offer an exceptional artistic and social experience, remain in the theatregoer's memory, prompt much post-performance reflection, discussion, gossip and word-of-mouth publicity. They are usually accompanied by considerable media attention because of the outstanding effort of all involved.

Some successful marathon productions:

Ten Oorlog, inspired by Shakespeare's history chronicles, written by Tom Lanoye, for Toneelhuis Antwerp (www.toneelhuis.be), directed by Luk Perceval (1999), re-staged for Salzburger Festspiele (www.salzburgerfestspiele.at) and elsewhere.

Le Dernier Caravansérail, Le Théâtre du Soleil, Paris, directed by Ariane Mnouchkine (2003), a saga of refuge, flight and assault on "Fortress Europe," based on interviews with asylum seekers.

Tantalus, a 10-play cycle by John Burton, inspired by Greek mythology, staged in 2000 by Peter Hall in the Denver Centre for the Performing Arts (www.denvercenter.org), in association with the Royal Shakespeare Company (RSC) (www.rsc.org.uk); re-staged in 2003 by Toneelgroep De Appel in The Hague (www.deappel.nl) and so successful in returning the audience to this Dutch company that it created another mega-production, inspired by Ulysses in 2009.

Roman Tragedies, Shakespeare plays inspired by Roman history, staged as a cycle by Ivo van Hove in 2007 with Toneelgroep Amsterdam (www.tga.nl) and seen also at the Avignon Festival in 2008.

Peter Stein appears as the grandfather and consistent practitioner of the trend, with his nine-hour-long rendition of Aeschylus's *Oresteia* in 1980, revived after the fall of the Union of Soviet Socialist Republics with Russian actors; Goethe's *Faust I and II*, 21-hours long, without any cuts, performed in Hannover, Berlin and Vienna in 2000; via his own for-profit company Stein reinvested the €1m earnings from this production in Schiller's *Wallenstein* in 2007, co-produced with the subsidised Berliner Ensemble, as a mega-chronicle of the emerging idea of an integrated Europe, with Klaus Maria Brandauer and German actors, lasting 10 hours with a budget of €4.9m; most recently, in 2010, he did a stage version of Dostoevsky's novel *The Possessed* (I demoni), with Italian actors (www.idemoni.org).

Besides the staging of plays, there is also an increasing number of self-conceived pieces, where there is no play or other literary work at the beginning of the process. Such work makes it difficult to signal some familiar elements to the audience. And yet, even repertory ensembles seek to make such pieces, starting from the social reality in their own city, turning the cast into a research team, conducting interviews with citizens, focusing on specific neighbourhoods, assembling memories of some emblematic moments of urban history and ultimately creating a production that has a documentary structure and a strong local inspiration, in the hope that such a work will appeal to local city-dwellers.

Programming in larger templates

The programming of venues, productions houses and companies could acquire some coherence and become more intelligible to potential audiences if the prevailing *smorgasbord* of titles and names is replaced by a distinct series and larger programming templates, series or clusters. Instead of an alphabet soup that cannot signal the programme features and those who could/should be interested in its components, larger programming templates provide a clarifying framework to individual productions and performances. Programming in large templates, sometimes practised by festivals that highlight thematic or conceptual clusters and enable audiences to follow the thread through the programme, should be tested as a plausible method for theatre companies and venues to address multiple and sometimes contradicting interests and constituencies, at the same time probing their own collaborative talents and impulses. The most obvious examples are monographic series, presenting the work of a prominent artist in a cluster of productions and other related events, such as interviews, lectures, debates, screenings of film versions of his or her works, documentaries, etc.

Teatro Scandicci (www.scandiccicultura.eu) in a suburban community on the outskirts of Florence dedicated its entire 2005–2006 season to Samuel Beckett in the year of the 100th anniversary of his birth, bringing in prominent personalities who had a historic role in introducing Beckett to the Italian stage, as well as several foreign guests. In 2006, for the 250th anniversary of Mozart's birth and at the invitation of the City of Vienna, Peter Sellars curated a festival of new work by upcoming artists from all over the world, inspired by Mozart's opus, under the title New Crowned Hope (the name of Mozart's Masonic lodge in Vienna), working not from an existing theatre organisation but on an improvised festival platform (www.newcrownedhope.org). He was thematically profiling Mozart's rich opus as a cue, a stimulus, rough material for the new artistic rendering of hope (Aspden 2007). In spring 2009 the Royal Court created a small cluster of productions by and with Wallace Shawn. Outside Europe, in the United States, the Guthrie Theatre in Minneapolis (www.guthrietheater.org/) staged a Toni Kushner festival in 2009 with a preview of his new play *The Intelligent Homosexual's Guide to Capitalism and Socialism With a Key to the Scriptures* followed by stagings of his other plays, lectures and debates (Stevens 2009). Back in Europe, a series of productions based on Heiner Müller's plays or a season of new Irish drama come to mind as obvious programming options.

Another approach is to create a cluster of productions and related events around a cultural icon, such as Hamlet, Faust, Don Juan or Medea, who have inspired many original artistic versions, dramatic and musical, extending from literature to the performing arts and then to film. These cultural paradigms, quite well known, with an echo of rich associations, can be recalled and reconnected with contemporary issues and developments, actualised and localised.

In 2006–2007 Staatstheater Stuttgart (www.staatstheater-stuttgart.de) created a cluster of productions and events around Faust, including a parallel youth production. Choreographer Sascha Waltz created a new *Medea* opera (2006) at the Radialsystem (www.radialsystem.de), a new cultural space in Berlin, which is the primary platform of her company; in the autumn of 2007 her manager and Radial programmer Jochen Sandig created a comprehensive two-month-long thematic programme around Medea, with other artistic work, invited productions, seminars, films, debates, a whole artistic and intellectual context emerging around Sascha Waltz's new piece, connecting Medea as a myth and literary motif with current concerns about battered and abandoned women and traumatised refugees.

Various anniversaries offer opportunities to develop a cluster of productions and related events geared to one historic moment or emblematic event. Very few theatres used the opportunity in 2008 to look back at the student revolt in Europe and North America in 1968 as an anti-authoritarian and utopian outburst of critical energy and alternative imagination, worth reconsidering in our cynical and anxiety-ridden times 40 years later. In the same way 2009 offered an opportunity to focus on the counterculture of the 1960s and its peak with the Woodstock festival in 1969 or to dwell on the historic experience and sudden collapse of communism, marked by the breach in the Berlin Wall in 1989. Koninklijke Vlaamse Schouwburg (Royal Flemish Theatre) in Brussels and De Balie in Amsterdam (www.debalie.nl) created a complex programme in 2010 around the anniversary of the independence of Congo. Such anniversaries provide a peg, not so much for a superficial celebratory sentiment, but rather to affirm public theatre as an intergenerational platform, capable of exploring collective memory and challenge its regular, broadly accepted narrative versions with new facts, insights and interpretative approaches.

Besides anniversaries, there are always many large burning issues that a theatre can address in a concentrated manner, creating a template and filling it with various productions and other related events. Testing such an approach, a theatre could first organise a series of intensive internal debates with a small group of journalists, researchers, politicians, businessmen, artists and intellectuals, in order to define a complex and significant theme that has some global proportions and a specific local manifestation. That theme is elaborated and taken as a framework for a forthcoming season. The repertoire is then composed from plays, old and new, that contribute to the understanding and exploration of the theme, in addition to commissions, adaptations and other programmatic components. The theme is prominently integrated into the theatre's communications and marketing, and the public is prepared to engage with a thematic framework throughout the season. Educational programmes are developed along this thematic line. In a programming venue that does not produce its own stage work but invites already-existing productions, the same approach is possible within some time restraints. If a theatre plans its thematic framework well in advance, it can approach local partners and solicit their own contribution to the elaboration of the same theme: museums, galleries, cultural centres, smaller theatre venues and groups, music ensembles, art-film houses, institutes and learned societies, professional organisations, interest groups and platforms could all take part. With enough time for preparation the theme could be further integrated into the courses of universities and other educational organisations. Book publishers and magazines can find their own way to contribute to the theme. Local press, radio and television stations could develop special programming units. Various NGOs could also get involved.

In this way, the theme put forward by the theatre is not only an artistic choice or line but a well-orchestrated, intellectual and civic adventure with the objective to create a specific temporary *coalition of concern* in the city and an inclusive, dynamic deliberative process that reinforces cultural democracy and advances the quality of public debate. As the initiator of this thematic exploration and a key player, theatre overcomes its structural marginalisation, imposed by the cultural industry of entertainment. Instead, theatre regains a central role in the local constellation and amplifies its own impact through several simultaneous partnerships.

The chosen theme has to be prone to exploration on various levels of complexity, appeal to more than one narrow target group, not lose its urgency quickly or be surpassed by the course of events, convey a sense of challenge, refer to those experiences and developments that make many people curious, concerned and engaged. The advantages are not only in communications and marketing but in the enhanced capacity of the theatre company or venue to create allies and partners and shape a discursive community with them and the interested public, thus enhancing the role of theatre as a key platform of civil society.

Planning requires 12–24 months in advance – not only for dramaturgs to find convenient plays in the library, but also to commission new work and invite other productions available for touring in the country and abroad and allow partner organisations to define their role and contribution. Theatre needs to induce and stimulate cooperation from other local partners, but not impose or force it – rather inspire and encourage, respecting institutional identities and the programming autonomy of others while seeking to synchronise, connect and intertwine multiple engagements. A joint logo of the thematic framework and some shared communication and marketing instruments could be developed and applied to all who participate. The thematic package should also be used for special fund-raising and additional sponsorship campaigns. An international dimension is highly desirable and could be realised through inviting guests and guest productions and some international cooperation projects.

An orchestrated programming in large thematic templates brings multiple advantages: more visibility and an opportunity to recruit new audiences and turn them into recurring visitors; the capacity to communicate effectively the theatre's orientation, identity and specific output; the expansion of the theatre's engagement through cooperation with multiple partners; a peg for extra fund-raising and the creation of more national and international attention; renewal of local cultural climate, enriching it with extra vibrancy and concentration, thus confirming the merit of theatre as a public institution subsidised from public budgets for the pivotal role it plays in civil society. Through cooperation within the thematic framework, theatre and its partners learn to appreciate each other better and create additional social capital (trust), broaden the usual circles of societal debate and make cultural life more inclusive and diverse.

There are many large and significant developments that can prompt the formulation of a thematic framework. One thinks first of all of ongoing climate change and its consequences, with the initial denial shifting towards acknowledgement, a growing ecological consciousness requiring changes in behaviour, values, lifestyles and consumption patterns that must be translated into political, economic, technological and cultural strategies. Or consider migratory processes bringing an altered demography to many places and regions and provoking concerns about social cohesion and the preservation of harmonious cohabitation among various social groups. With Europe turning into a continent of senior citizens, intergenerational relations, ageing, longevity and the meaning of extended life spans gain prominence. Illnesses, old and new, from plague to polio to HIV/AIDS and Alzheimer's, invoke healing and death, isolation and solidarity, mortality and transcendence, a sense of wellness and health, as well as spirituality.

De-industrialisation, the disappearance of production and service jobs and their displacement to distant places, where the labour force is cheaper, impose consideration of the future of work in Europe, the logic of the traditional division of labour, a sense of occupation and career, the separation of leisure and work, the temporary job-holding pattern interspersed with periods of unemployment replacing the pattern of long-term employment. Collective identities have become less self-evident and thus exposed to feverish reconsideration, reinforcement and delineation, creating new individual and collective dilemmas of belonging and drawing new dividing lines across societies. With our information hunger chasing us on the electronic highway, speed and acceleration create new sorts of blindness, numbness and indifference, an informational overload as well as addiction, ego-tripping and obsessive quests for more and faster. Fanaticism and terror have rephrased violence and rendered its perception as imminent and ubiquitous, spreading anxiety and aiding the marketers of fear. Security and safety have become priority concerns and encroach on the values of individual and collective life, as an obsession as well as a source of manipulation, control and restriction of civil liberties.

Painful historical episodes have been transplanted into traumatic collective memories of specific groups that seek empathy, recognition and compensation. Contentious memories escalate in the memory wars; a suffering in the past is invoked in the present, connected with a sense of entitlement and repentance, so that the perception of time collapses like an old accordion. With the notion of progress written off, a plea for retribution takes the place of aspirations and hope. The economic crisis, which exploded in 2008, has shaken the tenets of neo-liberal ideology, brought back state capitalism for a while and generated deep anxieties and uncertainties about the long-range impact of lost capital and accumulated debt; joblessness, homelessness, loss of savings and pension destroy the career planning of middle-aged people and the early retirement dreams of the baby boomers. The young discover that entry into the job market might be more complicated than expected. Frustrated, short-changed and disoriented people can easily be manipulated into outbursts of chauvinism and racism. The victims to blame are self-evident and available.

All these thematic clusters could each become the theme for a season or a thematic line marking its path over a few weeks or months. But are there some examples of such programming in larger thematic templates? Yes, there are some tentative cases, indicating that producers and programmers do think along thematic template lines to react promptly to major societal debates.

Teatro Maria Matos, one of two Lisbon municipal venues (www.teatromariamatos.pt), has been working with trimester themes since the beginning of the 2009–2010 season. Governance, time, biography, abundance, origin ... each of these themes is the focal point of an autumn, winter or spring part of the season, with its own visual identity and programme brochure. In addition to his own productions, the director Mark Deputter invites other artists and their work, organises discussions and special events, gradually broadening the range of partners who join in with their own artistic and intellectual contributions.

In the past the Tricycle Theatre in Kilburn, North London (www.tricycle.co.uk), has created several coherent series of new dramatic works, usually commissioned. In April – June 2009 Tricycle ran a series called Great Game: Afghanistan, invoked as a "festival" in the publicity material, consisting of premieres of 12 newly commissioned plays by UK authors, documentary and feature film screenings, exhibits and discussions. In its three chronological parts, covering 1842–1930, 1979–1996 and 1996–2009, the producer Nicholas Kent sought to re-examine not only the tumultuous and largely unknown history of Afghanistan, a country where British soldiers are currently being killed every week, but also to go beyond the front-page news and recall the long-standing connection of this distant and obscure territory with British and Russian imperialism. While a debate heats up in the UK public about the political, ethical and military rationale of UK involvement in the Afghanistan war against the Taliban, the Tricycle series offers a deepening of insights, a multitude of perspectives, an imaginative transfer to contemporary and historical situations, a personalisation of cultural clashes and the deconstruction of repeated instances of political opportunism, together with a discussion forum for concerned, informed and outspoken theatregoing citizens. It is a rich, intensive and quickly prepared series that embodies the unique function of public theatre in a democracy, caught in dramatic soul-searching (Straaten 2009).

In 2009 the RSC created a season of post-Soviet theatre under the title "Revolutions," consisting of two newly commissioned plays, *The Grain Store* by Ukrainian playwright Natalia Vorozhbit on the *holodmor*, the Ukrainian mass famine of the 1930s, and *The Drunks* by the Durnenkov brothers, Russian playwrights, about a soldier returning from the Chechen war, accompanied by a package of discussions and seminars, as well as public readings of new Russian plays in English translations; a new version of *Boris Godunov* and an adaptation of Gogol's *Dead Souls* are to follow later (Aspden 2009).

Facing the menacing proportions of the economic recession, the London Soho Theatre (www.sohotheatre.com) commissioned ten plays in April 2009 and staged them in June as a series called *Everything Must Go!* (Hemming 2009).

While many theatre companies and venues remain reluctant to give up their traditional *smorgasbord* programming method, fearing politicisation or loss of diversity, other types of cultural organisation might find it easier to think in these integrative programming terms. Cultural centres, which are always struggling to give the multitude of their programmatic output some coherence, might find such template programming rather convenient to set up larger series, which will be better noticed by the public and attract a recurring audience.

Vrede van Utrecht (www.vredevanutrecht2013.nl) is a fluid cultural organisation, funded by the city and the province of Utrecht (NL) to create each year until 2013 (the celebration of the 300th anniversary of the Treaty of Utrecht) several programme packages, lasting from one to four weeks, on various pressing themes, and in cooperation with local institutions and resources, including venues and theatre groups. The organisation has only a core team and works with guest curators of thematic blocs, which have so far included explorations of art production in war conditions, migration and acculturation, changes in specific urban neighbourhoods, the suburban landscape, and common threads among major monotheistic religions. The organisation is gradually preparing resources, networks and partnerships, which are expected to reinforce Utrecht's candidacy to become the European Capital of Culture in 2018 and broaden the support base to develop its programming.

What needs to happen in theatres to switch them to a larger template programming? The change will not be imposed from the outside, by the subsidy providers, at least not for some time. Artists working either within the organisation or outside are also unlikely to plead for a broader and more complex programming formula since they tend to think of their *own* project only. The artistic and managerial leadership of performing arts organisations might instigate such a change, realising that the organisation has more chance of pulling through the tough times ahead with the reinforced partnerships, which such a programming method requires and stimulates, than without them. In the rep companies, dramaturgs might appear as initial agents of change – they are equipped to think conceptually, and even though larger templates might make them busier, they would also foreground their role in conceptualisation, planning and realisation. But arrayed against them they would have individual artists, concerned about their own new roles for the next season, directors fixed on a specific play, marketing departments fearful that they might alienate more target groups than win new audiences. So it would be a difficult, slow and uncertain process of institutional change, requiring as it does the re-imagining of an organisation and its position in the immediate context – from a provider of a diverse package of artistic offer to an instigator of complex ideas, probed in multiple partnerships, from a self-perception driven by artistic impulses to an idea of theatre as a forum for social debate and analysis stimulated by artistic gestures and artefacts. Inevitably, calls for the defence of artistic autonomy will also be deployed to block a shift to larger templates.

Venue programmers might realise that larger series could bring them distinction and a unique programming offer, putting them ahead of the competitors even if they had to rely to some extent on the same pool of available artists and their productions. They could learn from festival directors, who think conceptually and invent themes and slogans to stress the unique features of their selection and mutual connections among the work featured. Curators of large exhibits in museums and galleries also develop and offer diverse auxiliary programmes and activities. Isolated instances of larger thematic template programming, even if they cover just a few weeks and not the entire season, will work as an encouragement. And yet, *smorgasbord* programming is deeply entrenched in European theatres, reflecting the variety and richness of the offer available but also the pervasive anti-intellectual climate of many performing arts organisations, suspicious of concepts and conceptualisation while at the same time – paradoxically – trusting blindly marketing mix formulas, and perpetuating the conviction that they have something to offer to everyone – every target group and interest – every week and every month.

Chapter 6

A Sense of Place

Theatre activity is at first glance associated with the disposition of a theatre venue. Yet a building made specifically to accommodate performances is a relatively recent phenomenon in the 2500-year-long history of theatre: it was only towards the end of the sixteenth century that playhouses evolved from Spanish urban courtyards (*corrales*), Elizabethan inn-courtyards and the improvised stages of banqueting halls and courtyards in Italian Renaissance palaces. The first venues – the Theatre built on the outskirts of London in 1576, the Madrid *corrales* turned into permanent venues between 1575 and 1585, the Teatro Olimpico in Vicenza, built during 1580–1585 – were followed by the Italian court theatres of Sabbionetta and Farnese in Parma. After a century of consolidation in the application of Renaissance notions of space, a standard format emerged in the late seventeenth century, primarily supporting the performing practice and needs of opera, accompanied by an orchestra, placed below the stage. The spectacle of the opera was framed by a proscenium arch and separated by it from the audience in the auditorium. The audience was placed in circular or semi-elliptical rows of seats, with the distinctions of social status and wealth reflected in the comfort and quality of vision. This separation was less rigid in many drama theatres, where the thrust stage was gradually reduced to a less deep proscenium and the fops who preferred to sit on the stage rather than in the auditorium were chased away in London and Paris only at the end of the eighteenth century.

Failed reforms, some accomplishments

The eighteenth and nineteenth centuries were marked by the growth in the size of theatres (up to 3,600 places), the embellishment of the proscenium arch, an increase in the width and depth of the box stage (the Italian stage), an advancement in sophisticated technical equipment (movable sets, sliding sideways in grooves, splendid effects, flying machines, a rotation stage), and constant improvements in lighting (from torches and candles to oil and then gas lamps, and finally electricity). In parallel, the comfort of the spectators and safety were improved, with stringent anti-fire precautions. With boxes turned into small luxury salons for reception, banqueting and even amorous pursuits, with splendid foyers and salons, monumental vestibules and galleries, the theatre became a place of socialisation, encounters, parading, gossip, a favourite location for the display of social status and power, a privileged circumstance for the making and propagation of fashion, as well as a place for flirting and prostitution. From the outside, eighteenth- and nineteenth-century theatres were constructed as temples of arts, placed in privileged positions in the city centre, with elaborate, embellished façades, splendid entrances and grandiose staircases (Leacroft and Leacroft 1984).

The history of twentieth-century theatre architecture could be seen as a series of mainly failed attempts to overcome these traditional patterns of theatre space. The twentieth-century theatre-makers, producers, architects and financiers hardly altered the predominance of the frontal positioning of performers towards the audience, and the sharp distinction between the stage and the auditorium, stressed by the proscenium arch. Futuristic renditions of what a theatre would look like were grandiose, even megalomaniac, intended for mass audiences of many thousands, with gigantic movable screens envisaged by Edward Gordon Craig, graded stage floors designed by Adolph Appia, and the double-triple rotation stage of Gropius, aided by Piscator, and Barchin, inspired by Meyerhold. These were far-reaching but never realised futuristic dreams. Instead we have today large sports stadiums for 100,000 spectators – with beams of blinding light, large digital screens, the overwhelming presence of advertising – used for sports events and occasionally for large concerts of popular music, but not for theatre performances.

Since the end of the nineteenth century, significant theatre innovations have taken place not on such a grand scale but in small improvised theatre spaces, for an audience of 100–250 people, without special comfort but with much intimacy, uniting the performers and the spectators despite the dogma of the fourth wall. Antoine's Théâtre Libre, Théâtre de l'Œuvre, The Independent Theatre, Freie Bühne, Strindberg's Intimate Theatre – all these small-size, non-commercial theatres brought about the reform of subject matter and style, language and visualisation, while respecting the norm of the proscenium arch between the performers and the audience. After World War II they inspired the proliferation of pocket and chamber theatres, of studio theatres with the audience seated in a few rows on two or three sides or in a circle, and then of the black box theatres with flat floor stage and the public seated on elevated stands.

While advanced stage technology made changes of set quick and easy, the trend towards simplicity and abstract forms, compensated by sophisticated lighting, marked the modernism of the twentieth century. The rotation stage was practically discarded, except in rare opera and musical productions. In order to stress the centrality of actors and their performance over other visual elements, Copeau introduced a permanent set in the Vieux Colombier theatre in Paris in the 1920s. It was expected to work in all productions – a solution taken over to some extent by the much larger thrust stages of Stratford (Ontario) and the Guthrie Theatre in Minneapolis, constructed in the 1950s. The Olivier stage in the National Theatre in London (1976), and the Shakespeare Memorial Theatre in Stratford-upon-Avon, remodeled in 2010 (Dinulović 2009; Heathcote 2010) opted for the thrust stage in order to improve visibility and reinforce intimacy and the proximity of the audience to the action. The thrust stage demands a semicircular auditorium and imposes specific demands on the mise-en-scène and acting style, as Tyrone Guthrie discovered in his late productions. Despite experiments with an arena, and the placing of the audience almost full circle or on three to four sides in larger and smaller venues, the frontal juxtaposition of the box stage and semicircular auditorium, separated by the proscenium arch, remained the norm throughout the twentieth century. Never have more theatres been built in Europe than in the decade or two after 1945 and never has the implemented spatial innovation been of a more cosmetic nature (Dinulović 2009).

A matter of context

Theatre architecture has its own strong tradition, but *where* theatres come to be built is usually decided by politicians and urban planners. The public value of a theatre is not only determined by how its building looks and what it has to offer, but also how it fits into the urban context. A theatre building inscribes itself with its programme, facilities, shape, structure and audience within the urban texture of a city and the neighbourhood in which it is situated. Historically, the first London theatres were built after 1576 just beyond the city limits, signalling the liminality of theatre activities, their implicit sinfulness or at least moral ambiguity as judged by the prevailing puritan views of the urban middle class. In Madrid, *corrales* could function in the city centre under the strong surveillance of religious authorities but had to expiate their presumed sinfulness by channelling part of their earnings into charitable purposes. From the early eighteenth century, theatres were commonly erected in the city centre, next to other edifices that radiated power and prestige, so that theatre implicitly also claimed social influence, cultural clout and a prescriptive role in matters of taste and judgement of the arts. Such claims would not be sustainable today and the central position of the venue usually means that it is situated in an intensive commercial context of retail infrastructure and places for going out. A theatre building in a central urban spot draws certain advantages from such a privileged location, but needs to interact with its neighbours and signal an open-door policy of hospitality and welcome to all passers-by, whether they enter the building to attend a performance or just have some fun in its public zone.

Today's theatre managers in downtown locations tend to worry about the parking provision for visitors, the quality of street lighting as a factor in feeling safe and the timetable of late-evening public transport. Certainly, these are all legitimate concerns, but eminently solvable if there is an attitude of cooperation rather than of institutional jealousy and competitiveness in a cluster of centrally located cultural organisations and facilities, supported by surrounding cafés, restaurants, bookshops and other related commercial outlets. Theatres and museums, for instance, have more shared concerns and interests than what separates them as public cultural organisations, and yet it is rare for them to cooperate – even when they are situated next door to each other. Cultural clusters have been emerging in bigger cities as a result of the efforts of urban planners to concentrate and connect the existing cultural infrastructure and add additional facilities, thus hopefully increasing their appeal and effectiveness. The real benefits of a cluster emerge only if the cultural organisations themselves find ways to collaborate – in signposting, marketing and common concerns for the safety, comfort and cleanliness of the area – and preferably if they also share some expertise (like ICT) and services (catering, merchandising) and coordinate their programming schedules and opening times. Most theatres tend to open their doors only an hour or two after the surrounding stores and cultural facilities (such as museums) close, but this does not have to be the case. Modifications in working hours can keep the dynamic life within the cluster going until late in the evening.

If plurality of diverse functions is integrated into the operation and programming of a theatre venue, if the building is made accessible to the public not just during a few evening hours but throughout the day, theatre has a chance of becoming one of the crucial points of socialisation for various groups that use it as a resource for their diverse needs. In theatres that have understood this dynamic, one can watch various groups come in at different times of the day to attend a performance, a guided tour, a lecture, a public discussion or a children's workshop, or to drop into the bookshop, have lunch, tea or drinks and appear again for the evening performance and a late-night snack and drink. Several hundred people of various generations and interests pass through such an inviting, hospitable playhouse throughout the day. A theatre that contains a gallery, a library, a bookshop, an Internet café, one or more restaurants and cafeterias and a comfortable lounge/lobby appeals to citizens to come in from mid-morning on, to have fun, to meet someone or simply to work. A free Wi-Fi access to the Internet turns a theatre lobby into a meeting and working space.

> People who come to the London South Bank complex of cultural organisations during the day can work for hours on their laptops in a quiet corner, meet other people and network, schedule appointments, go with someone for lunch, a walk or a concert, and perhaps, as an extra option, see a performance, a film or attend a concert at the end of a productive and diverse day. In contrast, most other theatre buildings remain closed to the public throughout the day and open one hour before the performance, closing again half an hour after it ends, thus fulfilling their public function in a minimal time span instead of seeking to extend it and attract people throughout the day and the evening.

If a new theatre is erected in some peripheral urban zone or established there through the conversion of an existing building, the usual expectation is that it will serve local needs but also act as a magnet, help develop the surrounding district, initiate the revival of commercial activity, increase sociability and the intensity of pedestrian traffic, and, in time, attract other cultural, educational and social initiatives and organisations to settle in the neighbourhood. This might indeed happen, but not as quickly as urban planners and community activists usually expect. For years the theatre or cultural centre may be rather lonely, even isolated, perceived by those who live in the central urban zones to be too far away, too difficult to access. Even good public transport – always essential for a theatre's well-being – may not be able to alter those negative perceptions. If a theatre is placed in a distant, underprivileged community, it could also be perceived by the local inhabitants as an arrogant and wealthy bastion of distant elitist culture. And indeed, people working in this theatre might commit the folly of living up to this negative image and remain aloof, unconnected and indifferent to the social and cultural realities in front of their doors and yearning for their audience to come from the central and wealthier parts of the city. Or they can take the time and energy to engage with the surrounding community and prove that they are eager to serve it and involve it. It is a matter of patiently building trust, which should ultimately result in mutual benefits.

The Theatre Royal Stratford, on the eastern outskirts of London (www.stratfordeast.com), has a venerable history as the Theatre Workshop of Joan Littlewood, who produced the premieres of well-known British plays there in the 1950s and 1960s. When Philip Hedley took over the leadership of the theatre in 1979 he gradually attuned the theatre with the surrounding area, much altered by migration, and built it over the next 25 years into a key force for interculturalism by programming new productions and education, as well as a change in the composition of the staff, management and board. Today, Hedley's successors at the Theatre Royal take cultural diversity as its main asset, run educational programmes, develop new plays and new musical theatre, give voice to exiled authors and run a complex cooperation scheme with Birkbeck University.

In contrast, MC 93 Bobigny (www.mc93.com), in the north-eastern outskirts of Paris, is a result of the French policy of cultural decentralisation, which in this case has worked out as dumping. Set at the crossroads of Blvd Maurice Thorez and Blvd Lénine, in a former working-class Communist stronghold, this venue has a distinguished record for its innovative music and dance programming and many international guest appearances, especially of the US avant-garde, but has little connection with its surroundings. The demography of the area has been altered, together with its political orientation, and most residents nearby have their cultural consumption habits conditioned by the cultural industry and not by a provident state offering cultural emancipation. MC 93 has displayed little sensitivity to the cultural affinities and needs of the community in the immediate vicinity and its lasting dependence on the central Paris audience has made it quite vulnerable. In 2008, the French Ministry of Culture sought to stabilise the venue by bringing it under the management of the Comédie-Française, the oldest state company in Europe, located in the very centre of Paris, but abandoned the idea under loud protests from performing arts circles. The local integration of MC 93 cannot be improved by centralist directives or by managerial takeover since it is an issue of local politics and intercultural openness in a concrete urban zone.

The cultural and social synergy of theatre and its neighbourhood is achievable only if the playhouse asserts itself as a public facility of the local community, as well as of the entire city and painstakingly explores the micro-structure of the civil society in its neighbourhood in order to identify possible allies and partners and develop a relationship with them finding informal ambassadors who will spread the word about the theatre and instigate interest in it and goodwill towards it.

Space markers

Public theatres seek to draw the attention of passers-by to their programme as much as commercial venues do, with large panels, banners, posters and blinking electric advertising but they could go a step further by revealing their internal working process. The inside of the theatre has become more transparent for those outside thanks to ample usage of glass panels in modern building construction but the large-size video screens on the façade could also show excerpts from past and present productions, sequences from rehearsals, shots of the stage while a crew is building a set, or ongoing work in the theatre workshops or leisure scenes from the lobby. If the exterior of a commercial venue screams out how entertaining, hilarious or thrilling its currently running show is, a public venue could use its exterior not just to advertise its running production but also to reveal its multiple working processes and make itself more intriguing and inviting for those who have never taken the trouble to enter. Small scenes, acts and musical moments performed outside the venue reinforce the inside/outside dialectics and prompt passers-by to dare to come in.

The fluidity of theatre space also requires attention, both in the front of the house and in the auditorium. The younger zapping public, rock-concert and club visitors and shopping-mall regulars have difficulty accepting the rigidity of spatial lines, barriers and behaviour conventions of late nineteenth-century theatre at the beginning of the twenty-first century. One can mingle in the foyer before and after the performance and in the intermission, but otherwise must sit still in the darkness during the show, be quiet and applaud politely at the end. That is the ruling convention. In some parts of Southern Europe, in the whole Mediterranean basin in fact, as well as on the Indian subcontinent, on the islands of Indonesia, in China and in some traditional Japanese playhouses, the audience eats, drinks, comments during the performance, addresses the performers, goes in and out, takes a nap, and sits with babies and small children. The old prints and caricatures from the English and French theatres of the eighteenth and nineteenth centuries indicate that such behaviour was once a normal part of Western European theatre life as well, but was eliminated as theatre ceased to be a form of popular entertainment and turned into a stronghold of high culture, ruled by the norms of middle-class decency and restraint. New norms of propriety, imposed on more prestigious houses, dominated by middle-class audiences, sought to differentiate them from the more unruly, bawdy popular playhouses of working-class entertainment (Ehrenreich 2007).

The dominant organisation of the auditorium, with slightly elevated seats in rows or on stands, is not very suitable for those who would like to go in and out, shift perspective, come closer or go further away from the performers – as many youngsters would like to do in the theatre. They resent being forced to sit silently without moving throughout the performance, or at least until the intermission, if there is one. Increasingly, theatres have been learning from incidents with bored young audiences causing disturbances. Free seating and short performances without intermission have become more frequent, not only in theatre for children and young people.

As a step further in the same direction, the company Het Waterhuis (www. theatergroepsiberia.nl) performed *Atalanta* (2006) in an emerging cultural centre in Rotterdam harbour, converted from a former warehouse, where all 100 spectators stood around a central platform for the entire performance, as at a rock concert. Large video panels were on all four walls. A 55-minute-long performance enabled individual spectators to move around the space among other spectators, standing closer or further away from the central platform or focusing more on the video screens.

In his long production of the *Roman Tragedies* for Toneelgroep Amsterdam, Ivo van Hove made allowances for the audience's fatigue and restlessness by making it possible for them to leave the auditorium, go out for a drink, a snack or a cigarette, but stay connected with the progress of the performance via large screens and loudspeakers, placed in the cafeteria and other public places in the theatre. Upon return, the viewers could take another seat in the auditorium or decide to sit on the stage.

In some other instances, spectators who leave the auditorium during the performance can stay in touch with it by listening to its live audio-stream on earphones with a transmitter. Obviously, in a large auditorium with long rows of densely packaged seating with little space between them, anyone who wants to leave or come back to the performance inevitably disturbs other spectators. In its recent renovation, the Berlin Volksbühne (www.volksbuehne-berlin.de) eliminated its fixed rows of seats and replaced them with large cushions on the floor, offering more fluidity in the space for going in and out, as well as more options for how the audience wants to watch the performance, sitting up straight or reclining. But it also reduced the capacity of its large hall.

Whoever buys a £5 ticket for the pit of the arbitrary and hypothetical replica of the Globe Theatre (originally from 1599, rebuilt 1614), erected in 1997 in London, on the south bank of the Thames, comes to stand in an inner space that is seductive and intimate, with good vision. It allows the audience to move around during the performance and watch it from shifting points of view. The groundlings in the pit used to have more freedom in Shakespeare's day, however; now the pit audience is under the close surveillance of strict, grumpy stewards. Nevertheless, spectators seated in the galleries and those in the pit can look at each other in the daylight and the sense that they are together taking part in a public event is much stronger than in the usual darkened auditorium of a conventional playhouse. Notwithstanding the far-fetched claim that the Globe faithfully reproduces the conventions and stylistic features of performances in Shakespeare's time, this is a fine space, flexible and unusual, albeit firmly entrenched in the mass-tourism industry: its gift shops and eating and drinking facilities compete with the educational impact or cultural significance of the productions. The Globe, a non-subsidised private endeavour, is part of the broad revival of the south bank of the Thames, with elegant office buildings, luxurious apartments and many restaurants and bars, flanked by a pedestrian path with stunning vistas running for miles, connecting the Design Museum, the Tate Modern and the South Bank Centre, a remarkable cultural cluster that reiterates the significance of the context for theatre. Encouraged by the Globe's success, the Shakespeare Festival in Gdansk, Poland, plans to erect a theatre venue inspired by the Elizabethan playhouse (www.festiwalszekspirowski.pl).

Artists also expect flexibility and fluidity from a venue but are in practice confronted with legal regulations and standards, house rules and sometimes a lack of cooperation and goodwill from the house staff. Coming to rehearse or to perform, artists expect to find an inspiring, challenging space, which can be adjusted to fit their vision, as well as the needs and specific demands of the production, or a work in progress. In practice, they sometimes find indifference, constraints, discomfort, and even dangerous spots and situations. Every season news items appear about stage accidents, occurring even in the most respectable European theatres and opera houses in performance and in rehearsal (BBC 2007). In 2009 performers complained about the dismal condition of the dressing rooms in some West End theatres, leaking toilets and even rats running along the backstage corridors. Years earlier, the association of West End theatre owners calculated how many million pounds they would need to refurbish their old, heavily used venues and increase audience comfort. They were claiming that, as a major factor of the London tourist industry, they deserved some public support for the improvements, a small percentage of the value added tax earned with ticket sales (Baluch 2009).

A public theatre facility has an even stronger obligation than a commercial venue to respond to the expectations of both the audience and the artists, as well as all the staff members who work there. The EU public and occupational safety standards are slowly being introduced all over Europe. In Central and Eastern Europe one sees recently renovated theatre buildings with many improvements made, but also venues still in a dismal state, ripe for radical refurbishment, waiting to have the ugly elements from the 1970s peeled away and taken out, and some comfort and style introduced into the drab lobby and hall, shabby workshops, offices and dressing rooms. These venues show years of neglect and insufficient maintenance due to inadequate subsidy, but also to the withdrawal of care and goodwill by the demoralised, disgruntled staff, visible in dusty corners, forgotten pieces of furniture, twisted light features and missing electric bulbs. Such a state of decay usually signals the waning of artistic energies, a drop in the production rate and the overall loss of the theatre's ability to engage and thrill its audience. Therefore, just pumping EU structural funds subsidies into theatre renovation will not automatically make them into vibrant artistic spaces or popular social hubs unless there is a major investment of creativity and hospitality on the part of the employees, unless attitudes change and an internalised sense of a public service is gained.

An artistic vision projects its own spatial desiderata, hence the understandable striving of an increasing number of artists and companies to have their own venue, however small. Nevertheless, the argument could be made that public facilities should not be monopolised by one group of artists, especially as many groups, which have finally secured their own venue, have difficulties sustaining it financially and filling the capacity with their own productions alone. Touring groups prefer staying for a few days in a selected number of playhouses, affiliated by kinship, appreciation, warm hospitality and comfort, rather than touring in a routine series of one- or two-night stands in many cities, using dozens of uninviting venues where they are received with indifference.

Big or small?

Big theatres, with 1,000 or more seats, are potentially suitable for commercial exploitation and can compensate with the sense of spectacle for what they lack in intimacy. They can increase their average seat occupancy by discounting the price of tickets for seats with restricted view, offer reductions for early bookings and sell the last few dozen available tickets at last-minute prices. Such theatres prosper if they are strategically located in big cities or organise an exquisite group-marketing strategy to bus in larger groups of people from further away. Small theatres, whether with an Italian stage or a flat floor, with 100–400 seats, need some – but not much – operating and programming subsidy, especially if they are open to performing artists and various cultural and educational organisations, audience groups and subgroups. Such venues are most suitable for the tasks of a public theatre – exploring, experimenting, creating and challenging the audience and instigating a debate.

Medium-sized theatres, with 500–1,000 seats, many of them built in the 1950s–1970s, now need modernisation, aesthetic redesign, upgrading of functions and facilities and expensive technological improvements, also in order to adjust to new workplace and fire protection rules. But this type of theatre seems to be in serious trouble. Not big enough to go commercial, with running costs too high to be properly subsidised, of little attraction to artists of whatever discipline and imposing an uneasy anonymity on the audience, such theatres are common problem cases, especially in cities of under 100,000 inhabitants, where it is usually difficult to gather more than 400 people for anything a non-commercial venue would offer. Consequently, managers and programmers of such theatres are forced to make compromises and book productions that, properly speaking, belong to commercial venues, such as popular singers, stand-up comedians and magicians, light comedies, whodunits, tribute shows and similar standard entertainments. In this way, they undermine their own quality programming, poach in the commercial theatre fishpond of hits, but also make some extra money at the box office by having the venue full at least a few times a year.

Luck smiles on those theatres that can offer some flexibility in the size of the auditorium, thanks to expandable stands accommodating, for instance, 450 or 900 spectators, so that the venue does not have to look half-empty even if, in reality, it is because its auditorium shrinks and expands according to the size of the production and the public it can generate. An additional convenience appears if the venue has a big stage and a smaller stage under the same roof, or if a smaller stage has been created later on through the conversion of a rehearsal room or a workshop, as long as the separate audience streams can be managed smoothly and there is no noise interference between the two performance zones. In this way a theatre can acquire more flexibility in programming and can better match audience interest to the available space. If this double-track programming is impossible in the same building, a smaller offshoot can be created elsewhere in the city, such as Milan's Piccolo Teatro or the Budapest Katona József Színhás (katonajozsefszinhaz.hu) possess. The new building of the Drama Section of the Royal Danish Theatre in Copenhagen (www.kglteater. dk) has three stages. Kungliga Dramatiska Teatern (www.dramaten.se) goes to extremes with seven different spaces in the main building and elsewhere around Stockholm, practically competing with itself and luring the audience from one of its own stages to another, a constellation whose rationale is difficult to grasp.

Smaller theatres clearly have lower overheads and are easier to maintain. They are also easier to make ecologically sustainable, while large venues function as insatiable energy guzzlers with their high ceilings, broad corridors and staircases, spacious lobbies, heating and air-conditioning systems and extensive lighting equipment. Ecological concerns have become a hot issue in venue construction and management and are rising on the attention list of festival organisers.

The Arcola Theatre in Dalston, East London (www.arcolatheatre.com), has been recognised as a pioneer in the reduction of carbon dioxide emissions through recycling, solar panels on the roof, a biomass boiler in the cellar and radical retooling of its lighting instruments, enabling it to run performances in its 200-seat hall with 5 kW only, instead of the usual 30–50 kW. The leadership of Arcola, with an energy engineer as Executive Director, seeks to make it the first carbon-neutral theatre and to develop with artists and engineers such energy-saving strategies as will also benefit the surrounding community. With 70,000 visitors a year, Arcola contemplates developing and selling ecologically sound products to the public alongside theatre tickets. This environmentalist commitment has brought Arcola distinction among similar-size venues and some new valuable partnerships (www.arcolaenergy.com).

In autumn 2010 Jellyfish Theatre on a Southwark playground in London became the United Kingdom's first fully functioning theatre made entirely from recycled and reclaimed materials (ACE 2010), but it remains a curiosity, an exception to force the issue onto the agenda. With the fossil fuel energy shortage set only to become worse in the future, it is realistic to expect that all public cultural facilities will seek to reduce their energy bills in the next ten years and that many will generate at least some of their own energy. Energy costs and the generally sluggish growth of European economies might slow down the building of large venues and tighten the environmental requirements for all new construction projects, big or small. Besides waste reduction, it is quite probable that all public cultural facilities will grow some food on the roof, balconies or adjacent plots of land, at least for their own cafeteria consumption.

Newly built or recycled?

Many municipalities, determined to build new theatre venues and expand and renovate the existing ones, do not pose the crucial questions: Who is it for? Who is the target audience? How many evenings a year can the capacity be sold out? What orientation will the programme have? What demands and expectations must this facility satisfy?

Politicians rarely think about such essential questions, since they are seeking to leave a trace in stone of their glorious term in office. Powerful construction lobbies smell money and play on the ambitions of municipal politics to reach distinction with impressive edifices. Architects hope to earn fame with a prominent public building. Numerous consultants and specialists look for well-paid assignments for feasibility studies and advice in various complex technical matters. This constellation of enmeshed interests and aspirations too often results in a cultural infrastructure intended for twenty-first-century usage, but derived from anachronistic images and notions of nineteenth-century theatre practice and architecture. Driven by prestige objectives, the construction of a new theatre gets entangled in incompatible desires to create a multifunctional space that will be suitable for a symphonic concert, dramatic theatre, dance and musicals, but also serve for professional conventions and conferences. An overambitious list of demands sinks into a sea of obscure technical questions of acoustics, movable sets of seats, lighting facilities and noise isolation. Vital social, cultural and aesthetic issues that will determine the usage and functioning of these spaces in future decades are ignored or sidelined. Artists are not asked what they want and need, or what their dreams are. Architects with little theatre experience and a limited understanding of the changes that have been occurring in performing arts practice think they know better and reproduce traditionalist models, which fit the expectation pattern of politicians but disappoint the artists and the public as users.

Theatres are built or renovated to expand their audience capacity even in cities where no significant population growth is expected, where there are no recognisable artistic resources to run them properly and where a huge audience development process needs to be undertaken at an early stage to ensure public acceptance of a new facility. Otherwise, newly built oversized theatres and old, oversized and old-fashioned theatres, renovated and recklessly extended at great cost, lose money despite optimistic income predictions. Or, during a slump in the construction industry, politicians find money to build structures, but fail to provide them with an adequate operating subsidy and programming budget, as happened in the early 1990s, when 300 historic theatres in Spain were renovated with the aid of EU structural funds, but not endowed by the public authorities with an adequate running budget and thus left dark for most nights or used only as cinemas.

Among hundreds of theatres built in Europe since 1980 there are few architectural successes. Top architects are rarely engaged for theatre construction projects and new theatres do not make architects famous, as museums do nowadays. Once built, theatre buildings become an issue of public controversy and much criticism, especially if the artistic output is also mediocre. Municipal politicians and civil servants miss the opportunity to consult with sociologists, demographers and cultural analysts about the dynamics and patterns of the employment of free time in the surrounding community. They would do better to ask the theatre-makers about their aspirations and references and talk to teachers and teenagers, send the architect to a club and a rock-concert hall to observe the dynamics of sociability, the patterns of movement, the concentration and fragmentation of attention, the atmosphere. They should look at theatres that are doing well and especially at the newly built playhouses that have failed to work properly, such as the Millennium Centre in Cardiff, Wales (www.wmc.org.uk), with its £16m deficit in two years of operation and plastic buckets in the lobby to catch the rain from the leaking roof! Building a new theatre can take years, even decades if the funds run out, so that when the venue finally opens it may well appear as an anachronism in relation to altered circumstances and needs. A year of debugging, trouble-shooting and adjustment of the building and its technology should be envisaged before a smooth mode of operation is reached.

> For 170 years, building a proper venue for the National Theatre (www.nemzetiszinhaz. hu) has been a major cultural and political project of the Hungarians, since the time when they wanted to assert themselves against the dominance of the German-speaking inhabitants of Budapest. For some reason or other, the National Theatre has always been quartered in some temporary, improvised structure, even after many fine theatre buildings were erected in the last third of the nineteenth century and afterwards for other companies and when the city's theatre life became rich and diverse, encompassing everything from boulevard to avant-garde, from opera to cabaret. Under communism, and especially from the late 1960s, the National Theatre was not the dominant artistic force, but yielded that role to several repertory companies, such as the Katona József or the regional rep ensemble in Kaposvár (www.csiky.hu). The project of a proper building remained on the political agenda even after the end of communism, as a kind of historical debt of the nation and, after one more public call, a left-wing government approved an architectural plan in the mid-1990s. Work started in the very centre of the city. A subsequent right-wing government decided to turn the hole excavated into an underground garage cum club, changed the architect and assigned a new location, a few kilometres outside the centre, in a non-descript area near the banks of the Danube. There, a new proper theatre building designed by architect Mária Siklós opened in spring 2002.
>
> A visitor walks several hundred metres from the tram stop or from a car park, passes under a concrete portal in the middle of a meadow that serves as a parody of a triumphal gate, and sees a whole pediment lying in puddles of water as a reminder of previous National Theatre buildings, surrounded by hyper-realist statues of famous actors from the past. The theatre building seeks to imitate a ship, including an extended deck ending in a wooden bowsprit, pointing in the wrong direction. The view of the Danube is spoilt by a Babylonian ziggurat nearby, whose function is enigmatic. The venue is an inelegant colossus, an eclectic mixture of forms, materials and proportions, difficult to take in.

Inside, ostentatious kitsch reigns, with expensive fixtures and fittings: the carpets, lamps, chairs, and even the washbasin taps in the toilets are all in eminently bad taste. The main hall has 700 seats, including one gallery, and there are old-fashioned boxes, the stalls are split in half, with a barrier resembling those in eighteenth-century venues, where the rabble in the first rows had to be kept at bay from *la bonne bourgeoisie* seated behind them. Outside, there is a small open-air stage and in the basement a decent studio-stage of 150 seats. Years after the opening, many Budapest theatregoers stubbornly refuse to approach this architectural monster.

While in some cities plans are being made to build a new theatre, in others everyone is at a loss about what to do with the existing one. As industrial entertainment products gain a broad public and fewer people go to the theatre, theatre buildings come to stand abandoned for years because they are too big and too expensive to exploit or upgrade technically. To make them usable again would require a major renovation, especially delicate and more expensive if the requirements of cultural monument protection have to be matched with mandatory safety requirements. The Bourla Theatre in Antwerp (1827), abandoned as unusable in the 1980s, thoroughly and exquisitely renovated in 1993 when Antwerp was the European Capital of Culture, is now again running up against the limits of usability because of rapidly changing safety standards, to which the playhouse can no longer respond. There are several theatre buildings of great cultural heritage value that are practically impossible to use for their original performing purpose, except for some very exceptional occasion. These include the Teatro Olimpico in Vicenza (1580–1585), Teatro Farnese in Parma (1628), the castle theatre in Česky Krumlov (1689) and the Drottningholms slottsteater (1766) near Stockholm. They are fragile monuments to the history of the performing arts and the history of theatre architecture, not live venues any longer. But some more recently built theatres might also be decommissioned in the future for lack of public interest or public subsidy and turned into … what exactly? That is quite difficult to say, the options not being self-evident. How many concert halls, how many conference centres can still survive in Europe?

At the same time, former factories are being converted into cultural centres and theatres. An argument could be made that creating a performing art space today through the conversion of a former industrial plant, military barracks or bus depot makes more sense than building a new structure from scratch. In most cases, performing arts facilities are incorporated into an interdisciplinary cultural centre that offers concerts, film, exhibitions, discussions and lectures and ample space for socialisation in lounges, cafés, bars and restaurants.

Here is a list of some successful performing arts spaces in Europe created through conversion:

Former factories: Kampnagel in Hamburg (www.kampnagel.de), Muffathalle in Munich (www.muffatwerk.de), Radialsystem in Berlin (www.radialsystem.de), Westergasfabriek in Amsterdam (www.westergasfabriek.nl), Cable factory in Helsinki (www.kaapelitehdas. fi) and Millenaris in Budapest (www.millenaris.hu)

Former engine sheds/tram depots: The Roundhouse in London (www.roundhouse.org. uk), the Tramway in Glasgow (www.tramway.org) and Theater im Depot in Dortmund (www.depotdortmund.de)

Former slaughterhouses: Several stages in the Parc de la Villette in Paris

Former tannery: Teatro India in Rome (www.teatrodiroma.net)

Brewery complex: Dansehallerne on the Carlsberg site, Copenhagen (www. dansehallerne. dk)

Former military barracks: Kanonhallen in Copenhagen (www.kanonhallen.dk) and Metelkova in Ljubljana (www.metelkovamesto.org)

Former electricity plants: Trafó (www.trafo.hu) in Budapest and Stara Elektrarna in Ljubljana (www.bunker.si)

Former milk-processing plant: Melkweg in Amsterdam (www.melkweg.nl)

Former printing plant: Arts Printing House in Vilnius (www.menuspaustuve.lt)

Former wine vaults in an underground labyrinth of railway tracks near London Bridge: Shunt, London (www.shunt.co.uk)

Former imperial stables: MuseumsQuartier in Vienna (www.mqw.at)

Former luxury cruise ship: De Rotterdam (www.ssrotterdam.nl), converted into a hotel and theatre and docked in the Rotterdam Maas port; and MS Stubnitz (ms.stubnitz.com), former refrigerator ship of the German Baltic herring fleet: converted into a travelling arts centre with film screenings, concerts and performances given in one harbour after another

Some of these places are relatively small, others are huge cultural complexes with many different cultural organisations as tenants (Cable factory, MQ, La Villette) and there is a great divergence in the governance models and the degree of coordination among the various programming lines and units. The location may be quite central (MQ) or peripheral. In the architectural sense, these spaces preserve some memory of their original function and remind us of the drama of de-industrialisation as the prevailing European process of the late twentieth century. They offer simple comfort, much fluidity and flexibility of usage, smaller and larger studios, and at least one larger place with a flat-floor stage and steep stands for the public. Several events can run in parallel. There is an unpretentious sociability, reasonable traffic of people coming in and out at various times of the day, and usually the cool, alternative look of the space matches the relaxed behaviour of the staff. Each space is quite special and unique, so that those facilities can be seen as strongholds of cultural resistance to the uniforming pressures of globalisation. The advantage of creating a cultural, and especially a performing arts space through the recycling of a building that has lost its primary purpose is that it can be carried out in several phases, whereby habits and needs articulated during usage suggest further renovation interventions, without having them externally invented and imposed in advance from a single blueprint.

Away from the theatre

With all the disappointments and frustrations linked to new and old theatre buildings, it is not so strange that a search for alternative places of theatre action, in a dense urban context or in natural surroundings, mark the entire twentieth century. Among the great directors, Max Reinhardt was the first to take flight from the playhouse and explore the spectacular potentials of a circus, park, city bridge, busy square or sports hall even before World War I, and then systematically in Salzburg from 1918 to 1937. For him, theatre was a big social feast of neo-baroque opulence for at least 5,000 spectators, who could anyway not be squeezed adequately into the existing theatre building. Russian theatre directors after the October Revolution also went outside to celebrate the revolution and amplify its messages to between 10,000 and 30,000 spectators on the streets and squares of Moscow and St Petersburg, using thousands of performers, field telephones and dozens of assistants to orchestrate the movements of an entire army of performers. These spectacles about the glory of the revolution, staged between 1918 and 1920, revived the tradition of popular ideological feasts of the French Revolution of 1789–1794, and followed Gémier's arrangements of thousands of amateur performers on the shores of Lake Geneva at the beginning of the twentieth century. In some features and desired functions they also revived medieval mystery plays in a secularised mode.

Theatre on location has remained an artistic passion, emerging in the historic sites of ancient ruins and medieval edifices, rediscovered and theatricalised, such as the Terme di Caracalla in Rome, La Cour d' Honneur in the Palais des Papes in Avignon (www.palais-des-papes.com), the medieval ramparts, squares and palaces of Dubrovnik, but also on beaches, in harbours, former factories, garages, and countryside estates. This sort of fascinating performance implies the question: Is a theatre building still required? Before giving a categorical answer, the typology of performance on location deserves a closer look.

The relationship between the environment and the production is not uniform – a production displays varying degrees of dependence on its location. One sort of location that theatre-makers seek to penetrate are places where the audience is already concentrated, instead of staging productions at a place where the audience might or might not turn up on purpose. Thus shopping malls, lobbies of office buildings and hospitals, airports and train stations, parks and large squares are temporarily appropriated for a performance, or invaded unexpectedly by the performers, who in the form of a parade or procession, or indeed a happening, suspend the daily rhythm of the place, overwhelm it with spectacularity and surprise, but only for a short time. The French companies Royal de Luxe and Generik Vapeur (www.generikvapeur.com) excel in such interventions of merriment and ironic historical consciousness. Paul Koek's Veenfabriek (www.veenfabriek.nl) played Martin Crimp's *Attempts on Her Life* in the V&D department store in Leiden during regular opening hours in 2008, mixing theatregoers with shoppers (Wensink 2008), and Zurich Opera (www.opernhaus.ch) staged *Traviata* in the main railway station (*Le Monde* 2008). On YouTube one can watch funny mini-operas, concerts and performances staged as abrupt, unexpected events at airports (www.youtube.com/watch?v=RgZuHlDuulk and other sites).

Here the spectacle is more important than the parameters of the location, which is taken over, or invaded so to speak, without much engagement of its specific qualities and features. Otherwise, productions are staged in squares or parks, in front of palaces and churches, all being used simply as a spectacular backdrop, a found piece of monumental set opposite an audience seated on stands. Wonderful places serve as an inspiration for a production and, if successful, a production can be displaced to another similar environment, or even taken on tour. This is not the case for opera productions staged every summer in Bregenz, on Lake Konstanz, where 7,000 spectators watch performers on a floating stage in the lake from the shore. In Graham Vick's *Aida*, both Ethiopians and Egyptians washed, splashed and swam in the lake while giant cranes moved chunks of the set (Apthorp 2009).

The Italian group Motus (www.motusonline.com) performed Jean Genet's play *Splendid's* (1948) in a series of luxury hotels, since the play invokes the siege of a hotel by a group of terrorists, a prophetic anticipation of the terrorist attack on the Taj Mahal Hotel in Mumbai in November 2008. Productions inspired by a concrete environment but so integrated into it that they cannot be displaced anywhere else are the only ones to be justifiably called site-specific, like Dogtroep (www.dogtroep.nl) made for the inauguration of the new regional hospital in Groningen in 1995, in order to present this facility to the local population. The choice of locations European artists discover and use for productions is quite mind-boggling. Most productions invite the audience on a journey of adventure, merging it with the alteration of a familiar site into an enigmatic performing environment or by an expedition to an unknown location that would otherwise never be visited.

Dogtroep (www.dogtroep.nl) played on Red Square in Moscow, in the ship passenger terminal in Amsterdam, then on a plot of cleared land near Utrecht, just before it became a construction site for 30,000 housing units.

Hollandia (www.zthollandia.nl) made a long trajectory through pig farms, junk yards, scientific laboratories and factories and ran a production in the KLM Cargo hangars at Schiphol airport, before disbanding.

Krétakör played in a secret underground hospital under Buda Castle, built in the 1950s to be ready for nuclear war and still managed by the Janos Hospital of Budapest as a stand-by facility.

Punchdrunk (www.punchdrunk.org.uk) staged an elusive *Faust* in the corridors and rooms of an abandoned tobacco factory in Wapping, East London.

PeerGroup (www.peergroup.nl) erected a 12 m-high castle of 12,000 straw bales in the countryside of the province of Drenthe in the Netherlands and used it for two years for performances, workshops and conferences.

A Polish staging of the return of Ulysses to Ithaca was performed in the dilapidated halls of the former Lenin shipyard in Gdansk, where the Solidarity movement was born.

In an early phase, the Danish Hotel Pro Forma staged several site-specific productions in various emblematic public buildings in Copenhagen.

Theater Ulysses (www.ulysses.hr) started a performance of *King Lear* (2000) on two ships, which take the audience from the coast of Istria (Croatia) with the King of France and the Duke of Burgundy, on their way to ask for Cordelia's hand, to the island of Mali Brijun, where the rest of the tragedy unfurls in several ambiences in a former Austro-Hungarian naval fortress and in natural surroundings left undisturbed for decades.

The Four Days in Motion (www.ctyridny.cz) festival in Prague started with mime performances in a former water-processing plant dating from the beginning of the 1900s.

Shadow Casters (shadowcasters.blogspot.com) staged originally their performance *Vacation from History* in 2008 in a Zagreb downtown public library turned during off-hours into an improvised dormitory for 16 visitors/dreamers, transferred the production from 2009 on to the former Zagreb Mosor cinema where the dormitory can accommodate 35 people, and toured extensively abroad with it performing in various spaces such as a gallery, former printing house, two dance halls, former synagogue etc.

In summer 2009 Willy Decker staged Schoenberg's opera *Moses und Aron* in the Bundeshalle, a huge post-industrial space near Bochum for the Ruhr-Triennale (www.ruhrtriennale.de), Beer 2009).

In the same summer Shakespeare's *The Tempest* was staged in the Wilhelmina polder, a huge piece of agricultural land reclaimed 200 years ago in Goes, the Netherlands (Jansen 2009).

An environmental Malta Festival in Poznan (www.malta-festival.pl) gave a huge boost to the development of street theatre and theatre on location in Poland.

Three types of environment appear most frequently. The first is former factories, with depressing industrial debris, and huge enclosed spaces extending the vista for visitors and imposing a sense of a vanished past, the only palpable trace of which is junk and scrap metal, broken glass windows and roofs. The second environment consists of productions set in natural surroundings, appropriating their beauty and unpredictability, including shifts of light, rain, wind and mud, as well as testing the goodwill, preparedness and endurance of the public. Third, there are productions incorporated into buildings, which form part of the cultural heritage – in monasteries, palaces and fortresses – seeking to contradict, efface or rewrite the history those environments represent.

With the explosion of new or expanded museums and the steady rise in visitors, these complex and carefully guarded environments beg to be inducted into performative practice, which in turn needs to be adjusted in shape and time to the logic of the museum space and the patterns of visitor movement through it, with the production thematically linked to the temporary exhibitions held in the museum, staged in the exhibition galleries, adjacent lecture rooms, halls, vestibules and courtyards. The Centre Pompidou in Paris (www. centrepompidou.fr), Kiasma contemporary arts museum in Helsinki (www.kiasma.fi) and the Museum of Contemporary Arts in Zagreb (www.msu.hr) have a regular performing arts programme, but it is not fully integrated into the exhibitions' programme on offer.

Increasingly, productions are being made in prisons, with prisoners and occasionally guards in the cast, but these are not necessarily environmentally challenging interventions, even though the outside visitors pass through an initiation ritual of identity control and metal-detector checks. In the Volterra (Italy) prison, productions have been made for years with high-security prisoners performing plays by Genet and Peter Weiss. In the Bruges prison in 2002 Dogtroep made it impossible for the 80 spectators in a processional performance to work out who was a prisoner, a guard or a professional actor (Baumeister et al. 2002). Similar restricted environments in which productions have been made are asylum-seeker detention centres and refugee camps, but usually here, too, the environmental dimension is less accentuated than the trauma, acculturation and the uncertainty of the target population, who both perform their own experience and receive it mirrored as a signal of interest, empathy and support, in contrast to the institutionalised indifference or outright hostility of everyday life there.

As for the audience, it is invited into the performative zone, seated and escorted at the end; or moved through several environments by guides and scouts who monitor the safety of passage and watch the timing of displacement; or the public is left to rummage freely around the environment and compose their own dramaturgical sequence of scenes; or the audience is split into several groups, which are then taken through a series of the same, repeatedly performed scenes but in a different sequence; or the audience is prompted and steered through the environment by some digital device that each spectator receives. Such strategies can produce a multiplicity of experiences, spatial memories and sequential variants that each spectator and group take from such a performance.

Especially summer festivals are keen to embrace environmental theatre as a special feature, helping them to claim that their operation boosts tourism and contributes to urban revitalisation. This is certainly true for Avignon with some 40 urban sites used by the festival but not necessarily for all other summer festivals. Environmental performance offers limited comfort and imposes additional safety concerns and precautions, coupled with additional expenses. The Oerol festival (www.oerol.nl) stages dozens of productions on beaches, in forests, on dunes, in barns, almost everywhere and anywhere on the island of Terschelling, off the Frisian coast, but the festival also takes the trouble to repair the environmental damage inflicted by the throngs of 65,000 spectators in sensitive nature spots. The recovery of tourism in Dubrovnik after the 1991–1995 war made it practically impossible for productions in the Dubrovnik Summer Festival (est. 1950) to use the historic palaces, fortresses and the medieval city walls. The noise and the crowds pushed the performances out to the suburbs, away from the city's emblematic urban core and the intensity of urban movement. A five-hour-long production of *Troilus and Cressida* in the summer of 2009 on a historic site in Skopje, Macedonia, resulted in the angry appearance of neighbouring residents in pyjamas, interrupting the performance with protests about the loud performance noise keeping them awake.

Commercial theatre avoids this experimental drift and prefers to stick to large playhouses, where the safety and standardised procedures, repeated several times a week, can easily be guaranteed. Environmental exploration is part of the public theatre mission and function – to create short-term experimental zones of arts and sociability, to expand the public space by shaping its surprising pockets, to induce urban revitalisation in decaying post-industrial zones, to pioneer the conversion of former military facilities to civilian usage, and to bring urban dwellers to ravishing natural surroundings while sharpening their environmentalist consciousness.

Just as the traditional subsidised playhouses suffer from the competition with larger commercial theatres, often concentrated in particular entertainment zones, such as London's West End or along the Paris boulevards, location theatre also faces specific commercial competition in the form of increasingly popular and sophisticated theme parks. They offer a complex marketing formula of densely packaged attractions, entertainment, hospitality, family-oriented fun and a capacity to process millions of visitors throughout the whole day and in the summer until late into the night. Theme parks require huge investment but offer long exploitation prospects. In comparison with them, environmental theatre – as a rule non-commercial, that is, subsidised – is always a temporary occurrence, an incident, a short adventure. The great outdoors is not so suitable for performance in parts of Europe with a high rainfall, even in warmer summer months. Indoor location performances sometimes excite so much enthusiasm for the found environment that plans are made to turn this temporarily appropriated space into a permanent performing arts facility, with renovation paid for by public funds, as well as perhaps partially by private means; this is how a flight from the playhouse ultimately yields another playhouse or an arts centre.

Chapter 7

Finding the Audience, Making the Audience

M ost public theatres in Europe complain of a stagnating or even shrinking audience, a worrisome trend because it reduces their own income and weakens the legitimacy of the subsidy they receive. Such a trend has many objective causes, as analysed in Chapter 2 and affects entire categories of non-commercial performing arts organisations; yet it should not be accepted as inevitable.

That many public theatres – and other publicly supported cultural facilities as well – fail to reach a bigger audience and achieve a degree of cultural diversity that comes close to the demographic diversity of their surroundings has become a serious political concern, shared by municipalities, regions and ministries. The European Commission has also set up a platform of professional operators to come up with recommendations on how to improve access to culture (Access to Culture 2009). Public authorities increasingly demand to see how their investment is working and what results it yields. They also want to rebut possible charges of implicit elitism in cultural policy and in cultural subsidy flows, and thus scrutinise the audience figures of public theatres more critically.

Audiences: Limited, elusive and unstable

Standardised parameters, articulating some correlation between audience size and a level of subsidy, are impossible to develop and impose, since big and small performing arts organisations, with and without their own playhouse, live in parallel but markedly different realities. It would seem that securing an audience is easier in smaller towns with less cultural offer than in big cities; but there are also advantages of scale that big cities allow, especially in comparison with performing arts organisations in smaller towns of less than 50,000 inhabitants, where a venue might give 50–60 performances a year, for 10,000–15,000 visitors, and stay dark for over 300 evenings: clearly, a low intensity of facility usage, difficult to justify on economic terms. A political argument could be set against this economic reasoning: it is a matter of cultural democracy that citizens have access to a diversified and quality theatre offer in their own town throughout the season, without having to travel to a bigger city. But will politicians be willing to listen?

In Italy, many small towns of even less than 25,000 inhabitants have an old historic theatre, restored with care as the object of much community pride thanks to EU structural funds and the contribution of the Italian banking foundations. Such a facility is expected to serve all local needs, including amateur associations, educational projects and visiting performers but in practice performances are given only once or twice a week, and even then the average occupancy is quite low because a 500-seat theatre has become too big for the town. The annual overheads and even the most modest programming budget are hardly covered by the municipal subsidy and the box-office intake. Another solution, characteristic of Italy, is a dramatic shortening of the theatre season, which both reduces overheads and programming expenditure but results in the house standing dark and locked for months, although some employees are still kept on a permanent payroll despite having little work to do. In countries with a low population density, as in the Nordic region, both touring companies and venues in small places that receive them need to be heavily subsidised, an economic impossibility for the poorer cultural systems of Eastern Europe, where a large part of the population outside bigger urban centres depends primarily on television and radio for its cultural consumption.

Pressured by the competition of endless alternative leisure options that lure potential audience away, leaders of public theatres now understand that more publicity and more sophisticated marketing is not the key to bringing them more spectators. If they want to increase audience volume *and* audience loyalty – that is, the frequency of return visits – if they care about the audience's appreciation of the work shown *and* about the cultural diversity of the audience, they need multiple simultaneous strategies that will reinforce each other. There are no ready-made solutions since contextual circumstances tend to be quite specific. Marketing textbooks contain some standardised approaches, often confirmed in practice, but as helpful as they might be, the challenge is more complex, with too many variables in play: from the theatre's artistic identity and its perception, surrounding demography and intensity of performing arts competition to funding conditions, media attention and the overall sociability of a place. Programming, marketing, education and communication need to reinforce each other in order to achieve some audience development.

If there is some point of agreement among different approaches to audience development, it is the priority assigned to the young public, both as a political legitimisation of the subsidy received and as a sustainability factor – an investment in a stable future audience. Concrete steps beyond this habitual politically correct stance are less obvious and the match between the theatre's artistic product and the interests, temperament, patience and curiosity of any young audience is difficult to make and sustain. Especially as the youngsters of today socialise in a solipsistic manner, with laptops and mobile phones. On the other hand, with the entire European population ageing rapidly – especially in Spain, Italy, Bulgaria, the Baltic countries, Ukraine and Russia – there are enough good reasons to pay more attention to the recruitment of older theatregoers, those over 50, who might have more time and inclination to attend performances. This demographic "silver tsunami" hitting Europe could be seen as a precious opportunity to increase the audience with representatives of the generation that engaged in the cultural revolution of the 1960s and 1970s, arguing, criticising and struggling, and thus could constitute even today, at an older age, a committed, argumentative and discriminating theatre public.

Whether a theatre production can command the same degree of concentrated attention and appreciation from a young and an older audience is debatable, especially in Western European societies, where the generation gap is manifested as a social and cultural differentiation and distance. In Budapest, Krakow or Moscow, however, one can still see three, even perhaps four generations of spectators sitting together in the auditorium, with seemingly the same degree of attention for the performance (even if an SMS occasionally flickers on mobile-phone screens in the dark).

Commitment to education

The seriousness of theatre's commitment to audience development is best visible in the range of educational activities it deploys, both for adults and youngsters. The more ambitious and sophisticated the production output, the more educational support it requires. That is why public theatres routinely organise pre-performance introductions and post-performance discussions with artists and experts. Guided tours round a theatre help the audience grasp the interdependence of simultaneous working processes in a complex performing arts organisation.

Educational activities run on a double track, one for youngsters and one for adults. For the first category, they need to be tailored to several age groups and placed in a school context, thus ensuring the cooperation of teachers and school leadership. Schools are – much more than theatres – highly regularised systems, with standard operations, firm programmes and much advance planning, so theatre education activities cannot fit quickly or easily into such a dense and rigid environment. Most theatre companies prepare educational packages for youngsters and their teachers about the productions they believe will interest them. However, hands-on activities have, it seems, more impact, and elicit more interest and involvement than lessons and introduction presentations. Popular entertainment, mediated by the Internet and television, shapes the histrionic notions and aspirations of youngsters and these cannot be easily reconciled with the type of performativity that theatre companies practise and seek to convey in an educational programme. Hence cultural notions and values might be at odds, with frustration and disappointment on both sides. Since secondary school students have very little time at their disposal, programmes need to be stretched over a longer period, which in turn allows for youngsters' self-confidence to grow and their imagination to be freed. A commitment to cultural diversity prompts theatres to focus their educational programmes on schools with a larger percentage of students from an immigrant background, where cultural differences and prejudices might manifest themselves as an additional difficulty, a complicating variable, or as a provocative and stimulative point of contention.

That good intentions are not sufficient and that roles and prerogatives in an educational project must be defined with precision is the lesson one can draw from an incident with the production of *Bezhti* at the Birmingham Rep (www.birmingham-rep.co.uk) in 2004. The theatre invited a group of young British Sikhs to follow the production process of this play by a young British author, Gurpreet Kaur Bhatti, herself of Sikh background, hoping to stimulate interest among the local Sikh community. But some of the youngsters failed to grasp that their involvement did not include censorial prerogatives, so when they felt that some scenes involving rape in a Sikh temple offended their collective sense of honour, they reacted as vigilantes. When they could not force the theatre to purge the production or alter the scene, they threatened those who arrived at the premiere with violence. While some 60,000 Sikhs who live in the Birmingham area showed mainly indifference, here a few dozen angry youngsters and adult hotheads created a calamity that neither the police nor the theatre knew how to handle. Instead of enhancing discursive opportunities for such issues as religious pride and blasphemy, freedom of creativity and expression, art and reality, collective and individual identities, and making them a stepping stone in new educational programmes, the Rep capitulated to bigotry and cancelled the production. The extremists among the Sikhs could feel vindicated and any other disgruntled group in the UK population can now turn to anti-theatre vigilantism, expecting to replicate the shutting-down of *Bezhti* (Branigan and Dodd 2004). In 2009 some 300 Christians protested in front of a Glasgow theatre that portrayed Jesus Christ as a transsexual within the "Glasgay!" festival of queer culture. Their protest remained peaceful (BBC 2009).

In most cases theatre education efforts have a more satisfactory outcome, but there are no longitudinal studies to confirm their long-term effect, to establish whether the participation of teenagers in such projects makes them regular theatregoers in their adult life or not. Too many intervening variables and altered life circumstances can sway people away from the habit of theatregoing despite early exposure, enjoyment and appreciation. Some performance forms, considered especially difficult and even obsolete by certain youngsters, demand particular, intensive educational engagement. Opera, classical ballet and contemporary dance, for instance, can appear to teenagers as artificial, even absurd or incomprehensible, and that is why the best opera and dance companies display a great deal of ingenuity in designing educational projects. RESEO, the European Network for Opera and Dance Education (www.reseo.org), runs training courses for artists to take part in educational activities, works with teachers, collects and presents a suitable repertoire for young people, and maintains a database of articles on educational practices linked to these artistic forms. The relative coherence of the European standard opera repertoire makes it easier to recycle educational approaches and packages from one opera house education service to another. But RESEO does much more, including creative workshops for artist-animators to develop youth opera projects. In the Mozart anniversary year of 2005, RESEO ran a "Creative Ways to Mozart" project that reached 136,000 youngsters across Europe and, besides engaging them with Mozart's opus, it led to a rap *Hip H'Opera*.

During the 2009–2010 season, Stuttgart Opera (www.staatstheater-stuttgart.de) developed a new youth opera based on the successful German-Turkish film *Gegen die Wand* ("Against the Wall," 2004) by Fatih Akin, recruiting youngsters who were interested in music and singing and eager to appear on the stage. With weekly rehearsals throughout the school year and a more intensive schedule after Easter, the opera premiered in June 2010 with a remarkable, culturally diverse cast, and brought to the performances parents, relatives and friends of the protagonists, many of whom had never entered an opera house before. Stuttgart Opera carries opera education to a high degree of hands-on experience, as well as direct and complex engagement of youngsters. Moreover it also counters common views about opera as traditionalist and elitist by producing a series of Junge Oper (youth opera) with new works, specially developed for children, families and teenagers, and recently even a piece with the participation of opera-lovers aged 50+, *Memento Mori, Baby*, derived from a season-long series of workshops on baroque music. Here again programming originality and freshness of educational approach merge.

Theatre education for adults is also moving away from mere presentations and debates to experience-based occasions, where cognitive aspects merge with the expressive ones, where talks are replaced by workshops and creative acts. There is an emerging range of specialists involved in these activities, whether they are called educationalists, animators or facilitators; they often have an artistic background themselves, or have some training in education. Company artists are not always willing and eager to take part in educational activities, neither with youngsters nor with adults. Some artists consider such tasks a waste of their creative time and talent, even demeaning, or just not their job, something that is better left to education specialists. Most professional artists' training programmes still do not include educational aspects and ideologically reinforce a sharp dividing line between artistic creativity and education. In public theatre at least, this division is unsustainable and indefensible – insistence on the separation of realms imperils the very existence of public theatre, because one of its strongest claims to public support is anchored in the provision of educational benefits. It goes without saying that a public theatre is first and foremost an artistic organisation, but it is also an educational one by virtue of its dependence on public funding and the mandate shaped by such support.

Some impoverished theatre companies would rebut this stance, claiming that they suffer from such harsh public neglect that the subsidies they receive do not allow them to carry out even their core artistic tasks properly – performing in venues of some elementary comfort and making new productions. For them, engaging in educational activities is the utmost luxury, unimaginable for as long as they are unable to carry out their mission, albeit in a highly scaled-down manner. That complaint is not without merit, especially in some post-communist countries, where the extensive public theatre infrastructure, once benefiting from stable government support, has not been scaled down nor reformed, but simply left to decay, with miniscule subsidies. These are too high to let it collapse completely and too low to make it function properly. In the poorer countries of Eastern Europe – in some provincial cities of Ukraine, Moldova, Albania and Macedonia – such companies are experiencing the post-communist transition as a protracted agony. The opposite is also true, that many smaller groups in Western Europe assure the continuity of their creative work by a patchwork of small grants, given to them mainly for educational services in schools and communities. For them, creation and education are intertwined processes that involve all members, and ensure the continuity of their artistic endeavour.

In bigger and better-endowed companies of outstanding reputation, educational activities of great scale and diversity are carried out thanks to special public subsidies and grants from private foundations, even from sponsorship deals. Among them, the Royal Opera House (ROH) in London's Covent Garden displays a rich variety of educational programmes for young people from elementary school to university, for adults, families, special groups and local communities, covering tours, talks, seminars and creative workshops. A short dance piece placed on YouTube invites viewers to compose their own dance music. In dance, where many young aspiring dancers always seek opportunities to perform, learn and appear on the stage, ROH offers ample opportunities for collaboration including the Street Stories series of creations with youngsters from East London Dance (www. eastlondondance.org). Moreover, the charismatic and versatile persona of Wayne McGregor as resident choreographer embraces creation and education, arts and science, classical and contemporary dance idioms, movement and other artistic domains (Aspden 2008).

The intensive growth in educational programmes and offers on the part of large and small companies is a rather recent phenomenon and goes well beyond standard introduction-before-the-curtain and the post-show meet-the-artists format, especially by diversifying the target groups and multiplying the approach, method and content of the offer. Commitment to education, to life-long learning, is one of the key markers of public theatre.

Outreach strategies

Educational activities support a theatre's programming core output – a field in which audience development becomes connected with those format and template options discussed in Chapter 5. Theatres experiment with the structure of occasional complex events that fuse artistic experience, entertainment, socialisation, reflection and education. Once or several times in the season some performing arts organisations offer a rich cluster of programmes in various spaces of a larger venue so as to enable spectators to make their own itinerary and determine their own preferred sequence of attractions to be experienced. These broader time-frame formats, lasting a whole weekend, or all of Saturday or Sunday, or from early afternoon to the small hours, appeal to spectators with their rich menu of options – performances, talks, public interviews, guided tours, mini-concerts, improvised scenes, film screenings, workshops, cocktails, meals, exhibitions and so on. These are all included and yet not sequenced in any firm order; it is left open for the individual spectator to choose, order and structure. Such an extended event, which the spectator can join, leave and rejoin at any time, could be criticised as a theatre's efforts to recruit and bind spectators by overwhelming them and pampering them with an abundance of programming options. Yet they do work and enjoy considerable popularity, even offering additional socialising and networking opportunities that many spectators today expect from a public event. The degree of participation depends on the spectators themselves. The dramaturgy of these events is comparable to the one applied across Europe in Museum Nights, organised in many cities and keeping museums open until the late hours with a variety of special programme options, all in the hope of recruiting a new audience, which would otherwise live with the prejudice that visiting museums is boring.

Nothing enhances sociability as much as the shared consumption of food. Since the early 1960s Peter Schumann's Bread and Puppet Theater has shared bread with its public after the performance, reinforcing a sense of community. When nowadays theatre venues run restaurants or offer buffet meals before the show or in the intermission, they do that mainly for the comfort of the public. They treat it as a group of hungry consumers to be fed quickly, missing the opportunity of reinforcing the sense of community and shared experience around food and thanks to food. At the Théâtre du Soleil, however, meals offered in the intermission have always been part of the ritualised attention the performers give to the public, a sign of respect, care and appreciation. Not just a mere convenience devised to relieve hunger during a long show but a sensual experience that aims to imprint the entire visit in the memory (Cohen 2009). In 2007 LIFT (London International Festival of Theatre; www.liftfestival.com) created *Eat London* with the artists Alicia Rios and Barbara Ortiz. It was a huge participative performance where an edible mini-replica of London, created by 15 communities, was laid out over 60 m² of tables in Trafalgar Square and consumed with gusto in a big party.

In contrast to these mass public participation events, there is a visible growth in theatre experiences that pamper the audience, giving all the attention to a single individual spectator. These performances for an audience of one (and then another one and then another one …) became so numerous that the Battersea Arts Centre (www.bac.org.uk) in London held a whole festival, One To One, of this genre in 2010 – say something about the individualisation of society, the consumer's urge to create an impression of personalised service (a personal trainer in the gym, a personal performer in the theatre?), but while they pander to the narcissism of clients, they also destroy theatre as a social experience and wipe out its socialising potential (Lee 2010).

International Theatre Day on 27 March, introduced by the International Theatre Institute (www.iti-worldwide.org), a UNESCO affiliate, and celebrated for almost 60 years, and International Dance Day on 29 April, introduced by the International Dance Council (CID, www.cid-portal.org) in 1982, are ignored in many countries altogether or celebrated in some European towns in an unimaginative, cumbersome fashion by the reading of a message by some celebrated artist, selected by ITI or CID, in front of the curtain. Both days could be used for audience development and the celebration of theatre and dance but only if liberated from the worn-out formula and enhanced with a rich programme. If a company celebrates 20 or 30 years of existence, there is usually a dinner for the employees, awards and recognition for the veterans and a thick book of photos is commonly published to be given away as a depository of institutional memory. The occasion is frequently wasted as an opportunity to invest in the future, launch new initiatives benefiting emerging artists and new audiences, create a festive occasion marking out where the company wants to go; instead, it just consists of nostalgic and sentimental reminiscing. Another option is to share the fun with the public as Parc de la Villette (www.villette.com) did in September 2006 soliciting volunteers who, under the direction of Philippe Decouflé, paraded in 100 selected costumes from the warehouse of the Opéra and Comédie-Française. One cannot help wondering why the Opéra and Comédie-Française did not think of organising such an event themselves.

Amorphous programmes, excursions outside the theatre for loyal visitors, bus trips to a performance in a special location and other audience development inventions, whether they are seen as mere gimmicks or not, seek to treat the individual visitor as a member of a community formed around the theatre. Another strategy for a theatre is to invent and launch its own mini-festivals in the course of the season, thus conveying to the public a sense of business *not as usual*. A theatre director from Maastricht admits he needs several festivals each season as a way of attracting the young audience eager to attend a special event but also in order to secure much-needed sponsorship for programming some international artists (Embrechts 2008).

One step further is to approach the public as co-author of a new work. In Hamburg's Thalia Theatre (www.thalia-theater.de) teams of company members made expeditions to specific neighbourhoods to collect residents' stories and use them as material in productions with a strong local thematic character. These projects prompt a reflection on the dynamics of urban transformation, accelerate a change in lifestyles, interests and values, and also highlight the impact of migration. They are a convenient vehicle for collecting, processing and foregrounding the migrant experience in a city, as well as further intergenerational understanding among its residents.

In 2008 Theater a.d Ruhr in Mülheim made a production from collected citizens' memories, *Wer hat meine Schuhe vergraben? Eine Stadt erinnert sich* (Who buried my shoes? A City Remembers) and turned the entire venue into a "labyrinth of memories," full of installations, exhibits, lectures and film screenings about a town historically shaped by the Ruhr industrial complex and the German post-war economic miracle. At the end or at the beginning of the season this company organises "White Nights," a special open-air programme in the park surrounding its playhouse, on the edges of Mülheim and Duisburg, a fusion of garden party and mini-festival with specially invited artists. NNT in Groningen (www.nnt.nl) used to organise once a year, usually during the autumn or winter school break, a week called "Dichterbij" (Closer) during which all the resources of the company and of the venue were made available to teenagers, who created their own production with the assistance of professional artists. In 2010 this changed to a series of weekend and evening workshops linked to the company's production of *Alice in Wonderland*.

Other companies also create festivals at the beginning or end of the season, inviting other groups and productions to join them and thus create a broadened, international context for the reception of their own productions, pamper their audience with more diversity of offer and expect to attract some new visitors as well. Enlarging and diversifying the audience and enhancing the loyalty of the core audience are the key objectives of such programmes. Festivals are always great opportunities to initiate and develop partnerships, both local and international, to merge artistic goals and audience development objectives through programming.

> Again the ROH in Covent Garden offers an impressive example: a 3-day mini-festival at the opening of 2010–2011 season under the Deloitte Ignite label. Curated by the artist Joanna MacGregor, a versatile pianist, the programme lasted from 3 September to 5 September and was inspired by the concept of a forest reappearing in various spaces, in a range of artistic works and formats. That the daytime events were free-of-charge and only evening programmes were ticketed indicates clearly that this was an audience development endeavour for ROH. And the prominently displayed leitmotif of the forest signalled that ROH was experimenting with broader thematic template programming as discussed in Chapter 5.

Audience development actions could also rest on some cross-marketing schemes, offering mutual discounts between a theatre and a local museum, music venue or public library, especially if these incentives are linked to membership and loyalty cards. User-friendly arrangements with public transport companies, giving ticket holders free transport to and from a theatre, have already been mentioned. Discounts upon showing a theatre ticket are offered by some cafés and restaurants in the neighbourhood. An alliance with a club would also be worth considering. Hotels, especially hotel chains, are increasingly seeking to lure out-of-town spectators by partnering with theatres, commercial and public ones, offering package deals, including tickets, dinner and overnight accommodation, especially for festivals. Theatres are slow to link up with public libraries and bookshops, especially in offering a platform for better-known authors, forgetting that public readings by authors from Dickens to Mark Twain constituted one of the most popular stage forms of the nineteenth century (Harkin 2009).

In bigger cities companies seek to provide programmes for professional meetings, conferences and symposia, company dinners and other professional, civic and corporate events. In Amsterdam, some dance, dramatic theatre and music ensembles have formed a consortium called CultuurBox (www.cultuurbox.eu) to provide such programmes in four well-known venues – Concertgebouw (www.concertgebouw.nl), Stadsschouwburg municipal theatre (www.stadsschouwburgamsterdam.nl), the smaller Bellevue theatre (theaterbellevue.nl) and Muziekgebouw aan 't IJ (www.muziekgebouw.nl), a new hall for contemporary music. Such initiatives could be seen primarily as one more way of increasing income, but with proper framing they work for the purpose of audience development as well, with additional information and special offers for the participants. Companies that aspire to prove their regional status, or are funded by regional authorities, are expected to go on tour to nearby towns but find it cumbersome and too expensive to travel with their full sets. Instead, they develop several smaller productions that travel easily, are set up and struck in a short time and are technically not very demanding. Such productions could be seen as teasers that should encourage the audiences to consider a trip to the big city and its more complex theatre performances. La comédie de Saint-Etienne (www.lacomedie.fr) in central France has its own itinerant stage, le Piccolo, that can be quickly set up in gyms and community centres and for which every season a special travelling production is made and performed in surrounding locations.

To enhance the cultural diversity of their audience, performing arts organisations need to think beyond the limits of the playhouse. Even Broadway, the traditional stronghold of the white middle-class public, has increased its segment of Afro-American audience from 1.9 per cent in 1998–1999 to 6.7 per cent in 2006–2007 by systemic programming of productions about their experience and with well-known Afro-American casts (Staps 2008). Partnerships with specific NGOs, which, for instance, group people of immigrant background, might bring a culturally diverse public to the venue – but only if such a public can recognise specific programming options as related to their own experience, memory, interest and position. The results will not be spectacular and will remain isolated incidents, rare occurrences when the standard audience is visibly altered for an evening or two. For a lasting impact, a theatre company or group needs to venture to the city neighbourhoods where ethnic and cultural minorities live, in cooperation with and with the support of local community organisations that can provide a point of entry, lend networks and credibility. The range of a company's engagements in such places – usually cultural deserts, where there are no cultural facilities and hardly any continuity of cultural offer – may vary from a large site-specific spectacle or processional performance to workshops for youngsters and fully-fledged community theatre projects with adolescents or adults, stretching over a longer period of time. Performing artists need to acknowledge that they are not on their usual territory, that they are dependent on local intelligence and much intercultural competence, that they need to be both prudent and streetwise, engaging and unpretentious, in order to make any impact in places marked by poverty, high unemployment and low-quality housing, as well as perhaps drugs and street crime. An immersion exercise could in the first place challenge some of the professional beliefs and notions of performing artists and other accompanying professionals, question their middle-class assumptions and their entrenched notion of culture, just as theatre work in prisons, refugee centres and medical establishments does. Such activities can go far beyond audience development and result in mutual learning (Rowntree 2006) or even prompt significant modification in aesthetic predilections – or remain just an incidental excursion, almost a flirtation. Ultimately, outreach programmes – with all their risks, complications and expense – reflect how a performing arts organisation understands its own character as a public theatre, how it interprets and marks its own urban or regional territory, what kind of cultural benefit it wants to deliver, and ultimately – to whom.

More than half a century ago Roger Planchon settled his Théâtre de la Cité, later known as Théâtre National Populaire, in Villeurbanne, an industrial suburb of Lyon and the hub of working class, whom he primarily wanted to address. Over the subsequent years and decades, Planchon hosted a mainly middle-class audience in his theatre, coming from the wealthier neighbourhoods of Lyon, but in his long tenure he gave plausible artistic responses to such abstract notions of cultural policy as democratisation of culture, cultural decentralisation and *théâtre populaire*, recruiting and inspiring many followers, also outside France. Today, around Lyon and elsewhere in Europe, it is difficult to pinpoint the hubs of a working class that has almost disappeared as a coherent social group. Instead, European cities, especially their outskirts, have become predominantly housing zones for immigrants and their offspring. Their sense of citizenship, the scope of their integration, their rate of socio-economic advancement and cultural participation are today the key challenges of urban policy. The issue of class has not disappeared, as John Holden reminds us (Holden 2010), but has been rephrased in terms of both access to culture and authority to define what culture is as well as an opportunity to make it. In a much more diffuse and heterogeneous society than the one Planchon knew in the late 1950s and 1960s, it is less self-evident for public performing arts organisations where their primary lines of engagement lie. One thing that they know for certain is that, in today's media-dominated society, they have to communicate intensively about their work.

Communication: Create your own media outlets

Theatres frequently complain about the media's shrinking attention to their work. Even quality daily newspapers have reduced the space they devote to coverage of cultural affairs and run fewer and much shorter theatre reviews, if any at all. Critics are under pressure to act, not as discerning public intellectuals but as consumer guides who attach one to five stars to their reviews as a recommendation or a warning. The culture pages and arts of newspapers have been transformed into "lifestyle" and "leisure" sections stuffed with articles on fashion and exercise, food and dieting and restaurant reviews. News magazines and opinion weeklies struggle to survive and also cover less cultural production. In many newspapers, theatre enjoys some coverage only as gossip, or when caught up in scandal and conflict. In other media, the arts are covered through interviews with celebrities, so that stage actors, directors, playwrights and designers have to compete with film and television stars. Television, commercial or public, might cover the premiere of a musical in a commercial theatre, or the opening of a film festival as a society event, but not pay attention to ordinary premieres in the non-commercial theatre. Radio programmes display the same attitude.

In defence of the media, one can invoke their own threats and pressures. The traditional business model, according to which the paper keeps the circulation high so it can charge high advertising rates, no longer works. The demand for advertising space has shrunk considerably with the economic recession and many people do not buy a daily newspaper any more since they get their news free-of-charge from the Internet. With the circulation in free fall, papers charge less for advertising. They cut costs and rearrange their coverage priorities or switch to a tabloid format expecting that a more compact newspaper format will be cheaper to produce and distribute as well as being easier to handle for the readers. The cultural affairs coverage gets squeezed out. The same malaise affects the weeklies even more severely. Daily papers also suffer from the competition of the free distribution dailies that live on advertising and recycle a small dose of agency news, cover a few large commercial entertainment events and pay no attention to non-commercial culture – *Metro*, for instance, appears in 42 editions in 17 countries and 16 languages. Against this background, the future of print media, a steady feature of European public life over the last three centuries, has become uncertain, if not bleak.

The tremendous increase in cultural output has also affected its coverage. The number of theatre performances, concerts, lectures, conferences, exhibitions and other events taking place every week in most larger European cities is much bigger than ten years ago, and only a small segment of them receives any coverage in print. The Netherlands, for instance, enjoys a rather developed quality daily press with regular arts pages but, with over 2,500 performing arts premieres a year, only a few hundred can get at least one press review. If, despite the growth in media outlets, many performing arts organisations feel ignored by them, increased theatre output makes the competition for media attention only worse. Public theatre cannot afford much print media advertising and, in most countries, no television or radio ads at all. But in larger cities there is also a tremendous growth in free listing print media, the "what's on" type of magazine, using cheap paper or a pocket format, where the performing arts organisations can place their own programme data for no charge. These media have no journalists, only copy editors who will gladly place small text items and photos on theatre productions if delivered by their producers on time. Budapest, for instance, has three such weeklies and more monthlies, specialising in popular and classical music, all distributed free in venues, cafés, restaurants, universities and hotels. There is a growing number of local Internet portals with going-out options and current cultural events where theatre programme announcements and photos can also be placed free-of-charge; young people use them as their primary information source for going-out options.

Under competitive pressures, public performing arts organisations continue producing their own posters, leaflets and brochures for free distribution and free mailing. Most of them are quickly thrown away and a proportion of mass mailing never reaches the addressee, who has moved away. Some companies make sophisticated programme books for each production and sell them to the public well below the production cost. Instead of all this expensive print material they would be better off investing more in their website, where a practically unlimited amount of text and photos can be placed at very little cost, without print and mailing expenses. Yet theatres fear that by emphasising website communication, they will miss the older potential public that does not use computers or uses them in a very limited way. This could be a temporary dilemma that will resolve itself in a few years as the computer literacy of senior citizens grows and as computer penetration and the availability of fast ADSL connections improves in several Southern and Eastern European countries where it is still quite low. Even though one could speculate that the computer-illiterate part of the population contains probably only a very small number of people interested in going to the theatre, public performing arts organisations might be eager not to neglect them. The point is that unless they build up their websites with sophisticated and interactive platforms, they will miss the opportunity of connecting with their young potential audience and with the middle generation as well. Delayed investment in the quality of theatre websites has not only a temporary but also a lasting negative impact on the affiliation of a significant part of the current and future potential public.

To be effective, theatre websites need to differentiate among various categories of users: incidental and regular visitors, educators and students, professional colleagues, funders and potential sponsors. Websites are not only an information source on the current offer of productions and auxiliary programmes, including educational activities, but can maintain the cultural memory of the venue, company or group, with data about past productions and seasons, show work in progress, carry on material from tours and participation at festivals and offer links to partners. If theatre criticism has lost much space in the print media, it has moved in a modified form to Internet platforms including an exponentially expanding blogosphere to which theatre websites can provide some guidance. By creating discussion platforms on their websites, theatres can shape a community of core audience, of an eager, curious and discriminating public, stimulate a protracted echo of their own productions and a plurality of reactions and opinions. A good website becomes an extension of the crucial public sphere that the theatre creates with its productions and auxiliary programmes. The Vlaams Theater Instituut has dedicated part of its website to systemic fostering of theatre criticism as a compensation for the review space lost in the mainstream media (www.vti.be/nl/content/corpus-kunstkritiek). Of course, a website is also a digital box office where tickets can be purchased, a shop for the sale of merchandising, a social website and an archive of artistic accomplishments. The panoply of institutional partnerships, local or distant, that a theatre nurtures is also reflected on the website. And yet it is amazing to see how many theatre websites do not provide any opportunity for visitors to say anything, to send any message, even to pose a question. They can get information and perhaps buy a ticket but that is all. This is the digital face of entrenched institutional arrogance, typical of many publicly subsidised performing arts organisations that – rightly or wrongly – take their public subsidies for granted.

Even performing arts organisations with a highly sophisticated website should not ignore YouTube, which has become the major global depository of short videos. Without a regular YouTube presence, a theatre company, venue or festival loses much of its visibility. Today YouTube offers a unique anthology of video recordings of performing arts works, contemporary and historical, that no archive and no theatre museum could ever hope to collect and make available. These are short fragments, only a few minutes long, of uneven quality and interest, as befitting such an institution of grass-roots, global cyber-democracy, but there is a contextual density and search-machine precision that can satisfy even the most sophisticated and demanding surfer. In addition to its own website, a performing arts organisation should make sure it uploads fragments of all its output onto YouTube.

Theatres are increasingly sending SMS messages to a great number of registered visitors, creating fan groups on Facebook and other social networks and Twitter about work in progress, even challenging Twitter fans to create a libretto for a new opera, as the ROH in Covent Garden did in 2009. These means of communication are too new to allow some firm conclusions about their usefulness and yet Facebook, with 500 million registered users (in July 2010), cannot be ignored: "We set up a fan group for our festival on Facebook and within one hour, even before we had time to ask anyone to join it, we had over 100 registered fans," reports a Polish colleague, quite amazed. Theatres could gauge audience preferences by asking them to send an SMS as some orchestras do when deciding what to play for an encore (Wakin 2010a).

For festivals, where there is an abundance of events every day, these platforms offer a chance of keeping the potential audience abreast with what is happening and creating an overview of intensive festival proceedings for those who manage to catch one event a day but want to know more. Proximity is no longer a precondition for affiliation, for the bonds of the public with a company, a venue or a festival. Live streaming enables people to watch events tonight in another city, even another continent. The Metropolitan Opera in New York, benefiting from its strong reputation, has been broadcasting high-definition recordings of its productions in hundreds of cinemas worldwide. It was quickly followed by London's National Theatre doing the same. Strangely enough, leading European festivals and performing arts companies have not yet developed a cooperative model for feeding recordings of their programmes into a permanent cable television channel, analogous to the Mezzo music channel (www.mezzo. tv), conceived primarily as a public-service and audience-development tool, nor have they developed a joint DVD and CD label. The next frontier for performing arts organisations is to create applications for advanced mobile phones that will display the repertoire, show short scenes from the performance, offer a choice of reviews or audience comments, sell tickets and give clear instructions on how to come to the venue, where to park and where to have a drink or a meal in the neighbourhood.

Instead of deploring the indifference of the media, performing arts organisations should create their own media platforms and produce their own content. Instead of complaining about the lack of attention of established critics, they should nurture the posting of audience opinions, analysis and reactions on the Internet, respond to their questions with respect and without defensiveness and stimulate and record debates among members of the public. Dangers of populism? Arrogant opinions of self-proclaimed but ignorant pseudo-experts? Yes, certainly, but also an opportunity to solicit and mobilise a younger audience and catch some of its attention under the duress of intensive media competition, turning it into a community of fans. A way to get a sense of what the public thinks. And most importantly, a strategy to oppose the marginalisation of public theatre and the prevailing indifference to its creative work by making it a subject for debate.

Chapter 8

Theatre in a Globalised World

Theatre is affected by globalisation as all other fields of cultural production are, which means that it is exposed to a strong pressure to conform, follow certain worldwide trends, standardise its products and chase its own hits and fads in programme, style and publicity. This is certainly the policy of commercial theatres, which seek to reproduce successful artefacts precisely in order to multiply the profit they make. Public theatre is itself not immune to globalisation pressures but it is capable of devising resistance strategies that reinforce its unique features and local significance. By doing so, public theatre can enhance cultural diversity and at the same time legitimise the public subsidies it receives. And, conversely, the more public theatre succumbs to globalisation and fails to assert its own specific features, the more imitative and conventionalised its output, the less deserving it will be of public subsidy.

The changing role of festivals

The impact of globalisation on today's cultural production and consumption is clearly visible in the explosive growth of festivals of all sorts. So many festivals have been set up on an imitative impulse, just because everyone else is having a festival, without a specific concept or recognisably distinct features. These serial festivals, hardly distinguishable among themselves, confirm the globalised trend of playing to fashion, aping and reproducing. Neo-liberal ideology, which appreciates culture primarily for its economic value, unleashed an opportunistic avalanche of one-sided arguments for festivals because of their supposed economic benefits. If this may be true for mass rock-music festivals – with occasional tragic twists, as in the incidents at Roskilde (www.roskilde-festival.dk) in 2000 or in Duisburg in 2010 – it is hardly true for theatre festivals, which, with the notable exceptions of Salzburg, Edinburgh and Avignon, usually gather a much smaller public, and thus can have a very modest or no economic impact at all.

Festivals with strong local anchoring and conceptual clarity can be temporary platforms of resistance to globalisation with a capacity to integrate global issues and local circumstances, needs and aspirations. If early theatre festivals, such as Edinburgh (est. 1947, www.eif.co.uk) or the Holland Festival (est. 1948, www.hollandfestival.nl), had a clearly *compensatory* function – to offer a diverse international programme that could not be seen during the regular season, today the best festivals have a *developmental* function: to discover new talent, affirm emerging aesthetics, advance professional discourse, transfer skills and methods to younger artists, and initiate a broader and more diverse public. Festivals that establish a panoply of local partnerships, also including those beyond their own artistic domain, reach out to the educational and civic infrastructure and capture the attention of the media, mobilise volunteers and attract international guests, certainly amplify their local impact but can expect to accomplish their own artistic and social objectives only thanks to some subsidy from public authorities, even if they do well at the box office and enjoy some commercial sponsorship.

A proliferation of festivals of all sorts causes difficulties for providers of public subsidies, principally in sorting out which festival initiatives deserve public support and how much of it. And yet, most public authorities have not articulated a consistent festival policy (Ilcsuk and Kulikowska 2007) based on firm expectations, criteria and evaluation, but improvise in their decision-making often driven by habit and routine rather than by the merits of a specific festival concept, its past achievements and future prospects. If public authorities tend to support festivals because others are doing the same, they also expect that a festival will address a variety of diverse issues: enhancing the prestige of the place, bringing in tourists, creating jobs, attracting the attention of the media, stimulating cultural life, reinforcing art in education, setting high artistic standards for local artists and furthering citizen participation. Consequently, even the most successful festivals carry a burden of contradictory and escalating expectations, feel the pressure to do more and better each year and thus run the risk of overstretching themselves, which can be fatal (Autissier 2008).

Since the end of the Cold War, the European map of theatre festivals has become much denser, and in Central and Eastern Europe new self-propelled festival initiatives have replaced the crumbling official festivals of the rejected regimes. Several theatre festivals have succeeded in establishing themselves as vibrant occasions for gathering professionals together, as accelerators in the development of careers of artists and groups featured by them, as places with a capacity to articulate new insights and reveal upcoming artistic ideas. The Festival d'Avignon is the primary gathering place of the professional French and francophone performing arts world but increasingly also an occasion for European cultural debates (Banu and Tackels 2005). Kunstenfestivaldesarts in Brussels (www.kfda.be) enjoys much professional appreciation for its radical programming that reshapes the notions and concepts of the performing arts. Euro-scene in Leipzig (www. euro-scene.de), Dialogue in Wroclaw (www.dialogfestival.pl) and Divadelna Nitra in Nitra (Slovakia, www.nitrafest.sk) have become visibility enhancers for theatre in Central Europe. Festivals have been pioneers in introducing some types of performing arts into the Central and Eastern European theatre culture where they were previously practically unknown; they also recruited the initial audience for them. For instance, Tanec Praha in Prague (www.tanecpraha.cz) ushered contemporary dance into the Czech Republic, while Homo Novus (www.homonovus.lv) brought post-dramatic and ambiental theatre to Riga.

In addition to these well-known initiatives, there are hundreds of smaller theatre festivals with more limited international programming, fewer reverberations and prominence and numerous festivals whose programme is chiefly national or regional. Many older festivals programme theatre productions alongside dance and music work. There is a growing movement towards fringe festivals, run without any preliminary selection, thus open to all groups willing to take care of their own logistical requirements and secure their own performing spots, as pioneered by the Edinburgh Fringe (www.edfringe.com) with over 2,000 productions per edition and Avignon OFF (www.avignonleoff.com) with over 700. Showcases, densely packaged weekends showing much new work to a professional audience of foreign presenters and programmers rather than to the general public are also becoming a standard professional device for international promotion of the performing arts work of a country or region. Festival concepts and formulas are in quick development and performing arts works are increasingly programmed in festivals with eclectic concepts, addressing urban, digital and diasporic cultures, thematically focused on globalisation, migration, science, spirituality and other fields.

While international theatre festivals were a rarity, they were endowed almost automatically with a certain prestige, as extraordinary cultural events. Consequently, their audience was quite elitist and partially professional. With the multiplication of theatre festivals and increased diversity of programming concepts, festival audiences have become broader and more varied. In smaller places, festivals rely on outside visitors more than on locals whereas in larger cities it is the opposite. Unlike music festivals, theatre festivals have to cope with limitations imposed by the language barrier and they do so by providing some form of translation, mainly surtitling and opting for productions where movement and visual elements prevail over the spoken word. Here again the impact of globalisation becomes visible – in the growing number of productions conceived and made primarily in order to go on the festival circuit; they are entertaining, limited in complexity, spectacular but easy to pack and make ready for travel, with a small cast, not depending too much on the semantic nuances of a spoken language.

Festivals stimulate the mobility of artists and artistic work, of artistic concepts and ideas, but also increasingly appear as instigators and co-producers of new productions, usually putting exceptional artists in a position to create new work or collaborate with colleagues with whom they normally would not be able to work in regular theatre institutions. As co-producers, festivals pull resources with their partners, split the risk that the creation of a new work always entails and, with a guaranteed number of performances in the first series, they also increase the visibility and the shelf-life of a new production that might be seen by other programmers and consequently presented by them. In this way many festivals have gone from the role of programmer and presenter to that of (co)producer, a shift that is financially impossible to accomplish on box-office income and sponsorship alone but has become feasible only thanks to additional public subsidies, often combined from different levels of public authorities in several countries. These multiple subsidies brought together by partners are local, regional and national but also often engage modest sums from the cultural programme of the European Union.

International cooperation in the performing arts

The availability of EU grants for international consortia of partners from different countries has – despite strong competition, a complex and long selection procedure, stringent accounting regime and regular delays in payment – stimulated many performing arts organisations to seek partners across borders and to embark on international cultural cooperation in such consortia, carrying out projects of increased complexity, some running for three to four years. The requirement to construct the cooperation project among at least three partners from different countries (or at least six for multi-annual projects) has shifted the international cultural cooperation from bilateralism (exchange and cooperation between two parties), traditionally favoured by national governments, to a multilateral mode.

The European Union articulated its limited cultural competences fairly late when a cultural paragraph was introduced into the 1992 Maastricht Treaty. Kept in the subsequent revisions of the Treaty and now confirmed as article 167 of the Lisbon Constitutional Treaty (2009), it positions culture as the primary responsibility of national governments but allows the European Commission to instigate cultural actions and programmes if the member states agree. In practice, the European Commission has run small cultural programmes since the mid-1990s, encouraging international cultural cooperation among organisations from the member states and gradually expanding so as to encompass those from the countries of the European Economic Zone, such as Switzerland, Iceland or Norway, to states that are official candidate members (Turkey, Croatia, Macedonia, Montenegro) and some countries in the immediate neighbourhood of the EU. This expanded eligibility, together with EU enlargement with 12 new member states in 2004 and 2007, has in fact stretched the same modest budget across a growing geographical area. Within the seven-year-long budgetary cycle of the EU, the funds reserved for the cultural programme have always been pathetically small and disproportionate to steadily growing interests and ambitions. This modest sum, some €40m per year for all sorts of cultural projects, including cooperation in the field of cultural heritage, amounts to a mere 0.03 per cent of the EU budget of some €125bn. Only a few million euros are allocated to international cooperation projects in the performing arts (www.ec.europa. eu/culture).

Rather than just go on tours, performing artists are increasingly eager to work with their foreign peers, to experiment, discuss, learn and create new work together, testing the boundaries of their professional and institutional habits, traditions and routines. In music and dance, two heavily internationalised artistic domains, this is an everyday practice. In theatre, dominated for so long by the mode of dramatic theatre and thus by language, this is less self-evident and more difficult to achieve. Large theatre organisations, with the most resources and prestige, are in practice less able – but also usually less eager – to engage in complex international projects, since their planning, logistics and multiple-production schedule get disturbed by the displacement of artists and additional time investment such cooperation requires. They also resent the risk of failure that such projects entail.

In order to stimulate the international curiosity of German repertory companies, usually a rather insular and self-centred segment of the performing arts sector, the Bundeskulturstiftung (www.bundeskulturstiftung.net) launched a Wanderlust programme in 2009, offering a grant to 14 selected companies that have shaped a bilateral partnership abroad. These vary considerably, some barely going beyond symmetrical exchange, with parallel separate processes containing a minimum of real cooperation; others are quite ambitious and even risky, such as cooperation with a Palestinian collective on the Israeli-occupied West Bank. Despite their institutional differences, cooperation between a French and German company can rely on the rich tradition of Franco-German cultural cooperation in all fields; projects with a Russian company in Karelia or with colleagues in South America are more difficult because of evident asymmetries in institutional structure and public subsidy provision.

Smaller groups, festivals, venues and production houses are better able to design and take part in international projects, also in an extended time frame, than large structures. In a cooperation venture envisaged to last three years, much effort is inevitably required to sustain commonly agreed artistic objectives, keep the initial division of responsibilities among the partners and guard their mutual synergy, cope with the individual, group and institutional dynamics of change caused by re-framing, undermining or questioning some starting premises of the project. Such consortium-run projects build trust among the partners and also require it as starting capital. They demand much intercultural competence and enhance it at the same time. Organisations that have cooperated successfully on one project tend to work together again, also in a multilateral mode, with some inevitable change in the composition of the consortium. International networks in the performing arts, as in other artistic domains, remain the rudimentary infrastructure of international cultural cooperation. Their growth and vitality over the last 30 years have made possible the degree of sophistication and complexity that such cooperation ventures have acquired today (Klaic 2007a).

Longer, multilateral, complex cultural projects might be a way of creating a new European awareness and offer insight into the diverse simultaneous realities experienced by artists and audiences in Europe, as well as increasing their intercultural competence. Such a long-term process is the mission of SEAS (www.seas.se), marked by the metaphor of seas, surrounding the continent and connecting its ports as points of openness, exchange and intercultural communication. In the starting phase, artists from various countries joined each other to venture to a destination in a third country, to a port unknown and unfamiliar. Guided by a local partner, they were encouraged to explore, examine and absorb. In the following phases a series of artistic works was conceptualised and developed on the basis of these travel experiences, unexpected encounters and discoveries. Artistic work derived from several disciplines was then inserted in various places, brought to other shores and into other ports. The first series (2005–2007) connected the harbours of the Baltic and the Adriatic, the next and final one (2008–2010) connected the ports of the Black Sea and the North Sea. Neither a festival nor a conventional tour, SEAS is a collective adventure into the unknown, a joint effort to use cultural shock and cultural difference for creative purposes, for learning and enjoyment. Theatre, dance, music and sound, design, video and web art, photography and writing are the overlapping artistic fields, linked to workshops, debates and a series of Cityscape conferences on the role of culture in urban revitalisation. SEAS has been an initiative of Intercult (Stockholm, www.intercult.se) relying on numerous presenting and producing organisations, local authorities, private foundations and renewed three-year funding by the European Commission.

Professional training programmes in performing arts are still framed by national cultural policies, systems and institutional set-ups and do not sufficiently equip future professionals for the specific skills and know-how needed to work on an international scale. Therefore, international consortia are increasingly being set up to provide such training to young professionals with some experience and a strong interest in such work. The Theoreme consortium (2001–2006), initiated by the Avignon Festival, initially sought to introduce emerging new theatre directors from Central and Eastern Europe to the Western European public but soon realised that it needed to provide training in production and tour management. The consortium was not sustainable on its own after EU support came to an end, but other groupings took its place with EU support. In 2009, SPACE (www.theaterinstituut.nl) trained new performing arts leaders while Festivals in Transition (www.theatrefit.org) focused on upcoming festival professionals, Jardin d'Europe (www.danceweb.eu) on dance managers and Changing Room, run by Trans Europe Halles (www.teh.net) and its members, focused on managers of complex cultural centres in former industrial buildings.

As international cooperation in the performing arts has become frequent - continuous rather than incidental, regular and no longer exceptional, fed by the communication within expanding and dynamic networks, oriented at co-production and not only touring - some partnerships have become reoccurring and even strategic, driven both by an artistic and a co-financing rationale. In a field where aspirations and creative ideas always exceed the resources available, intensive international cooperation shapes not only skills but also some shared values, a specific ethic of co-production, internalised by professionals and their organisations and reinforced by the discourse of major networks. The European Festival Association (www.efa-aef.eu), originally set up by the philosopher and European cultural activist Denis de Rougemont in 1952 to connect festivals of classical music, today includes festivals with a variety of contents, mostly of a multidisciplinary character. IETM, initiated in 1981, is the largest and most diverse cultural network for interdisciplinary, contemporary performing arts in Europe, with a current membership of over 520 organisations (festivals, theatres and arts centres, performing companies, programmers and curators, independent producers and public authorities) from 54 countries, which means that some members are from North and South America, Asia, Africa and Australia. The network is a learning and discussion platform, encompassing at least four different generations of professionals, who benefit from an immense repository of collective knowledge, experience and memory. Other smaller performing arts networks, such as ETC, ETU/UTE and EON, specialising in dramatic theatre, dance, musical theatre or theatre for children, have their own membership profile and more specific objectives but what all these networks have in common is that they provide an informal exchange of information, facilitate the search for appropriate partners, instigate discussion and advocacy of cultural policy development at all levels, from municipalities to the EU, further mobility and cooperation, and contribute to the articulation of an integrated European cultural space.

An emerging European cultural space

To what extent such an integrated European cultural space exists is a matter of contention. There is an unprecedented degree of communication, flow of information, debate and discussion among performing arts professionals, facilitated by digital communication technology but also restrained by the language barriers that delineate linguistic cultural realms, mainly overlapping with the borders of national cultural systems. Polish theatre debates, for instance, are carried out in the Polish language, in the Polish-language media, referring to recent Polish productions, the institutional infrastructure and funding policies of the Polish national, regional and municipal governments. In Romania or Portugal or Finland it is the same, with the national language, media, production output, infrastructure and policies again determining the debate. This separation of cultural and linguistic realms is mitigated to some extent by the preponderance of English as a connecting factor and a common denominator as is clearly visible on the Internet and English-language web-debate platforms. Consequently, English-language professional periodicals and books can count on wider attention than their counterparts in other languages. Networks and festivals play a key interface function among the organisations belonging to different national theatre systems, again with English as the dominant language of communication.

There is an unprecedented degree and volume of circulation of works of art and artistic mobility aided in the performing arts not only by the abundance of festivals, but also by an increasing number of venues that programme international work with frequency and all together mark out an integrated European cultural space, both as an operational realm and as a platform that attracts Europe-wide attention. Numerous non-commercial groups and teams of artists are continuously on the move, appearing in various cities and countries. They include La Fura dels Baus or Rimini Protokoll and some individual artists who regularly shift their working context, as Robert Wilson and Peter Sellars do. Both are incidentally Americans, and both are prospering as directors in the European theatre constellation, kept vibrant by significant public subsidies on a level unimaginable in the United States.

But for how long? After the severe economic recession of 2007–2009 was declared over by politicians, bankers and corporate executives, savage budgetary cuts, announced by numerous European governments in 2010 in order to reduce the public deficit and the cost of its financing, now pose an unprecedented threat to European public theatre as it was known since 1945. Catalan theatre, strongly driven by international touring, was one of the first to send out an alarm signal about rapidly shrinking opportunities (Barranco 2009). The quality, continuity and diversity of the performing arts in several countries might be at stake, but the opportunities for international cultural cooperation will also be diminished, just when the economic crisis feeds isolationism, xenophobia and selfish nationalism as a counterweight to the ambitious integration agenda pursued by the European Union. One could argue that various forms of international cooperation, together with the existing provisions to stimulate artistic mobility and especially the international programming of theatre festivals, are more necessary today than ever before, since they all contribute to the emergence of a European cultural citizenship by celebrating cultural diversity and opposing the cultural uniformity imposed by commercial cultural products on the global market. Moreover, if Europe wants to become a political, not just an economic and monetary union, this goal cannot be achieved without some cultural integration as embodied in cross-border theatre cooperation, for instance. Integration is not to be interpreted as imposed uniformity but, on the contrary, as a widening of opportunities to explore and engage cultural diversity and create new cultural values in the interaction of cultural traditions, habits, values and features. This could only be a public project, supported by public authorities and contrary to the uniformity pressures the market exercises on commercial entertainment.

If the economic crisis is causing overall insecurity, feeding jingoistic emotions and prompting dangerous protectionist measures instead of shared European policies and solutions, the greater mobility of artefacts and artists and more international cultural cooperation could offer a much-needed counterweight. Such artistic endeavours reduce the cultural distance among the citizens of Europe, affirm cultural diversity as a common asset and teach audiences how to appreciate cultural differences rather than be intimidated by them or prompted to reject them as strange, incomprehensible and menacing. The internationalisation of theatre practices, especially after the removal of the Iron Curtain, has delivered not only artistic benefits but also cultural and political gains. It has achieved this by shaping the intercultural curiosity and competence of theatre professionals and the theatre public, as well as by expanding the capacity of audiences to understand social realities other than those in their own immediate surroundings. By working on an international scale, performing arts organisations create works that challenge the deeply entrenched prejudices and stereotypes held everywhere about fellow Europeans and migrants from outside Europe, sustained by widespread ignorance and manipulated by demagogical politics and nationalistic media.

Conversely, the question could also be posed about how European performing arts address Europe as a discursive reality, as a process of historical strife and nowadays of integration, as inter-related knots of collective memory. The question particularly arises why festivals and consortia of performing arts companies do not initiate more projects that seek to offer transnational and intercultural perspectives on the collective perceptions of Europe, on common European anxieties, concerns and aspirations?

If one looks for common European threads in the collective memory, experiences of World War II still play a major role. Successful plays, performed across Europe, about the Occupation and its effects on theatre (Slobodan Šnajder, *Hrvatski Faust/The Croat Faust* 1981), or about the Holocaust (an Israeli play, Joshua Sobol's *Ghetto* 1984), on collaboration with the occupier and Nazism (J. P. Sartre's *Morts sans sépulture* 1946, *Les Séquestrés d'Altona* 1959), the race for the atom bomb during the war (Michael Frayn's *Copenhagen* 1998) and artists under Nazism (Ronald Harwood's *Taking Sides*, about the conductor Furtwängler 1995) are in fact exceptional in European drama. The plays of Heiner Müller, much staged across Europe in the 1980s–1990s (*Der Auftrag, Quartett, Zement, Hamletmaschine*, etc.), which addressed European history with large, bold strokes and with powerful metaphors, have since faded away and disappeared from theatre repertoires. British authors addressing European topics, both historical and contemporary, such as Edward Bond, Tom Stoppard, Christopher Hampton, Howard Brenton, David Edgar, Caryl Churchill and Howard Barker, together form rather a strong cohort, unmatched in other European theatre cultures and performed quite frequently abroad – Bond and Barker even have a much higher standing on continental stages than in the United Kingdom.

Today, more than 20 years after the Berlin Wall came down, where are European cooperative initiatives to render the individual and collective experience of communism in the arts? Who is preparing a research symposium on theatre under communism, its allusive critique, games with censorship and vacillation between appeasement and dissent (Klaic 2009)? Where is an orchestrated international project on the changes in social fabric and prevailing values in Central and Eastern Europe since 1989? What about a comprehensive thematisation of the European history of patriarchal repression? Has the Magdalena Project – an initiative of feminist performance – died out? And what about a European effort to stage the experience of European colonisation and decolonisation? The KVS in Brussels has taken the fiftieth anniversary of Congo's independence as a challenge for its repertoire, but many other theatres in former colonial powers ignore colonial history and the half century since the beginning of decolonisation. These and other big European topics could be addressed on stage, preferably if a company decides to devote a season or part of it to one of them and commissions new works in a well-designed series; or if there is a consortium of companies, perhaps connected with venues and festivals, from different countries that function as co-commissioners and jointly develop, produce and tour such a series of inter-related work.

The dynamics of globalised financial capitalism, its onslaught on the European welfare state and its implicit values remain by and large outside the vision field of European theatres, even after the myth of the unfailing, self-correcting market has been discredited in the economic recession that exploded in the autumn of 2008. David Hare, who systematically analysed the power structures of contemporary British society in a series of plays, was quick to write a new piece, *The Power of Yes* (2009) but found no equivalent European counterparts nor followers. One should not blame the playwrights, but rather the theatres and the festivals for not seeking to commission and create, alone or in co-production with others, larger thematic packages of stage work exploring the recession but also the de-industrialisation and the future of work in Europe, migration and citizenship, rifts in contemporary urban life and ecological issues. European theatre networks, such as the ETC (Electronic Theatre Controls) and the UTE (The Union of the Theatres of Europe), which boast of their importance for European cultural integration, are missing a chance here to follow their promotion rhetoric with specific productions and contribute to the quality of debate in Europe. By pooling resources, they could commission new works on topics of pervasive European concern, as the Andersen Bicentenary in Denmark did when they commissioned 12 new productions, inspired by Andersen's opus, from some leading international theatre-makers in 2005.

Essen-Ruhr European Capital of Culture 2010 launched an ambitious project, going back to the common European mythological and literary tradition. Six European authors were each invited to write a play based on one episode of Homer's *Ulysses*. Their plays were produced by five theatre companies in the Ruhr area (Bochum, Dortmund, Essen, Mülheim, Oberhausen and Moers). On five weekends spectators could make a trip through the Ruhr area and see all the episodes of *Odyssey Europa* in various places, using buses, trains, boats and cars. Moreover, the connection between the European and local dimensions was reinforced by a scheme whereby the spectators could be hosted overnight, fed and guided through the area by local residents, who signed up as volunteers to offer hospitality and exchange stories with the visitors (www.essen-fuer-das-ruhrgebiet.ruhr2010.de/en/programme/changing-stages/odyssey-europa.html). Universal, pan-European and local dimensions intertwined in this truly unique project that resisted the faceless globalisation of standardised products and offered its public a unique exploratory adventure, even if they were residents of the Ruhr – where theatregoers are quite used to commuting from one place to another to a theatre performance and where a dense network of motorways and a well-synchronised regional system of public transport facilitated the mobility of spectators.

Another response to globalisation is a withdrawal to a remote rural setting and deeper exploration of a local environment before the results can be shared with the big world – as exemplified by Wlodzimierz Staniewski, who in 1976 established the Gardzienice theatre centre (www.gardzienice.art.pl) in the village of the same name near Lublin, on the eastern edge of Poland. At the time he was seeking some distance from the repressive atmosphere of the city, where communist authorities imposed their stifling ideological norms on creativity. In his voluntary rural exile, Staniewski and his followers hoped to find inspiration, to capture and integrate in their productions ancient rituals and customs, skills, songs and oral literature, a visual culture determined by the colours and rhythms of nature. From this village, Gardzienice became a well-known company, performing around the world and hosting hundreds of students in its rural workshops and on its stages. This is a remarkable story of globalisation, beaten at its own uniforming game, with a withdrawal to a specific remote location, leading in time to outreach to the world far away (Allen 1998). In a way, Staniewski followed the pattern pioneered by Eugenio Barba, who in 1964 founded his Odin Teatret in Norway and settled in 1968 in the small Danish town of Holstebro. There he ran the Nordic Theatre Laboratory that put Holstebro prominently on the world theatre map through hundreds of alumni of this training from across the continents, who in turn translated Barba's books into many languages.

Trans-European vistas

Productions from other continents are not often to be seen in Europe. In addition to major festivals as the main presenters of non-European productions, there are occasional tours sponsored by foreign governments and some commercial endeavours. American experimental companies, such as the Living Theatre, have been coming to Europe regularly since the mid-1960s, where they have found more generous support than at home. Quebec Canadians launched the Cirque du Soleil (www.cirquedusoleil.com) with government support before it became a global commercial enterprise with simultaneous runs of several productions in Europe and the United States and in parallel tours. The Canadian LaLaLa Human Steps (www.lalalahumansteps.com/new/) has also found a strong European dance following. In 2010 the Venice Biennial dance programme was dominated by dance work from the Canadian province of Quebec, whose government maintains an efficient, business-like promotional agency to secure an international market for its non-commercial companies. Japanese theatre, mainly the traditional *noh, kabuki* and *bunraku*, is to be seen in Europe thanks to the support of the governmental Japan Foundation and corporate sponsorship. The Chinese Ministry of Culture has created an Arts Service Centre, which operates like a commercial agency in organising tours of foreign companies to China and placing traditional Chinese performing arts productions, such as Beijing, Shaanxi and Cantonese opera, abroad. Since the end of the apartheid regime in South Africa there has been a vogue of township musicals on the trail across Europe, with professional and semi-professional performers, and a strong interest in William Kentridge and his Handspring Puppet Company (www.handspringpuppet.co.za).

Theatre groups from all parts of the world come to Europe only thanks to the curiosity and diligence of exceptional European festival directors. Outside the festival infrastructure, seasons and series of non-European theatre are a rarity. Again, Theater a.d. Ruhr in Mülheim, a frequent traveller group, is an exception in presenting foreign theatre companies in a systematic manner since 1981, bringing them to the Ruhr for several years in a row. They initially came from Poland and the former Yugoslavia, even before the end of the Cold War, then from Turkey and Iran (where Ciulli's theatre performed at festivals and where he directed Lorca's *House of Bernarda Alba*), but were later followed by almost unknown

Central Asian and African groups, never seen elsewhere, gradually shaping a committed, regular audience who became sophisticated in an intercultural sense. Eugenio Barba and his Odin Teatret have also been consistent in intercultural exploration, at home in Holstebro and across the world, and especially through the biannual School of Theatre Anthropology (Watson et al. 2002).

European theatre companies travel beyond the confines of their continent mainly on the commission and with the support of their own governments and their promotional agencies, such as the Goethe-Institut and the British Council, sometimes accompanying the head of state or Prime Minister on an official visit, or appearing within a broader programme of national cultural presentation, driven by what is nowadays fashionably called "cultural diplomacy" – the usual form of art presentation during the Cold War, deployed for political promotion and influence peddling. While British commercial productions regularly get transferred from London's West End to New York's Broadway, the cultural programme of the 1984 Los Angeles Olympics opened up the United States for tours of theatre productions in languages other than English. Access remains difficult because non-commercial American venues depend heavily on the box office and thus do not dare to experiment much, with the result that guest appearances from Europe are in practice possible only thanks to substantial subsidies from European governments, while the regular American outlets remain just a few. There are the Next Wave festival, in fact an extended season in the Brooklyn Academy of Music (www.bam.org), a summer festival in the Lincoln Center (lc.lincolncenter.org) and a more recent Under the Radar festival (www.publictheater.org) – all in New York – as well as a few scattered university-based arts centres and occasional, mainly short-lived, festivals of some international ambition outside New York. In 2010 the Royal Shakespeare Company announced plans to perform five of its productions for six weeks every year starting in 2011 in the Park Avenue Armory (www. armoryonpark.org) in New York, a huge space of over 5,000 square metres to be adapted for this residency (Healy 2010a).

An additional complicating factor is represented by the US authorities, which have often been difficult and slow with the issuance of visas for performers and musicians from Europe, especially after 9/11, leading to some tour cancellations and loud protests from presenters and artists (Kliment 2006). After Senate hearings, promises came from the government to create fast-track visa processing for visiting artists (Sisario 2010) but soon afterwards Peter Stein cancelled his scheduled directing of *Boris Godunov* at the New York Metropolitan Opera complaining of a lack of empathy by the Met leadership for his humiliating experiences in applying for a US work visa (Wakin 2010b).

Australia has for a long time been a regular destination for European companies, thanks to the international festivals in Sydney, Melbourne, Adelaide and Perth, especially after increases in government funding there. Since the 1970s, European companies have been going to the Cervantino Festival in Guanajuato, Mexico (www.festivalcervantino.gob.mx) and to the International Theatre Festival in Caracas, Venezuela, both now overshadowed by the large international programming of the Ibero-American Theatre Festival in Bogotá,

Colombia (www.festivaldeteatro.com.co). The rest of Latin America offers very limited hosting opportunities due to a structural lack of substantial public support in most countries.

In Africa there is a lack of facilities and resources for hosting and a dearth of autonomous programmers, except to some extent in South Africa – but there, too, a sharp reduction in arts budgets has thrown several festivals with an international outlook into considerable poverty. In some African countries, the hall in the French Cultural Centre is possibly the only well-equipped venue available, used by local semi-professional and amateur groups and rare foreign troupes. In the Gulf States, during the high oil-revenue times (2000–2008), several ambitious venues were built but left without consistent domestic or international programming, some even lacking core technical staff. In the Arab countries in general obsessive censorship more than lack of resources keeps foreign work out, except in short special moments, such as the Cairo International Festival for Experimental Theatre (www.cdf-eg.org/English/exp_theater/index_e.htm), for which the foreign embassies are asked to send a production of their choice, with modest hospitality offered by the host but no fee. Consequently, the programme is a hodgepodge of arbitrary and incidental choices, often made by diplomats or ministry bureaucrats back in Europe, without any sense of the Cairo context and the predilections of its audience. When they undertake some theatre projects in the Arab world, such as the Swedish Institute's expensive and paternalistic *Midsummer Night's Dream* in Egypt, and also in some projects in South Africa, European governmental agencies are driven more by their own political agenda and visibility concerns than by the needs and conditions of the theatre professionals whom they supposedly seek to support. When the initiative comes from theatre people, however, and is then followed up by government support, cooperative projects tend to be more effective, fair and better shaped to fit local circumstances.

Some Mediterranean governments outside Europe tend to see theatre as a tourist attraction in the first place. After the long civil war in Lebanon, the tentative revival of tourism initiated festivals in Beirut and Baalbek driven by private investment, more for music than theatre. Similarly, a month-long music and dance festival in Carthage, Tunisia, seeks to serve tourists in the first place. In Turkey, where the ministry is significantly called the Ministry of Tourism and Culture, it is a pioneer private foundation, the Istanbul Foundation for Culture and Arts (www.iksv.org) that has been the main advocate of festivals as platforms for international cooperation rather than tourism promotion. Among government initiatives, the Istanbul European Capital of Culture 2010 failed to generate any coherent cultural programme and from the early phase focused on the upgrading of urban real-estate value rather than on the formation of cultural capital. In the same region, Israel has a number of professionally run festivals of international outreach, with a dynamic and polemical receptive context.

Festivals and venues in Japan, South Korea, Hong Kong, Taiwan and Singapore invite European companies sparingly and see their own performing arts increasingly as an export article, especially in the case of South Korea. In China, a destination of rising popularity,

European visiting companies are expected to pay for everything themselves, or have their governments and corporations pay for the tour expenses as part of the overwhelming effort to impress the Chinese and strengthen a country's presence on Chinese markets. The Chinese must be assured that the foreign production will stay away from any of the standard sensitive issues (Klaic 2007b), and then organise the tours without investing anything. Consequently, European companies risk performing to small, uninformed audiences or simply to their own co-patriots, because the local presenter feels no involvement and no responsibility. Nevertheless, Expo 2010 prompted many European governments to set up ambitious cultural programmes, including performing arts, to show themselves off in Shanghai, without any clear benefits.

Cooperation between European and non-European performing artists remains rare. In recent years, the choreographers Akram Khan (UK) and Anouk van Dijk (NL) (www. anoukvandijk.nl) have worked with the Beijing Modern Dance Company (www.bmdc.com. cn) to create new work. Simon McBurney and his Théâtre de Complicité from the UK (www. complicite.org) worked with a Tokyo company on *The Elephant Vanishes* (2003), based on Murakami's prose, and *Shunkin* (2008), based on the literature of Junichiro Tanizaki, and brought these production to Europe. Rimini Protokoll worked in Calcutta at the invitation of the local branch of the Goethe-Institut, but also in Cairo, Buenos Aires, South Korea and elsewhere, always finding – just as in their Europe-inspired productions and projects – some local protagonists to invest their very own experiences in the production and endow it with a strong local character. The Moroccan-Belgian choreographer Sidi Larbi Cherkaoui created *Sutra* (2008) at Sadler's Wells in London with the sculptor Antony Gormley and a group of Chinese Buddhist monks from the Shaolin temple, known for their mastery of the art of self-defence, prompting *ballet-tanz* magazine to declare him the "Choreographer of the Year."

The stage has always been a privileged place to assert cultural values, to shape, foster and admire identity; but, at the same time, the stage has also functioned as a convenient vehicle for intercultural exploration, influence and appropriation, within Europe and increasingly on a global scale. *Pichet Klunchun and Myself* (2004) is just such an intercultural vehicle and it bravely focuses on dance, performers and their cultural determinants. The unpretentious approach of the self-referential characters in the production does not shut the world out but rather invokes it in its basic human frailty shared between the East and the West, making it palpable on the small bare stage, where the Belgian conceptual choreographer Jérôme Bel and Pichet Klunchun, a master of *khon* – a traditional Thai court dance facing extinction – question each other about their understanding of the profession and its cultural context. Klunchun and Bel seek to understand each other with sincerity and fairness. They recognise their kinship in both being professional dancers whilst at the same time despairing at the divergent cultural anchoring of the profession in Western Europe and South-East Asia, which makes them so different (Klaic 2008).

An antidote to complacency

Is there some professional solidarity among performing arts practitioners and institutions in Europe? If one looks at how slowly most performing arts organisations absorb professionals from migrant backgrounds into their teams, the answer is "no." In the United Kingdom several prominent artists from a migrant background have become very successful, much appreciated and in demand. Sweden can name two or three, Belgium perhaps four, the Netherlands three, Germany a few, likewise Norway and Austria, but nowhere in Europe is there anything to boast about. Theatre refugees from military dictatorships in Latin America in the 1970s–1980s found asylum and working conditions in France, followed by some exiled Iranians. In the 1990s Mladen Materić's Tattoo Theatre, in flight from a besieged Sarajevo, settled in Toulouse with considerable help from French colleagues and made a series of new productions with regular French cultural subsidies. Teatro di Nacosto in Italy and many other European companies have made productions about the plight of refugees and asylum seekers and have often succeeded in involving them as witnesses and performers and in carrying their sense of solidarity to refugee camps. Théâtre du Soleil's *Le Dernier Caravansérail* (2006) was an exemplary saga of contemporary forced migration across the continents. The same company also ran workshops in Afghanistan and strives to secure funding for continuous work by a group of colleagues they have trained there.

During the war in Bosnia-Herzegovina, Haris Pašović toured Europe from besieged Sarajevo with his young company in 1995, sustained by the considerable sense of solidarity of theatre colleagues who hosted them in their venues. Such a response was shaped by an initial gesture of artistic solidarity that set a precedent: Susan Sontag's war-time excursion to Sarajevo, where in 1993 she created a production of Beckett's *Waiting for Godot* with local professional actors, performed in candlelight and with solar batteries and perceived by the inhabitants as a major boost to their spirit of resistance to the attackers and the ravages daily inflicted by them. Sontag was followed by many other artists who went to Sarajevo during the war at considerable risk to their own lives. The international solidarity of European colleagues sustained Jeton Neziraj in Prishtinë in creating the Centre for Children's Development (www.qendra.org), a series of productions for children after the NATO intervention in Kosovo in 1999; he even developed community theatre projects in which Albanians and Serbs shared the pain about their family members who had disappeared in the conflict.

In 2007 theatre people reacted with outrage to the brutal and never-resolved murder of Mark Weil, director of the Ilkhom theatre company in Tashkent, Uzbekistan but this had little effect as in several similar cases of persecution of theatre artists in other parts of the world. The Free Theatre of Minsk, one of the very few autonomous artistic initiatives in Belarus, has so far managed to survive government harassment primarily thanks to the support and invitations it has received from abroad, as well as the willingness of such prominent personalities as Tom Stoppard and Václav Havel to appear as its patrons. Yet at home it is forced to operate practically underground, reaching out to only a very tiny part of the Belarus public whose cultural consumption is otherwise controlled by Lukashenko's regime and its nation-building propaganda. Occasional gestures of solidarity, incidental and short-lived, with Palestinian colleagues on the Israeli-occupied West Bank have been made: European artists have gone there despite the check-points and resistance of the Israeli authorities, to perform in Hebron, Ramallah and Yenin, working with Palestinian colleagues and running workshops with children and young people, especially in the IETM campaign "100 Artists for Palestine" (2001–2003). After the end of the apartheid regime, many European artists and theatre groups went to South Africa to connect, encourage, teach and perform, sometimes following up with an invitation for a return visit to Europe (Engelander and Klaic 1998). Roel Twijnstra of Het Waterhuis, Rotterdam, mounted a musical on teenage sexuality, lifestyles and HIV/AIDS prevention, and toured South African high schools with it. The Italian actor and director Marco Baliani went to Nairobi, Kenya, to work with two dozen of the 300,000 street children there and make a production, *Black Pinocchio*, with them. He then brought them to Europe for a series of performances in the Netherlands and Italy, as a group of fully acknowledged persons, each with their own Kenyan passport and a valid Schengen visa in it.

These examples of global theatre solidarity also indicate a desire to test the capacity of the performing arts in conflict zones and in societies that are attempting post-conflict reconstruction. However, significant local impact depends on continuous engagement and empowerment of local artistic and community groups rather than on the occasional short-term journeys of European artists. European networks, embassies and branches of governmental cultural promotion agencies can hardly be expected to provide such continuity. That is why the German branch of the International Theatre Institute (ITI) has opened an office in Khartoum, Sudan, to set up community theatre projects of longer duration. Or why the Theatre Embassy of Amsterdam (www.theatre-embassy.org) instigates two- to three-year theatre-in-development projects in Asia, Africa and South America. And why did the German artist Christoph Schlingensief (1960–2010) start building an opera venue in a small Burkina Fasso village, four hours' drive from Ouagadougou? For Schlingensief, working with an African architect, the project encompassed the creation of an entire opera village or rather the articulation of the opera production process as the developmental strategy for a village community and, hopefully, the prospect of its long-term sustainability, achieved paradoxically through opera as the most complex of all artistic endeavours (David 2010). The Theatre Department of the University of Manchester (www.arts.manchester. ac.uk) ran a multi-annual programme "In Place of War" to explore the preventive, mediating and rehabilitative capacity of theatre in conflict zones, through academic and field research, training and artistic productions (www.inplaceofwar.net). The outcome includes a database of documentation, a large international network and publications.

Venturing out of familiar constellations, to faraway places of conflict and strife, tensions, poverty and fear, European performing artists are testing their own stamina and the limits of their art; they are also conducting research, probing their own habits and limitations and gathering material for their future work; they are making gestures of solidarity, compassion, empathy and commitment, supporting their colleagues in distress, and engaging with troubled local communities and constituencies made fragile. While they are confirming their values as global artists and global citizens, they are at the same time seeking to bring to their audiences back home the sense of a wider world, together with its realms of turbulence, threat and trauma, so as to challenge the complacency into which the European public can so easily slide. The European awareness and curiosity of public theatre, its European cooperative experiences, should therefore be seen only as a stepping stone towards a sense of global citizenship, for the more complex engagements far away, resulting in a global critical awareness and productive modes of resistance to the standardisation, uniformity and superficiality imposed by the forces of globalisation. And here lies the substantial potential of public theatre: it can shape a critical look at the world – the big, wide world – and at its key challenges and threats, sharing its own experiences and insights with the domestic audience, pulling them away from the complacency and oblivion that the commercial theatre regularly seeks to engineer.

Chapter 9

Leadership, Governance and Cultural Policy

The rising pressures under which public theatres operate in Europe have been made much worse by the economic recession of 2008–2009 and the ensuing government subsidy cuts. Moreover, it seems that the recession and its implications are prompting a change of political attitude towards public arts subsidies in general. For some 60 years there has been a rather broad political and social consensus across Europe that quality art institutions deserve public subsidy for the public benefit they create. How much subsidy and under what conditions and according to what sort of procedural regime – these were matters of national and later of regional and municipal resources and arrangements, not of principle. Gradually, the efficiency and effectiveness of the allocation of subsidies have become a matter of concern, so that the financial performance indicators of subsidised arts institutions have preoccupied subsidy givers in most European countries. For performing arts organisations, this scrutiny has meant that their capacity to generate their own income on top of the subsidy received has become indicative of their merit; for venues it is the average seat occupancy that has come to constitute the key concern. Public authorities have introduced a growing set of additional expectations and demands for all subsidy recipients, earmarking part of the public money for educational and outreach activities, mobility, international profile, cultural diversity and so on. With the probability that the total volume of arts subsidies available will be sharply reduced in the ongoing slashing of public expenditure, one can imagine that arts organisations will be severely affected – much more than cultural heritage institutions, whose responsibility for minimal upkeep – of museum collections, for instance – can be questioned only up to a certain limit. Among all art disciplines, the performing arts as a rather costly collective activity may be hurt quite severely.

After the initial 5 per cent cut in Arts Council England subsidies in spring 2010, the new British Conservative-Liberal cabinet's intention to reduce the budgets of all departments by 40 per cent was a menacing writing-on-the-wall for all English performing arts organisations. It unleashed a lively column and blog debate in *The Guardian* and other media about the purpose of arts in a civilised society. The intensity of this debate showed that its participants realise that the very principle of public subsidy for the arts cannot be seen as self-evident any longer but needs to be ferociously defended and reinforced with fresh arguments. Mark Ravenhill argued that performing arts organisations should first cut down on their swollen communication, management and fund-raising staff in order to save money for the core business of staging productions (Ravenhill 2010). Others joined the debate, seeking to prove that the arts are good for the economy (Toynbee 2010) and even highlighting the VAT money generated by the sale of tickets but were quickly called to order by John Kay in *The Financial Times*, who exposed the humbug of economic thinking and endless flow of commissioned and well-paid economic impact studies that set costs made against benefit produced while ignoring the cultural effects of the artistic production (Kay 2010).

Simultaneously, in Bulgaria a clumsy manoeuvre by the Minister of Culture to cut some budgets by the mechanical merger of repertory companies in various cities caused a huge outcry, but brought forward no arguments of principle for the right of each city to have at least one public theatre company. No alternative proposals came from the profession on how to modernise an anachronistic theatre model inherited from communism, impoverished and depleted during the last 20 years of transition, and how to cure it of a prolonged institutional and systemic fatigue (Gavrilova 2010).

In Italy, where the Berlusconi media machinery cannot hide the evident meltdown of public finances, fatalism and stubborn survivalism prevail among performing arts professionals. There is no visible sense of responsibility on the part of the boards of opera houses for the accumulated deficit of almost half a billion euros over the years, nor any initiatives to improve cumbersome governance structures, enmeshing banking foundations and various levels of public authorities. All that exists is a tacit acceptance of continuously shrinking output, fewer productions, shorter seasons and more temporary contracts alongside the steadfast engagement of numerous fragile initiatives and organisations, especially in smaller places, where they rely on a tight informal network of family members, friends, supportive small business and community groups, on the grey economy and local solidarity.

In Greece, pressured by the European Union and International Monetary Fund into a gigantic overhaul of public finances, the plight of public theatres has remained unnoticed in the midst of a major upheaval caused by striking flight controllers, railway men, lorry drivers, ship and ferry staff, civil servants and everyone else opposing the government measures and making the economic prospects much worse by causing the flight of foreign tourists from Greece in the chaotic summer months of 2010. Meanwhile, theatre festivals in Athens, Epidaurus and elsewhere went on as scheduled, perhaps with a reduced audience.

Everywhere in Europe, performing arts professionals have ample reason to worry about whether the long-standing consensus on the public funding of the arts has only been temporarily weakened or whether it is perhaps broken. Even if this intervention is only short-term and panic-driven, caused by the politicians' fear of a double-dip recession and mounting debt, the damage inflicted on the arts could be serious and recovery uncertain and slow.[1] But if what we are witnessing at the exit from the 2008–2009 recession is a more far-reaching paradigm switch, marking politics' abdication of responsibility for public culture, if the shift reflects an ideological conviction held by liberal and conservative parties in power across Europe rather than just a manoeuvre of political pragmatism and diligent housekeeping, it entails the conscious sacrifice of public culture to the predominance of the commercial culture industry. In the United Kingdom, there are several reasons to believe that the recession is just an excuse to implement long-held ideological convictions about shrinking government and rendering the market predominant in the realm of cultural production as elsewhere. If so, this shift, inspired by American neo-liberal predilections, will probably be – as often in the past – further copied across Europe. Public theatre then has to grasp that its own very survival is at stake. The response required from performing arts leaders, boards, communities and networks is to reinvent and fine-tune political arguments but also to come up with some plausible policy proposals offered to politicians as an alternative to the mechanical subsidy-chopping and other arbitrary measures that bureaucracies are imposing and will continue to impose.

Leadership: Fantasies of a cultural Superman

The more a not-for-profit cultural organisation is expected to behave as a business, the more notions of leadership get imposed on it. The reliance on leadership and its magic problem-solving capacity originates from US politics and business, but was first embraced in the United Kingdom, spreading quickly to cultural sector discourse, and from there spilling out across Europe. The United Kingdom remains in the forefront of cultural leadership training programmes set up by public and private sources (Kahn 2009). The individualist, elitist and essentially anti-egalitarian connotations of leadership cover up a systemic crisis in non-profit cultural organisations, with their traditional authority and sense of direction weakened and confused by globalisation and migration, their output questioned by doubts about their representational authority and their eminence overshadowed by the propulsive commercial cultural industry and its star cults. The challenge to public cultural institutions, as described by Pachter and Landry (2001), cannot be reduced to the question of leadership alone and to the remedy that it supposedly offers: a leader imagined as some sort of cultural Superman, endowed with an artistic vision, suave with the media, inspiring the staff, excellent at fund-raising, connected to an impressive international network, a sponsors' darling. Such a hyperbolical, robot-like portrait can hardly match real people; moreover, exceptional individuals who may perhaps come close to this idealised picture will in all probability not apply for the top positions in public culture, nor be recruited by head-hunter agencies. It is more likely that such high-flyers will prefer top corporate jobs with their enormous salaries and innumerable perks or an elective public office with the clout of political power or the prominence, glamour and wealth guaranteed by a career in the media.

The contextualisation of leadership in performing arts organisations is chiefly determined by their typology and size. In opera houses as complex organisations, in large ensembles and large multi-venue complexes, in organisations that run an ensemble and a venue or even several venues, there is inevitably a managerial hierarchy that allows for a type of leadership associated with great concentration of power, high visibility and much authority, whether it is filled by an artist or by a producer, a manager or an intendant who combines artistic and financial responsibilities. In medium-sized and smaller performing arts organisations, there is less hierarchy and the leadership role is filled in a symbolic, less formal manner, with the collective nature of the creative process more easily experienced and appreciated – even if infatuations with collective creation, shared decision-making and strict egalitarianism, popular in the 1960s and 1970s, have been by and large discarded. Despite the increase in managerial functions and tasks as part of the professionalisation of performing arts organisations, with a proliferation of communication, marketing and development, that is, fund-raising jobs, there is still a collective awareness that artistic work remains at the very core of the organisation, determines its identity and value and cannot be subcontracted to some outside party. Even in festivals and programming venues without their own production, the foremost artistic choices to be made are concentrated in the role of the programmer, and acknowledged inside and outside the organisation as the crucial ones, thus as the remit of a leadership role.

Some performing arts organisations are entirely the creation of their individual founders, who remain in the leadership position for a long time and determine the artistic identity of the organisation in a lasting manner: the Théâtre du Soleil is unimaginable without Ariane Mnouchkine, as is the Odin Teatret without Eugenio Barba, and Rosas without Anne Teresa de Keersmaeker. The companies created by William Forsythe, Emma Dante, Pippo Delbono and many others unabashedly carry the name of their founders and permanent leaders. In festivals, a long tenure by founding fathers and mothers is still common but there is also ample evidence that this can curb growth, evolution and adjustment to contextual change, and ultimately jeopardise the continuity of the organisation.

A performing arts leader interacts with ensembles and stars, with teams and crews, with departments and services, with artists, artistic collaborators and boards, as well as managerial, administrative and technical staff. Despite all the inevitable delegation of responsibilities, he or she lives the structural tension of all the interdependence among those functions and tasks to the full, as well as being engaged in the continuous fine tuning of their responsibilities, motivations, predilections and understanding of the entire endeavour and their contribution to it. In today's media-obsessed culture, a performing arts leader is obliged to manifest his or her own leadership externally as well: to the public and the media, to funders, sponsors, major donors, peers, colleagues, supporters and competitors.

In the complex collective endeavour that the machinery of opera requires, top leaders do make a difference. Gerard Mortier propelled Brussels La Monnaie/De Munt into the top class of European opera houses. Then he turned the Opéra Bastille (opened in 1989) into a truly democratic cultural hub, engaging the most daring of artists, such as Peter Sellars, video artist Bill Viola, La Fura dels Baus, Robert Wilson and Anselm Kiefer. With his departure for Madrid in 2010 there is a chance he will repeat the De Munt adventure, making the Spanish capital a remarkable opera centre, which it currently is not. In Amsterdam, during an almost 20-year tenure, Pierre Audi has made De Nederlandse Opera (DNO, www.dno.nl) fill the Muziektheater (www.het-muziektheater.nl, opened 1986) to full capacity with his own productions and those of a cohort of formidable directors he has repeatedly invited back. Without an exceptional opera tradition, saddled with a new building that provoked much controversy and frustration, Amsterdam has become a privileged opera city with regular world premieres of new operas, memorable renderings of classic works, consistent Janáček, Mozart and Monteverdi lines and such logistical mega-endeavours as Wagner's *Ring* and Berlioz's *Les Troyens*. DNO's productivity is achieved with a relatively modest subsidy but with a very efficient business model: the house facilities, as well as the technical and public-service staff are shared with the National Ballet. Only the chorus is in permanent employment while soloists are engaged separately for a few weeks of rehearsals and eight to nine performances within a period of four weeks only; a different Dutch symphonic orchestra or occasionally a chamber ensemble is engaged to accompany them for each production. In Budapest, the director Balazs Kovalik has inserted new flair into the venerable but fatigued State Opera (www. opera.hu) with his directing of *Elektra, Fidelio* and *Turandot*, subsequently becoming its artistic director. Before he could instigate substantial changes, he was removed by the new right-wing government in 2010.

A respectable artistic leader connects intricate and invisible artistic processes with the society and surrounding communities rather than identifying the performing arts organisation with a business or accepting to be a fellow traveller of politics; hopefully, he or she is someone who sees artistic creation as a function of citizenship rather than a representation of political power or any sort of group identity. Desirable competences for an artistic leader would further include an ability to make the organisation sustainable and distinctive through a medium-term developmental strategy, an anticipative outlook that can recognise forthcoming challenges and opportunities, and a personal dialectics of local conditions and global trends. In a nutshell, a performing arts organisation looking for a leader should hope to find someone who possesses a sharp sense of time and space, looks five years ahead, understands the immediate environment and connects it with the wider world. Moreover, he or she should be able to inspire and motivate collaborators but also enhance the intercultural competence of the board, staff, associated artists and public and, last but not least, rather than just being handy with spreadsheets and merciless in budget revisions, a leader should be resolute in the hiring and firing of personnel.

Appointments to the artistic leadership of permanent ensembles, production houses, venues, festivals and other performing arts organisations carry with them the authority to control considerable public resources and should thus be made for a limited mandate of four years, renewable once only in the case of an extremely creditable and accomplished performance. In this way leadership positions would at least be a little more in alignment with the prevalent short-term engagement of most performing artists hired for a single production and its limited run or, at best, for an entire season. The practice of permanent contracts in repertory companies is being quickly abandoned in most European countries and a limited mandate for leaders in public performing arts organisations is emerging as standard in cultural governance.

Governance matters: Boards safeguarding autonomy

Even the strongest and most competent performing arts leader must be responsible to someone, especially in a public theatre depending on public subsidy and expected to deliver a regular public benefit. Leaders must be selected and appointed by someone who also has the authority to supervise and even fire them, and someone must take care of their legacy and the continuity of the organisation by planning their succession after the end of the mandate, retirement, or departure for whatever other reason. These key tasks should be the responsibility of an autonomous board of the performing arts organisation rather than the duty of the public authority that subsidises it, a decision made by a political body or by the holder of a political executive office. Why? Because an autonomous board will first and foremost have the interests of the organisation in view, whereas a political body or a political executive will be guided by primarily political considerations of their own office and their own power entrenchment. Because the board will, at least to some extent, insulate the creative process from political interference and vouch for its autonomy, while taking the responsibility for the institutional, organisational and financial matters that can provide optimal conditions for artistic creation.

It is impossible to generalise on the diversity of cultural governance in Europe and even on the governance models and practices prevailing in the performing arts. While corporate governance has received much attention in recent years with the introduction of EU and national regulation, cultural governance is a rather neglected and underdeveloped field. A quite common assumption is that the one who pays – decides. That means that a public authority dispensing subsidies appoints and fires the performing arts organisation's executive directly. In many countries public theatres do not have their own governing bodies because they are considered one of the public authority services, not an autonomous organisation. In such cases, the city alderman or the head of the regional department of culture or the minister of culture is directly in charge, making appointments, firing, controlling and calling to account. The politicisation of cultural office holding can go as far as allowing winning party leaders after an election to fire public theatre executives and appoint their own loyalists instead. In Central and Eastern Europe, for instance, most theatre boards – if they exist at all – have a formal or simply advisory role since the meddling of politicians has made them lame and superfluous. Until the end of the twentieth century it was common practice in Germany and Austria for prominent politicians to chair the boards of public theatres, under an assumption that the public money spent on them would not otherwise be safe. In many smaller performing arts organisations, set up in a legal sense as associations and surviving mainly on occasional public subsidy, the boards are composed of friends of the artistic leader and thus have a supportive role rather than a governing and supervisory one.

Boards of performing arts organisations and other cultural institutions come into being in various manners in Europe: in the case of an association, the assembly of association members elects the board, at least formally; if the theatre organisation has another type of legal status, a public body that is its founder and the key funder appoint the board members and even designate the chairperson; alternatively, various public bodies, private foundations and professional organisations, specified in the performing arts organisation's statutes, delegate members to the board; then again the sitting board members may co-opt a new member in the case of a vacancy. All these systems have their advantages and disadvantages and are entrenched in the cultural and political traditions of the country, with the result that they are perceived there as self-evident, as a norm. Gender equality in board-formation is advancing slowly – men dominate overwhelmingly, even though more women are increasingly being appointed to leadership positions. The infamous glass ceiling of corporate boardrooms exists in public culture as well (Schoot et al. 2000).

All these formation systems and size differences notwithstanding, the major competences of a public theatre board are the same: making strategic decisions, supervising their implementation and evaluating the functioning of the organisation and of its chief executive. Critical scrutiny of the working processes in the organisation and monitoring of its impact on the broader cultural constellation are continuous tasks.

Safeguarding the autonomy of the organisation and its creative process, as well as its alignment with the public interest, which the board represents, is a delicate balancing act. Autonomy is not a given status and should not be confused with independence, but seen as a relationship, dynamic and alterable, subject to continuous negotiation, re-affirmation and defence, acknowledging various aspects of interdependence of the organisation on other entities, such as funders, partners, competitors, collaborators, sponsors, media, audiences, etc. In the case of a performing arts organisation, institutional autonomy contains a delicate but crucial aspect of artistic autonomy related to the artistic decisions made in the composition of the programme, choice of collaborators, creative process and manner of presentation to the public. Since a theatre production is a complex work relying on artistic, financial and technical resources in addition to considerable logistics and planning, it is difficult to imagine artistic autonomy achieved and safeguarded without institutional autonomy. Artists are very sensitive to artistic autonomy issues, not only as outside interference but also as a tension between different individual ideas and approaches within the creative team or cast and from other services and departments of the organisation.

Boards of cultural organisations are expected to ensure institutional development and continuity – even though in a performing arts organisation continuity has a different meaning and value than it has in a museum, for instance. In the performing arts, continuity is not an absolute value and could mean condoning routine or even artistic stagnation. Discontinuity could have its own merits and might even be necessary in order to usher in a new artistic phase: the re-conceptualisation of a festival, the decision to build a new venue or renovate the existing one, a change in the production model of the company, the introduction of an intensive touring schedule, the company's relocation to another city offering more favourable conditions or a change in the leading artistic team could all be positive decisions of engineered and carefully articulated discontinuity rather than one imposed.

There are few examples of organisations deciding to go out of business without being pressured from the outside, by a de-funding threat for instance. In 1990, Ritsaert ten Cate, the legendary producer and presenter of international experimental performing arts, announced that he would close his Mickery organisation after splashing out on the Touch Time festival held in all the venues around Amsterdam's Leidseplein, invoking lack of political support for international cooperation and insufficient funding. In 2000, Rose Fenton and Lucy Neal decided to remove the LIFT festival that they initiated in 1981 from the festival model, feeling that they had accomplished their initial mission of making international theatre widely available in London. LIFT outgrew its festival framework and became instead an open exploratory platform for debate, research and production (Wend Fenton, Rose de and Lucy Neal 2005). In both cases the artistic decision was taken with the full backing of the respective boards.

The public interest that the board represents and safeguards is quite difficult to pinpoint and define because it is inevitably diffused and heterogeneous in a pluralist democracy and in a rich, diversified cultural constellation. Nevertheless, as applied to performing arts organisations, it means constant attention by the board to artistic and cultural diversity, socio-economic and cultural inclusiveness, operational and financial accountability and transparency, artistic excellence and distinction, as well as a steady commitment to audience development. In some crisis situations, the board has special responsibilities to safeguard artistic distinction and autonomy. Typical examples would be when the organisation is caught up in intensive controversy, usually caused by a production that antagonises some constituency and provokes strong negative reactions or ensuring continuity and consolidation in a financial crisis whether caused by a deficit, a loss of major funding or of a substantial sponsor.

Both a public controversy and a financial crisis require a strong and well-synchronised board, capable of a strategic response that will be picked up by the media and mobilise supporters and partners. Such crises have a destabilising and even crippling impact on a performing arts organisation, threatening it with a loss of reputation or alienation from some of its public. In a controversy, the board can help by supporting the creation of additional discursive opportunities to air different views, arguments and opinions and defend the freedom of artistic expression regardless of any constituencies that could declare themselves offended, hurt or misrepresented. In today's media society they have ample opportunities to project alternative views and narratives and create their own alternative variants of self-presentation but not the right to attempt to censure or silence a theatre or threaten the performers and the public with revenge and violence.

In a financial crisis, the board needs to look first at its own responsibilities – quite evident in the case of an accumulated, undetected deficit – and to stimulate a financial consolidation strategy that might be coupled with significant reorganisation, restructuring of the working processes and expenditure and with downsizing and dismissal of some employees, including the artistic and managerial leadership. For the executives, it is impossible to ride through a storm of controversy or to overcome a financial crisis and implement re-organisation without the strong support of the board – but the executives might be under pressure to recognise their own responsibilities for financial mismanagement and draw consequences. Whichever the case, the board might find itself in negotiations with public authorities about the terms of further funding. If this happens, it needs to remain fair and wise, to display solidarity with the staff yet be decisive: otherwise it might succeed in parting with an executive or the entire leadership team. In turn, it will have difficulty recruiting competent replacements if the institution has suffered damage to its reputation and the board has lost some of its own integrity.

It is not so difficult for a board to function in a smooth way in good times but for a crisis situation it is better to have written down a protocol for its own functioning and decision-making, have a limited time mandate rule for its members and specify in advance how it will handle situations in which it may find itself at odds with the executives and where organisational and financial issues could imperil core artistic processes.

If board members are appointed by a public authority or serve as delegates of various public authorities, foundations, cultural institutions and associations, the harmony and effectiveness of the board might be threatened in times of crisis, its discord becoming more probable. The crisis could acquire political implications beyond the welfare of the theatre organisation itself. Especially tricky are situations in which individual board members cannot function as autonomous subjects but are under pressure to advance the interest of the bodies that have delegated them. If these interests are divergent or if they reflect the interests of different political parties – one in charge of the ministry, another of the region, or of the region and of the city and both co-responsible for the funding of a theatre – a performing arts organisation could become a pawn in the political game of mighty opponents, sacrificed to their prestige protection manoeuvres. Acknowledged artistic merit and sound financing tend to reduce the risk of such political spillover but cannot exclude it.

The Bayreuther Festspiele (www.bayreuther-festspiele.de) is run by a foundation whose board includes the representatives of local public authorities, the state of Bavaria and the German federal government but the upper hand is reserved by the statutes for the representatives of the Wagner family. An institution deeply compromised by its collaboration with the Nazi regime (Hamman 2005) but revived with public funds after World War II in the democratic German state yielded by such a governance arrangement to the mystique of the founding family. Consequently, a family soap opera for the succession to the ailing Wolfgang Wagner became a boardroom drama, resolved in a meek compromise by the appointment of both of his rival daughters as directors (Clark 2008).

Minima moralia for a public theatre system

Besides leadership quality and strong and alert boards, there is a third component we should now consider. This is the architecture of a performing arts system and the cultural policy principles, instruments and processes determining the well-being of public theatre and its impact on a certain territory. Again, one is confronted with a great diversity of systemic solutions in various European countries, shaped by history, tradition, size, the cultural diversity of the population, wealth and ideological predilections (Maanen and Willmer 1998; Berg et al. 2008). Nevertheless, the performing arts enjoy some public support in *all* European countries, which practically means that everywhere there is some debate about the volume of this support, its conditions, expected returns, procedures of allocation and qualifications for the right to access these funds. Performing arts professionals tend to be dissatisfied and critical without necessarily putting forward alternative solutions and, while they might all be in accord that public theatre deserves more public funds, they will never agree among themselves for whom, for what and under what conditions these funds should be deployed. Most of them have only a vague idea how the funding of public theatre is regulated in other countries.

Looking at the key functions of public theatre, some common positions can be recognised, however. Public support is needed for new creation, the commissioning of new works, including new plays and their first productions, choreographies and new musical theatre compositions, which will both stimulate innovation and reduce the risk of artistic failure. Equally, quality programming of non-producing venues and of festivals also deserves public support in order to make sure experimental, demanding and complex creations have a chance to test audience reactions and win some of its loyalty. The regional, national and international mobility of artists and artistic works should be seen as an aspect of professional and institutional development and therefore subsidised. Subsidies for mobility would also ensure that demanding and daring works are seen in locations where they could not be brought on the strength of box-office returns only. And in order to widen, diversify and upgrade the audiences, public subsidies should be allocated to audience development strategies, educational activities for adults, adolescents and children and for special outreach efforts to recruit an audience in those specific groups of population which, on account of their socio-economic position, residence location, educational level or some cultural markers, are remote from public theatre. Simultaneous translation or surtitling of performances in multilingual communities is also in the public interest. And since the performing arts function as a complex system of institutions and provisions, production and distribution, there should be some public subsidy for specialised support services, for intermediaries, for promotion, information and documentation, research and development, training, debate and reflection tasks that specialised agencies or organisations undertake for the entire sector, or some of its important segments.

Regardless of the volume of public money available for the performing arts, some common principles of allocation could be singled out. One would be a diversity in grant length, so as to offer specific project grants, as well as annual, biannual, three-year and four-year institutional grants, assuming that performing arts organisations of a proven track record can apply for longer grant terms and that the grants are issued with firm contractual obligations, specifying the output and deliverables expected from the grant recipients. This makes sense only if the grant recipients can ensure conscientious self-assessment and some neutral external evaluation of their performance and if the grant-giving agency has a clear, fair, comprehensive monitoring system in place to see how its subsidies work in practice. The latter is a weak point in most national subsidy systems, especially as the grant-giving agencies or departments nowadays tend, for the sake of efficiency, to employ account managers who look at the financial reports only and miss all the qualitative indicators of grantees' output.

Access to grants is also a painful issue because public authorities appear historically as founders of many public theatres and feel a special, even legal responsibility for their continuity and for the welfare of their employees. While committing funds for their work with an almost automatic renewal from one year to the next, they lack resources to make awards to many new autonomous initiatives, which have emerged in the last few decades without the mediation of public authorities but which make a good artistic case for receiving grants. Thus the equal right of access to public subsidy would eliminate, or at least reduce, the classifying differentiation between privileged and underprivileged applicants, regular and exceptional ones, those who are traditional recipients and those who are more recent. Classifying equality is a precondition for merit-based subsidy allocation but could in practice endanger the continuity of some historic subsidy recipients who would lose their support if judged strictly on the present merit basis regardless of their tradition and accomplishments in the past. Yet dropping some long-standing recipients from the subsidy rolls in order to accommodate new initiatives, even if that implies the orderly liquidation of de-funded organisations, is a necessary occurrence in any performing arts system that seeks to be dynamic, open for new talent and artistic approaches, and thus obliged to sanction institutional fatigue and artistic stagnation.

Funding: Decision-makers and their criteria

The question to address is: Who should make subsidy allocation decisions? Among "arms length" bodies, created in order to isolate artistic funding decisions from political influence, the Arts Council England is the oldest, in operation since 1946. Today it provokes some criticism as a swollen, arrogant bureaucracy and enjoys little enthusiastic support among professionals and little respect among politicians. Elsewhere in Europe, however, the arts council model is still emulated as an advanced and sophisticated solution. Disappointments do occur: after a long campaign, an arts council was established in 2009 in Catalonia, a region of remarkable public spending and institutional cultural build-up, now quite difficult to sustain; but the remit of the new council turned out to be quite restricted and its budget tiny, with the new body saddled by its founding statute with some representative and formal tasks. And yet, in the rest of Spain, where such provision does not exist, neither on the national nor on the regional level, or in France, where subsidy allocations are also the privilege of bureaucrats, covered by the authority of political office holders, an arts council and the peer-review principle are invoked by theatre professionals as a desirable solution. Semi-autonomous funds, set up to distribute subsidies of all sorts for an artistic field, as in the Netherlands, arts councils or other sorts of agencies based on peer review in the advisory or decision-making phase are certainly preferable to funding decisions driven by political loyalty or made by bureaucrats who can scrutinise annual financial reports but not assess artistic merit.

The key difficulty with peer review is to establish and sustain a clear code of conduct that excludes cliquishness and eliminates any impression of conflict of interest, guaranteeing the transparency of the decision-making. Especially in smaller systems, where almost everyone knows everyone, there will be the inclination to do favours and avoid offending colleagues with a negative judgement. This difficulty could perhaps, at least in the case of larger applicants, be alleviated by international assessment committees involving foreign experts with their external viewpoint and freedom from local loyalties, in a similar way to the international mechanisms being implemented in the quality assessment of higher education institutions and their programmes within the Bologna Process. Occasional suggestions that audience members should also have a voice in subsidy allocation overlook the fact that the public already makes a choice by buying tickets, thus deciding in their capacity of consumers, and that in some Nordic countries associations of spectators exercise an influence in local programming decisions, with some subsequent subsidy implications. Efforts to involve the active part of the audience in defining programme preferences need more local experiments, especially as a tactic for enhancing the cultural diversity of programmes and of audiences.

The curatorial practice in visual arts has also inspired ideas to appoint intendants, who would have the specific mandate of dedicating some public money to specific purposes, allocating grants to individual artists or smaller theatre and dance initiatives, with some public accounting and a limited time mandate. In peer-review bodies a change of membership every two years is also essential in order to avoid monopolies of taste or association.

Those who make funding decisions or recommendations should be able to assess past record and consider elaborate future plans of the applicant organisations, presented in some standardised format, covering the artistic and institutional development, business aspects and contextual analysis that determine the place of the applicant in the performing arts system. As a whole, the system should provide quality, diversity and continuity but it has become impossible to ensure this from one single centralised place of decision-making without the specific responsibilities of regions and municipalities. Thus complementarity of funding sources becomes an important issue in the design of public systems of arts funding. *Quality* has become a problematic notion, however, a container term that can be filled with various arbitrary meanings and usually emerges from some intersubjective consensus of application assessors. Artistic excellence implies professionalism, originality, innovation, artistic development and persuasive power. And yet there is much searching in Europe for additional criteria that will help distinguish and calibrate the merits of an increased number of funding requests competing for shrinking or stagnating resources.

Among such *auxiliary criteria* could be the systematic engagement of the applicant organisation in the enhancement of the intercultural competence of artists, staff, management, boards and audiences, signalling that the applicant organisation takes cultural diversity and inclusiveness seriously and seeks to expand and enrich the experience of citizenship through the artistic, intellectual (discursive) and social activities deployed. Further criteria could address the sophistication and effectiveness of educational and outreach programmes or the collaborative attitude of the organisation and the richness of its creative and operational partnerships. A pattern of mobility (regional, national and international) could be considered if deployed as a developmental strategy rather than a politics of prestige and representation. Of course, good housekeeping, astute managerial standards and responsible governance would also count.

Not surprisingly, some performing arts organisations would resent such additional criteria, accusing public authorities of social engineering and instrumentalisation of artistic creativity, even claiming that such additional expectations interfere with artistic development. Public authorities are, however, perfectly entitled to set additional criteria for the dispensation of public money and in order to increase the public benefit generated by their support, especially if those subsidies are seen as an investment in social imagination through the arts but also in social cohesion and equality of opportunities, as long as those criteria are applied in a fair, consistent manner to all applicants.

Own income versus subsidy is a growing matter of controversy. It is impossible to standardise such expectations – not across Europe, because of variance in economic potential, buying power, cost of living and attendance habits, and not within a single country and among various types of public performing arts organisations, whose size, position, location and type of work determine their earning potential. Ultimately, the minimal earning norm is usually set in an arbitrary fashion by political decision-makers, whether it is 15 per cent, 20 per cent or 35 per cent of the budget or of the allocated subsidy. The oft-touted idea that a performing arts organisation should have one-third of its budget covered by public subsidy, one-third by private donations and sponsors and one-third by its own earned income is too neat to be plausible. Most performing arts organisations would never be able to find one third in donations and sponsorship, especially in poorer countries and in smaller places. One-third of own earned income as a norm also disregards variance in audience buying power, limited elasticity of ticket prices and the fact that many producing companies create work that inevitably addresses small audiences and rests on intimacy of communication between the performers and the public. Standards of own income and sponsorship contribution imaginable in large cities, especially in those with a concentration of corporate power and with many tourists, cannot be applied as a norm on organisations in smaller places and those with a decaying economy.

There are some performing arts activities that are practically inconceivable without public subsidies, such as production and distribution in minority languages and a demanding and ambitious theatre for children and adolescents, framed within educational programmes. This also applies to community theatre with specific underprivileged populations – including people with disabilities, performances and workshops in poorer urban zones and in remote areas of low population density, international activities causing extra cost of displacement and the development of young talent, even though occasionally some of these might benefit from a grant from a private foundation. These aspects of the performing arts will not be catered for by the market and market players and thus present a clear responsibility for public theatre and its funders.

Public theatre and public culture

After 60 years of public policy in support of the performing arts, practically every national subsidy system in Europe is overloaded with anachronistic schemes, obsolete solutions and accumulated obligations. Yet there is little political will to undertake a major, comprehensive redesign of the system, streamline it with the altered circumstances in which public culture operates today, exposed to the impact of globalisation, migration, European integration and digitisation of cultural production and consumption. Policymakers also know well that systemic change demands additional resources and cannot be carried out under their regime of budget reductions, nowadays on the agenda of many governments. Instead of an overhaul that would make public culture more vibrant and participatory, ideological precepts drive politicians to insist on efficiency improvements of dubious effect or seek to undertake a radical shrinking or even a dismantling of the public subsidy system for the arts and let the market take over, thus yielding the public space to commercial cultural industry.

Performing arts professionals are, of course, alarmed. Many are making a serious mistake when they repeat old, worn-out arguments about the value of the arts, or worse, dwell on dubious economic arguments – as if the public benefit of the theatre, for instance, can be reduced to a financial value and precisely calculated in millions of euros. Artists and their associates are not necessarily the best economists and, when they talk about the value of the arts, they come up with benefits and advantages that remain abstract and remote to outsiders, leaving them indifferent. John Holden has pointed out the self-perpetuating misunderstanding: artists and other culture professionals invoke the institutional value of culture, politicians expect a representational or economic value in return for subsidy and the audiences cherish the intrinsic value of the experience, whether it is derived from commercial or non-commercial culture (Holden 2006). These three constituencies might refer to the same concepts and notions and yet project very different value assumptions and expectations. Among cultural economists, David Throsby valiantly points out that cultural value achieved in cultural production stands above the economic value generated (Throsby 2010).

While performing arts professionals are quite good at displaying their outrage in public, they are less good at engaging in systematic advocacy that would mobilise support in the media and sway public opinion for alternative systemic solutions. In most countries, performing arts professionals perceive their interest in different ways, depending on their institutional affiliation and position in the existing system, so they advocate different and even incompatible alternatives. Too often the public pitch concerns one specific company or festival or venue under the threat of de-funding or subsidy reduction and not the matter of principle enshrined in public culture as a precious attribute of a deliberative democracy – in contrast to the commercial entertainment that prospers on the free market. The decision of the Italian government in 2010 to abolish Ente Teatrale Italiano (www.enteteatrale.it) caused much outrage and petition-writing in defence of this tired organisation, which stemmed from Mussolini's corporatist vision of culture and society that could never live up to its divergent and incompatible functions and operate free from political manipulation. Larger performing arts organisations can try to mobilise their associations of friends – if they have set up such associations of their most loyal core public – but most of the smaller organisations and artistic collectives do not have such resources, just a handful of friends and devoted followers that have a limited mobilisation potential.

In several countries of Europe the debate on the public value of theatre is sidetracked in the debate about the desirability of a specific theatre law and its provisions – as if some legislative action will be able to change an unsatisfactory reality overnight. From all the efforts to create such a law, as well as from the few laws that have in fact been passed, one can conclude that those pieces of legislation attempt to safeguard existing monopolies and prevailing production models, even if they are anachronistic and unsustainable, and to entrench some accumulated privileges and reinforce the gatekeepers against newcomers and competitors. Even if such pieces of legislation prescribe some subsidy flows to the earmarked recipients, the ministries of finance carry out the ultimate reality check and can block or reduce the budgets available. Public theatre will not be stabilised by any theatre law – such laws are in fact not necessary.

What is needed in Europe instead of new theatre laws is a redefinition of public interest in culture and the articulation of instruments, criteria, procedures and resources that will implement these interests through the existing and emerging cultural infrastructure, drawing clear demarcation lines between commercial and non-commercial cultural production and distribution. This redefinition cannot be just a matter of national policy but needs strong regional and local anchoring. It cannot be carried out through an arts policy and certainly not through a performing arts policy alone, but requires instead a cultural policy that intertwines cultural diversity and inclusiveness, urban and rural development, integration of migrants and quality of citizenship, erasure of boundaries between arts and education and between culture and education, and affirms the public space, local and European, physical and digital. To advance such an ambitious agenda, types of voicing organisation are needed other than the prevailing models of arts advocacy or arts and culture advocacy platforms. What is required are broad coalitions of culture professionals and their institutions, of educators and schools and universities, allied with the public, or at least its most motivated, engaged core, supported by business, initiated on the local level but with a firm European, rather than national outlook. Public theatre and public culture cannot be revitalised by professionals and their artistic and cultural organisations alone or in cohort with politicians – they need to embrace and take along the public, as heterogeneous and amorphous as it is, starting in their immediate surroundings, on the local level. It is not difficult to sketch the principles and provisions of public theatre as a system, but such a system cannot be put in place without a broad professional, political and social commitment to public culture as an essential feature of democracy. This commitment has been substantially weakened throughout the last few decades by the market cult of neo-liberal ideology, the drive towards privatisation and managerial efficiency mantras. It now needs to be re-affirmed, despite the crisis and budget deficits, as an essential investment in democracy and a decent, reflective society.

Note

1 At the time of writing the author could not have foreseen the financial and economical crisis the world would be confronted with in 2011 and 2012 and the dire consequences it has for the arts.

In Place of an Epilogue: The Prospects for Public Theatre in Europe

- Commercial theatre is strong and successful while public (i.e. subsidised) theatre is under stress and disoriented. The vitality of commercial theatre and its profitability are nourished by the talent, ideas, products and styles developed in public theatre, thanks to public subsidies. Political neglect of public theatre will prevent it from stimulating the collective imagination and supporting deliberative democracy and also reduce its capacity to feed and enhance commercial theatre and other forms of entertainment.
- Serious cultural, political and financial challenges pressure non-commercial theatre, yet it has very limited capacities to respond, caught between the market competition for audience, sponsors and media attention and dependence on increasingly indifferent politicians for subsidies.
- Prevailing production and distribution models need reconsideration: the historic repertory company model of public theatre has a chance to survive only as a minority option, not as the dominant one. Groups, short-term initiatives, programmed venues and production houses, festivals, studios and research facilities complete the public theatre landscape. All these production and distribution models have a functional merit and deserve equal access to public subsidy, determined by recent achievements and plans for the future, not by tradition, prestige and historically established privileges. With the more rigorous competition of a growing number of artistic initiatives for shrinking public subsidies, all historic monopolies and automatic subsidy renewals have become politically unsustainable.
- In return for public subsidy, non-commercial theatre is expected to explore and revitalise classical drama and to instigate new playwriting; to invest in post-dramatic theatre, in the renewal of musical theatre and the re-imagining of the canonical opera repertoire; to build talent and an audience for various dance theatre forms; to provide young audiences with a socialising theatre experience; to insert performative events in various urban and rural contexts and address the needs of underprivileged groups and ethnic and linguistic minorities. That is a tall order. To achieve it, performing arts organisations need to specialise and specify their mission but also develop a range of partnerships and alliances, not imitate commercial show business and its perennial quest for hits.
- In their programming, theatres rely on name recognition of titles, authors and star performers on the part of the potential audience. Yet *smorgasbord* programming overwhelms and confuses potential theatregoers. Programming in larger templates and series would appeal to the audience, help create temporary communities of concern and strengthen the partnership of theatres with other structures of civil society.

- Playhouses can affirm their value as public spaces if they reconfigure them and run them as hubs of sociability, networking, leisure, debate and work. Public theatre should be an instigator of local and neighbourhood development, becoming an economic and social magnet. In performing arts facilities, small is beautiful and also more efficient while big is most frequently representational, expensive and ultimately unsustainable in the public sphere, feasible only under a regime of commercial exploitation. Spatial proximity can foster partnerships and improve the context of the playhouse. Recycling existing structures, inherited from the industrial era, for performing purposes is less risky than building new playhouses.
- A ready-made audience does not exist. It needs to be continuously discovered, developed and fostered. Without a continuous educational engagement and demonstrated work on interculturalisation and inclusiveness, no performing art deserves public subsidy.
- Public theatre cannot force the media to take a serious interest in it but it can shape and articulate its own media output, creating a deliberative community of core theatregoers around its own websites.
- International engagement is a developmental dimension of public theatre, not a matter of self-representation and prestige enhancement. As a learning and inspirational experience, international cooperative projects test and advance intercultural competence, articulating a specific dialectic of the local and global, and reinforcing a global critical awareness in the audience.
- Festivals thrive when they fuse local and global dimensions. The best festivals advance professional discourse, affirm innovative practices, initiate adventurous coalitions and continuously engage their audiences between two editions. With the proliferation of festival initiatives of all sorts, public authorities need to develop coherent policies of festival support.
- European theatre systems need a comprehensive overhaul, with clarified objectives, criteria and standards of subsidy allocation. Enhancement of intercultural competence, mobility and demonstrated collaborative attitudes should be included as criteria, alongside artistic excellence. Such systemic changes can be implemented only if there is a commitment to public culture as essential for functional democracy and the exercise of citizenship, in contrast to the entertainment market dominated by the commercial cultural industry. Re-affirmation of public culture requires broad advocacy coalitions that unite theatre professionals and the core public, social movements, education, politics and business from the bottom up – from local circumstances to the European public space.

Sources

Access to Culture (2009) (ec.europa.eu/culture/documents/platform_access_culture_july09. pdf). Last accessed July 1, 2012.

Allen, Paul (1998). *Gardzienice. Polish Theatre in Transition*. London: Routledge.

Allen, Woody (1975). *Without Feathers*. New York: Random House.

Anheier, Helmut (2009). "How can the cultural sector survive the financial crisis" (www. labforculture.org; January 2009). Last accessed July 1, 2012.

Apthorp, Shirley (2009). "Opera. Aida. Bregenz Festival, Austria", *Financial Times* (July 24, 2009). Last accessed July 1, 2012.

Arts Council England (2010). "UK's first recycled theatre opens in Southwark" (www.artscouncil. org.uk; August 9, 2010). Last accessed July 1, 2012.

Aspden, Peter (2007). "The world has to be changed by pleasure!" *Financial Times* (July 21/22, 2007).

Aspden, Peter (2008). "The Body from inside out". *Financial Times* (April 5–6, 2008).

——— (2009). "Revolutions in the Round". *Financial Times* (August 15–16, 2009).

Autissier, Anne-Marie (ed.) (2008). *The Europe of Festivals: From Zagreb to Edinburgh, Intersecting Viewpoints*. Toulouse-Paris: Éditions de l'Attribut and Culture Europe Internationale.

Balfour, Michael (ed.) (2004). *Theater in Prison. Theory and Practice*. Bristol, UK and Portland, OR: Intellect.

Balme, Christopher (2008). *Introduction to Theatre Studies*. Cambridge: Cambridge University Press.

Baluch, Lalayn (2009). "Culture Minister Follett joins calls for backstage improvements". *The Stage* (June 18, 2009).

Banu, George and Bruno Tackels (eds) (2005). *Le cas Avignon 2005*. Vic-la-Gardiol: Éditions Entretemps.

Barker, Howard (1989). *Arguments for a Theatre*. London: John Calder.

Barranco, Justo (2009). "El teatro catalan da la voz de alarma", *La Vanguardia* (October 20, 2009).

Barghouti, Sanae and Yohann Floch (2010). *Circostrada Network. Encouraging European Cooperation Projects*. Marseille: HorsLesMurs.

Barnett, Dennis and Arthur Skelton (2010). *Theatre and Performance in Eastern Europe. The Changing Scene*. Lanham, MD: The Scarecrow Press, Inc.

Baugh, Christopher (2005). *Theatre, Performance and Technology*. London: Palgrave Macmillan.

Bauman, Zygmunt (1998). *Globalization: The Human Consequences*. New York: Columbia University Press.

——— (2007). *Consuming Lives*. Cambridge: Polity.

Baumeister, Titia et al. (2002). *The Need for Imagination. Four Dissertations on the Dogtroep Performance in the Bruges Penitentiary Complex.* Amsterdam: Dogtroep.

Baumol, William J. and Wiliam G. Bowen (1966). *Performing Arts: The Economic Dilemma.* New York: Twentieth Century Fund.

BBC News (2007). "Dutch stars hurt in *Grease* mishap" (February 27, 2007).

—— (2009). "Transsexual Jesus sparks protests" (November 4, 2009).

Beer, Ronald de (2009). "Opera met Gods adem in je nek". *De Volkskrant* (August 25, 2009).

Beemsterboer, Toon. "Een Duitse (*sic*) laboratorium voor de kunsten vaart door Europa". *NRC Handelsblad* (November 19, 2007).

Bennett, T., L. Grossberg and L. Morris (eds) (2005). *New Key Words. A Revised Vocabulary of Culture and Society.* Oxford: Blackwell.

Berg, Hans Onno van den et al. (2008). *State on Stage. The Impact of Public Policies on the Performing Arts in Europe.* Amsterdam: Boekman.

Berg, Therese and Lise Amy Hansen (2009). *Program to Perform. Exploring Dance and New Media.* Oslo: Oslo School of Architecture and Design and Dance Information Norway.

Bodo, Carla, Dragan Klaic and Fabio Severino (eds) (2009). *Zone grigie nell' economia dei festival. Economia della Cultura.* 2009:3.

Bleeker, Maaike and Lucia van Heteren, Chiel Kattenbelt en Kees Vuyk (eds) (2005). *Multicultureel Drama? Theater Topics.* Amsterdam: Amsterdam University Press.

Boer, Noortje et al. (2008). *Dogtroep. 33 jaar beeldend locatietheater.* Amsterdam: Lava.

Bogusz, Tanja (2007). *Institution und Utopie. Ost-West Transformationen an der Berliner Volksbühne.* Bielefeld: Transcript.

Bots, Pieter (2010). "Requiem voor de filmbewerking op toneel". *TM* 14.6 (September, 114–117).

Bourdieu, Pierre (1984). *Distinction. A Social Critique of the Judgment of Taste.* London: Routledge.

Branigan, Tanja and Vikram Dodd. "Writer in hiding as violence closes Sikh play". *The Guardian* (December 21, 2004).

Brault, Simon (2010). *Le facteur C. L'avenir passe par la culture.* Montréal: Les Éditions Voix parallèles.

Brook, Peter (1968, Pelican edn 1978). *The Empty Space.* Harmondsworth, UK: Pinguin.

Brown, Frederick (1980). *Theater and Revolution. The Culture of the French Stage.* New York: The Viking Press.

Cate, Ritsaert ten (1996). *Man Looking for Words.* Amsterdam: TIN.

Canaries in the Coalmine. Masterplan for Dance in Flanders and Brussels (2007). Brussels: VTI.

Clark, Andrew (2008). "Half-sisters must beat the course to save Bayreuth's Wagner festival". *Financial Times* (September 6–7, 2008).

Cleveland, William (2000). *Art in Other Places.* Amherst, MA. University of Massachussetts Press.

Greater Copenhagen Theater Board (2006). *Copenhagen Theater Strategy 2006/7–2010/11.*

Cohen, Patricia (2009). "Troupe's communal vision includes lunch". *The New York Times* (July 6, 2009).

David, Thomas (2010). "A nanosecond of happiness. An Interview with Christoph Schlingensief" (www.signandsight.com; July 30, 2007). Last accessed July 1, 2012. Originally in *Neue Zürcher Zeitung* (July 17, 2010).

Delgado, Maria and Caridad Svich (eds) (2002). *Theatre in Crisis.* Manchester: Manchester University Press.

Dienderen, An van, Joris Janssens and Katrien Smits (2007). *Tracks. Artistic Practice in a Diverse Society.* Brussels: VTI.

Dinulović, Radivoje (2009). *Arhitektura pozorišta XX veka.* Belgrade: Clio.

Djian, Jean-Michel (2005). *Politique culturelle: la fin d'un mythe.* Paris: Gallimard.

Dragićević Šešić, Milena and Sanjin Dragojević (2005). *Art Management in Turbulent Times.* Amsterdam: ECF and Boekman Stichting.

Edgecliffe-Johnson, Andrew (2010). "Tangled web". *The Financial Times* (November 27–28, 2010).

Ehrenreich, Barbara (2007). *Dancing on the Streets.* London: Granta.

Ellis, Adrian and Russell Willis Taylor (2010). "Performing arts in lean times; opportunities for reinvention". Report 468 of the Salzburg Seminar February 2010 (www.salzburgglobal.org). Last accessed July 1, 2012.

Ellmeier, Andrea and Bela Rasky (2006). *Differing Diversities. East. European perspectives.* Strasbourg: Council of Europe.

Embrechts, Annette (2008). "Ik heb festivalreuring nodig. Interview Guido Wevers". *De Volkskrant* (February 28, 2008).

Engelander, Rudy and Dragan Klaic (1998) *Shifting Gears. Reflections and Reports on the Contemporary Performing Arts.* Amsterdam: TIN.

Epskamp, Kees (2006). *Theatre for Development.* London: Zed Books.

Erven, Eugen Van (2001). *Community Theater. Global Perspectives.* London and New York: Routledge.

Eurostat yearbook (2010). *Europe in Figures.* European Commission: Eurostat Statistical Books.

Fabiani, Jean-Louis (2008). *L'Éducation populaire et le théâtre: le public d'Avignon en action.* Grenoble: Presses universitaires de Grenoble.

Farano, Adriano and Laëtitia Manach, Olivia Pisano, Leïla Badis, Mary Ann DeVlieg (eds) (2007) *Made in the Med.* Paris: Roberto Cimetta Fund. www.cimettafund.org/~cimettaf/content/upload/file/Made-in-the-Med-FRC-En.pdf. Last accessed July 1, 2012.

Fischer-Lichte, Erika (2005). *Theatre, Sacrifice, Ritual. Exploring forms of Political Theatre.* London: Routledge.

Floch, Yohann (2008) (ed.) *Art in the Urban Space: Contemporary Creation as a Tool.* Marseille: Circostrada and HorsLesMurs.

Frame, Murray (2006). *School for Citizens. Theatre and Civil Society in Imperial Russia.* New Haven and London: Yale University Press.

Fry, Chris (2007). *The Way of Magdalena. A Chronicle of the First Ten Years of The Magdalena Project. An International Network of Women in Contemporary Theatre.* Holstebro: Open Page Publications.

Gaber, Floriane (2009) *40 Years of Street Arts and How It All Started. Street Arts in the Context of the 1970's.* Paris: Éditions Ici et là.

Gavrilova, Dessi (2010) "Da spasim publikata, posle teatrite". *24 casa* (August 2, 2010).

Goehler, Adrienne (2006). *Verflüssigungen. Wege und Umwege vom Sozialstaat zur Kulturgesellschaft.* Frankfurt and New York: Campus Verlag.

Gompes, Loes (2007). *Spiegel van Amsterdam*. Amsterdam: Stichting Felix Meritis.

Goossens, Jan with Danny Op de Beeck, Bruno De Lille , and all employees at KVS (2005). "KVS is zo Vlaams als Brussel maar kan zijn". *De Morgen* (March 12, 2005).

Grandage, Michael (2008). "West End Story". *Financial Times* (July 6/7, 2008).

Habermas, Jürgen (1989). *The Structural Transformation of the Public Sphere: An Inquiry into a Category of Bourgeois Society*. Cambridge: Polity (orig. in German 1962).

Haedicke, Susan C. and Tobin Nellhaus (eds) (2001). *Performing Democracy*. Ann Arbor, MI.: University of Michigan Press.

Hamman, Brigitte (2005). *Winifred Wagner. A Life at the Heart of Hitler's Bayreuth*. London: Granta (orig. in German 2002).

Harkin, James (2009). "All talk, plenty of action". *Financial Times* (June 20/21, 2009).

Hauptfleisch, Temple, Shulamith Lev-Alagdem, Jacqueline Martin, Willmar Sauter and Henri Schoenmakers (eds) (2007). *Festivalising!: Theatrical Events, Politics and Culture*. Amsterdam and New York, NY: Rodopi.

Havens, Henk and Chiel Kattenbelt, Eric de Ruijter, Kees Vuyk (2006). *Theater en Technologie*. Maastricht and Amsterdam: Toneelacademie Maastricht/TIN.

Healy, Patrick (2010a). "Shakespeare troupe plans residency in New York". *The New York Times* (February 9, 2010).

——— (2010b). "How Cirque slipped on Shpeel?" *The New York Times* (June 26, 2010).

——— (2010c). "Costly Spider-Man can't get off the ground". *The New York Times* (November 5, 2011).

——— (2010d). "'Spider-Man' starts to emerge from secrecy". *The New York Times,* (November 23, 2010).

——— (2010e). "Spider-Man takes off, with some bumps". *The New York Times* (November 28, 2010).

——— (2010f). "A Spider-Man actress is injured backstage". *The New York Times* (December 3, 2010).

——— (2010g) "Spider-Woman is leaving troubled Spider-Man". *The New York Times* (December 28, 2010).

Healy, Patrick and Kevin Flynn (2011). "A broadway superlative for all the wrong reasons". *The New York Times* (March 13, 2011).

Heathcote, Edwin (2010). "All's not so well". *Financial Times* (November 27–28, 2010).

Hemming, Sarah (2009). "Prompt reactions". *Financial Times* (July 18–19, 2009).

Henry, Philippe (ed.) (2007). *Art vivants en France: Trop de compagnies?* Paris: L'espace d'un instant.

Holden, John (2006). *Cultural Value and the Crisis of Legitimacy*. London: Demos.

——— (2010). *Culture and Class*. London: Counterpoint – British Council.

Hübner, Zygmunt (1992). *Theater and Politics*. Tr. Jadwiga Kosicka. Evanston, IL: Northwestern University Press.

Ilczuk, D. and M. Kulikowska (2007). *Festival Jungle, Policy Desert? Festival Policies of Public Authorities In Europe: Comparative Report.* Warsaw: CIRCLE (see: www.efa-aef.eu/en/activities/efrp/). Last accessed July 1, 2012.

Inkei, Peter (2009). "Culture and development 20 years after the fall of Communism in Europe". Background paper for the Krakow conference (June 2009). (www.coe.int/t/dg4/cultureheritage/cwe/CracowBackgroundPaper_en.pdf.) Last accessed July 1, 2012.

Jans, Erwin (2006). *Interculturele intoxicaties. Over kunst, cultuur en verschil*. Berchem: EPO.

Jansen, Kaspar (2009). "Moderne Kalibaan is mooie zwarte man met dreadlocks". *NRC Handelsblad* (August 25, 2009).

Janssens, Joris and Dries Moreels (2007). *Metamorphoses. Performing Arts in Flanders since 1993*. Brussels: VTI.

Jeschonnek, Günter (ed.) (2010). *Report Darstellende Künste. Wirtschaftliche, soziale und arbeitsrechtliche Lage der Theater- und Tanzschaffenden in Deutschland. Fonds Darstellende Künste*. Bonn and Essen: Kulturpolitische Gesellschaft and Klartext Verlag.

Johnson, Karen and Kristina Nelson (eds) (2004). *Staging Independence. Mutual Strategies for Directors and Theatermakers in Europe and the Arab World*. London: Directors Guild of the UK.

Julie's Bicycle (2010). "Moving arts, managing the carbon impacts of our touring". V 3. Theatre. London (www.juliesbicycle.com/media/research/MovingArts-THEATRE-df.pdf). Last accessed July 1, 2012.

Kalb, Jonathan, "Thirty Years War, All 10 hours of it". *The New York Times* (July 1, 2007).

Kay, John. 2010 "A good economist knows the true value of the arts". *Financial Times* (August 1, 2010).

Kahn, Nasseem (2009). *On Leadership*. London: ACE.

Klaic, Dragan (ed.) (1997). *Reform or Transition. The Future of the Repertory Theatre in Central and Eastern Europe*. New York: Open Society Institute.

Klaic, Dragan (2005). *Europe as a Cultural Project*. The final report of the Reflection Group of the European Cultural Foundation. Amsterdam: ECF (also on www.eurocult.org/uploads/docs/712.pdf. Last accessed July 1, 2012).

—— (2007a). *Mobility of Imagination*. A Companion guide to international cultural cooperation. Budapest: CAC CEU.

—— (2007b). "Chinese performing arts: From communist to globalized kitsch". IIAS *Newsletter* 44 (summer, 18–19).

—— (2008). "A small feast of intercultural dialogue". In Hanneloes Weeda and O. Chenal, G. Chierchia, L. Mathol, G. Wagner (eds) *Managing Diversity?* Amsterdam: European Cultural Foundation, pp. 43–46.

—— (2009). "Retrieved from oblivion", a critical introduction to an anthology of plays from the end of Communism. *Playwrights Before the Fall*. Ed. Daniel Gerould. New York: M. Segall Theater Center, Graduate Center CUNY, pp. xi–xxi.

Klamer, Arjo (2010). "Weg met de slechte excuses". *NRC* Cultureel supplement (August 27, 2010).

Kliment, Alexandar (2006). "Visa hurdles bar cultural dialogue, says Yo-Yo Ma". *Financial Times* (April 5, 2006).

Kustow, Michael (2005). *Peter Brook: A Biography*. London: Bloomsbury.

Lacombe, Robert (2004): *Le spectacle vivant en Europe, modèles d'organisation et politiques de soutien*. Paris: La documentation française.

Larrochelle, Jean-Jacques, "Une Traviata va-t-en-gare pour Arte". *Le Monde* (September 30, 2008).

Lazin, Miloš (2008). "La nouvelle écriture théâtrale des Balkans et d'ailleurs, version actualisée" (retors.net/spip.php?auteur52). Last accessed July 22, 2012.

Leacroft, Richard and Helen Leacroft (1984). *Theatre and Playhouse. An Illustrated Survey of Theatre Building from Ancient Greece to the Present Day.* London and New York: Methuen.

Lee, Felicia R. (2010). "Theater for Audiences of One". *The New York Times* (July 28, 2010).

Lehmann, Hans-Thies (1999). *Postdramatic Theatre.* Tr. Karen Jürs-Munby. London and New York: Routledge (2006).

Maanen, H. van and S. E. Wilmer (1998). *Theatre Worlds in Motion.* Amsterdam: Rodopi.

Martel, Frederic (2006). *Theater, Sur le declin du théâtre en Amerique (et comment il peut resister en France).* Paris: La Decouverte .

Mathews, DeHart Jane (1967). *Federal Theatre, 1935–1939: Plays, Relief, and Politics.* New Jersey: Princeton University Press.

McMaster, Brian (2008). *Supporting Excellence in the Arts.* London: Department for Culture, Media and Sport.

Meyer, Dennis (ed.) (1994). *Tomaat in perspectief.* Amsterdam: TIN.

NEA (2008). *All America's a Stage. Growth and Challenges in Non-Profit Theater.* Washington, DC: NEA.

Needcompany (2009). *Newsletter* (September 2, 2009).

Nicholson, Helen (2005). *Applied Drama.* London: Palgrave Macmillan.

"Opera House komt met Twitter-opera" (2009). *NRC Handelsblad* (August 11, 2009).

Pachter, Mark and Charles Landry (2001). *Culture at the Crossroads. Culture and Cultural Institutions at the Beginning of the 21st Century.* Stroud: Comedia.

Pearson, Mike (2006). *In Comes I. Performance, Memory and Landscape.* Exeter: Exeter University Press.

Polacek, Richard (2007) "A study on impediments to mobility in the EU Live Performance sector and possible solutions" (www.cultureactioneurope.org/images/stories/polacekstudy-impedimentstomobility-2007-en.pdf).

Popescu, Marian (2000). *The Stage and the Carnival. Romanian Theatre after Censorship.* Bucharest: Mediana.

Purcell, Julius (2009). "The sound and la Fura". *Financial Times* (August 1–2, 2009).

Ravenhill, Mark (2010). "Let's cut the arts budget". *The Guardian* (July 25, 2010).

Rengers, Merijn and John Schoorl (2008). "Joop van den Ende stapt uit vastgoed" and "'Ik ben enorm in de maling genomen.' Interview Joop van den Ende". *De Volkskrant* (April 17, 2008).

Rowntree, Julia (2006). *Changing the Performance.* London and New York: NESTA and Routledge.

Rimini Protokoll (2007). *Experten des Alltags: Das Theater von Rimini Protokoll.* Berlin: Alexander Verlag.

Schindler, Barbara (ed.) (2005, 2009) *Tanzplan Deutschland* (also: www.tanzplan-deutschland.de). Last accessed July 22, 2012.

Schino, Mirelle (2009). *Alchemists of the Stage. Theater Laboratories in Europe.* Holstebro Malta Wroclaw: Icarus.

Schoot, Carolien van der, Cecile Brommer and Sonja van der Valk (2000). *Dynamiek van veranderingen: ambities en loopbanen en de cultuur van het theaterbedrijf.* Amsterdam: TIN.

Sisario, Ben (2010). "U.S. pledges to speed up visa process for artists". *The New York Times* (July 22, 2010).

Slevogt, Esther (2007). "Wallenstein – Peter Steins Schiller-Marathon in der Neuköllner Kindlhalle. Überwältigungsästhetik im Breitwandformat" (www.nachtkritik.de; May 19, 2007). Last accessed July 1, 2012.

Slonim, Marc (1962). *Russian Theater from the Empire to the Soviets.* New York: Collier.

Smeliansky, Anatoly (1999). *Russian Theatre after Stalin.* Tr. Patrick Miles. Cambridge: Cambridge University Press.

Staines, Judith (2004, 2007). *Tax and Social Security, a Basic Guide for Artists and Cultural Operators.* Brussels: IETM.

Staps, Freek (2008). "Broadwaypubliek minder 'aan de blanke kant'". *NRC Handelsblad* (September 13, 2008).

Stefanova, Kalina (2000). *Eastern European Theater after the Iron Curtain.* Amsterdam: Harwood Academic Publisher.

Steinberg, Michael P. (2000[1990]). *Austria as Theater and Ideology. The Meaning of the Salzburg Festival.* Ithaca, NY and London: Cornell University Press.

Stevens, Andrea (2009). "Cosmos of Kushner, Spinning Forward". *The New York Times* (June 14, 2009).

Straaten, Floris van (2009). "Afghanistan in 13 toneelstukken". *NRC Handelsblad* (May 28, 2009).

Throsby, David (2010). *The Economics of Cultural Policy.* Cambridge: Cambridge University Press.

Toynbee, Polly (2010). "Arts for everyone is cheap considering its rich returns". *The Guardian* (July 28, 2010).

VTI (2007). *Metamorfose in podiumland. Een veldanalyse.* Brussels: VTI.

Wakin, Daniel J. (2010a). "Orchestras seek BFF by cellphone texts". *The New York Times* (July 21, 2010).

Wakin, Daniel J. (2010b). "Director says he left Met production in visa spat". *The New York Times* (September 3, 2010).

Walter, Birgit (2010). "Das Geld der Theater". *Berliner Zeitung* (November 29, 2010).

Watson, Ian et al. (eds) (2002). *Negotiating Cultures. Eugenio Barba and Intercultural Debate.* Manchester and New York: Manchester University Press.

Wend Fenton, Rose de and Lucy Neal (2005). *Turning Worlds.* London: Calouste Gulbenkian Foundation UK.

Wensink, Herien (2008). "Afdeling beenmode blijkt gedroomde locatie". *NRC Handelsblad* (October 19, 2008).

Williams, Raymond (1958). *Culture and Society 1780–1950.* London: Chatto and Windus.

Wilmer, Stephen (ed.) (2008). *National Theatres in a Changing Europe.* London: Palgrave Macmillan.

—— (1966). *Long Revolution.* New York: Harper and Row.

—— (1966). *Modern Tragedy.* London: Chatto and Windus.

—— (1978). *Keywords. A Vocabulary of Culture and Society.* London: Fontana.

About the Author

Dragan Klaic, renowned theatrologist, cultural analyst, lecturer at several European universities, long-time Director of the Netherlands Theatre Institute, theatre critic and essayist, was born in 1950 in Sarajevo. Klaic obtained his BA degree in Dramaturgy in 1973 in Belgrade at the Faculty of Dramatic Arts (former Academy of Dramatic Arts) and his PhD in Theatre History and Dramatic Criticism in 1977 at Yale University, USA.

From 1978 to 1991 he was Professor of History of World Drama and Theatre at the Faculty of Dramatic Arts in Belgrade. Klaic was also one of the most important theatre critics in the former Yugoslavia in the 80s, a long-time moderator of round table discussions at the renowned Belgrade International Theatre Festival BITEF and worked as dramaturg with some of the most renowned theatre artists, most notably with Ljubiša Ristić and his company KPGT. Together with Slovenian theatre director and playwright Dušan Jovanović and graphic designer Matjaž Vipotnik he was co-founder of European theatre quarterly *Euromaske*, which ceased to be published at the outbreak of war in 1991, the same year in which Klaic left Yugoslavia.

From 1992 to 2001 Klaic was Director of the Theater Instituut Nederland (Netherlands Theatre Institute). From 1998 to 2003 he was teaching at Amsterdam University. From 2001 to 2011 he was a regular lecturer at universities in Leiden, Budapest, Istanbul, Belgrade and Bologna. His lecturing activities also included numerous workshops and summer schools that he conceived and carried out worldwide in nine languages that he fluently spoke.

Klaic was President of European Network of Information Centres for Performing Arts – ENICPA – and European Forum for Arts and Heritage – EFAH – as well as member of various boards and networks (among other, OSI /Open Society Institute, IETM /Informal European Theatre Meeting, ECF /European Cultural Foundation and Erasmus) and a Permanent Fellow of Felix Meritis Foundation in Amsterdam.

Another essential part of Klaic's work were his research activities: thus he performed in 2005 in Istanbul extensive research on alternative cultural infrastructure in the context of EU, in Budapest and Barcelona researches on cultural policy and management, while he collaborated twice with the Dutch Ministry of Agriculture – in 2003 and 2008 – on researching the cultural dimensions of that institution. As Board Member of European Cultural Foundation (ECF), he was author of a significant study "Europe as Cultural

Project" in 2005. In 2004 he launched and was head of the ongoing European Festivals Research Project (EFRP) and was one of main consultants in the preparation process for candidateship of the Polish city of Lublin for 2016 European Cultural Capital.

Apart from books and collections published in Serbo-Croatian in former Yugoslavia until 1991, Klaic was author of books published in Great Britain, USA, the Netherlands and Norway, including: *Terrorism and Modern Drama* (with John Orr, Edinburgh University Press, 1990), *The Plot of The Future: Utopia and Dystopia in Modern Drama* (Michigan University Press,1991), *Shifting Gears/ Changer de vitesse* (with Rudy Engelander, TIN Amsterdam, 1998), as well as memoires on his life in exile *Exercises in Exile*, published in Dutch ("Thuis is waar je vrienden zijn. Ballingschap tussen Internet en Ikeatafel", Amsterdam: Cossee 2004) and Croatian ("Vježbanje egzila", 2006, Zagreb).

Klaic's reviews and columns have been published in numerous periodicals in several languages as well as in over 60 books by different editors.

His latest published work (before *Resetting the Stage*) was *Mobility of Imagination: A Companion Guide to International Cultural Cooperation* in 2007.

Dragan Klaic died on 25 August 2011, in Amsterdam.

Katarina Pejović

Afterword

On May 14, 2011 I received a disturbing e-mail from Dragan Klaic. He had been in an Amsterdam hospital since a couple of weeks. He wrote: "In the worse case, I'd like to ask you to act as my literary executor in the matter of my last book."

I was shocked: I knew he was sick, but I did not know that he seriously considered the possibility that he would not make it. I wrote back and said something like: "Of course you can count on me, but you'll see, in a few weeks we will have lunch in our regular restaurant again."

But I was wrong. Dragan, a long time friend and colleague, passed away on August 25, 2011, just over three months after he sent his e-mail.

I must admit that it took me a few weeks to turn to the task he had left for me. I felt awkward about reading the second version of his manuscript in his absence, knowing that any remarks I would have I would not be able to discuss with him anymore, as had been the case when he had sent me the first version, in the autumn of 2010. But I also knew that I had to do something, because I had promised him I would.

So I started reading. I encountered some issues that I was not sure about how to solve, several questions that I was hesitant to answer all by myself. I invited four of Dragan's old friends and collaborators, all extremely knowledgeable as far as the book's subject is concerned, to be my sounding board. I am grateful for their assistance to Vesna Čopič, Milena Dragićević Šešić, Sanja Jovićević and Katarina Pejović, who patiently (and rapidly) answered my mail messages. In the end it turned out that the issues and questions I discovered were not that problematic after all and that there was no need to do any drastic editing. The book does not differ in essence and in detail from the manuscript Dragan Klaic left behind, although during the fine-tuning that Katarina Pejović and I took upon ourselves we corrected some obvious errors and clarified one or two passages.

However, in the 18 months since Dragan Klaic finished his manuscript and the moment of publication inevitably several things and situations have changed. We decided not to update or correct most little inconsistencies, since they do not affect the essence of the book: a polemic analysis of the here and now of public theatre.

This book would not exist without the financial support of IETM (International Network for Contemporary Performing Arts), TIN (Theater Instituut Nederland) and VTI (Vlaams Theater Instituut) – organisations that Dragan had a long history with.

Rudy Engelander